Praise for the first edition of *Jesus, the Bible, and Homosexuality*

"Rogers adds immensely to those who argue for the full inclusion of gay and lesbian people in the church and in the clergy. His experience in and reflections on the Presbyterian Church (U.S.A.) will be useful to people of ALL mainline denominations. For those who truly wish to know what the Bible does and does not say, this is a real find."

—The Right Reverend V. Gene Robinson,
Bishop of New Hampshire, Episcopal Church

"This book offers a rare opportunity to see why one of America's leading evangelical scholars and a former Moderator of the General Assembly of the Presbyterian Church (U.S.A.) changed his mind about homosexuality. What Jack Rogers discovered by reviewing the biblical, creedal, and historical evidence for himself just might change your mind as well."

—Mel White, Founder, Soulforce

"This book is simply wonderful—an intelligent, well-researched, amazingly helpful contribution by a person of faith to one of the most difficult debates of our time. Jack Rogers just might change both the tenor and the content of the argument over homosexuality in the Christian church."

—Joanna M. Adams, Pastor, Morningside
Presbyterian Church, Atlanta

"All Christians, but especially blacks and women, will appreciate Jack Rogers's argument from history showing how and why mainstream Presbyterians changed their minds about race and gender equality. This plain-spoken but scholarly work teaches not only that we can change our minds about homosexuality, but that we must."

—Gayraud S. Wilmore, Emeritus Professor of Church History,
Interdenominational Theological Center, Atlanta

"Jack Rogers is an honest man who has changed his mind about homosexuality so that he is now convinced it is not a sin. He tells with clarity and passion the story of how he changed his mind."

—William C. Placher, LaFollette Distinguished Professor
in the Humanities, Wabash College

Jesus, the Bible,
and Homosexuality
Revised and Expanded Edition

Jesus, the Bible, and Homosexuality

Revised and Expanded Edition

Explode the Myths, Heal the Church

JACK ROGERS

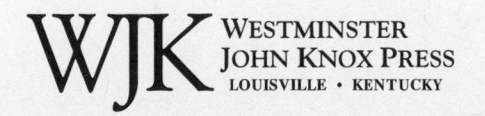

WJK WESTMINSTER
JOHN KNOX PRESS
LOUISVILLE · KENTUCKY

Book design by Drew Stevens
Cover design by Eric Walljasper, Minneapolis, MN

First edition
Published by Westminster John Knox Press
Louisville, Kentucky

This book is printed on acid-free paper that meets the American National Standards Institute Z39.48 standard. ∞

PRINTED IN THE UNITED STATES OF AMERICA

    11 12 13 14 15 16 17 18—10 9 8 7 6 5 4 3

Library of Congress Cataloging-in-Publication Data

Rogers, Jack Bartlett.
  Jesus, the Bible, and homosexuality : explode the myths, heal the church / Jack Rogers.
— Rev. and expanded ed.
        p. cm.
  "Jack Rogers study guide."
  Includes bibliographical references and index.
  ISBN 978-0-664-23397-6 (alk. paper)
  1. Bible and homosexuality.   2. Homosexuality—Religious aspects—Presbyterian Church (U.S.A.)   3. Presbyterian Church (U.S.A.)—Doctrines.   I. Title.
  BS680.H67R64   2009
  241'.66—dc22

                                                                2009006554

To my son, Toby Rogers—
with whom it is a privilege to work

Contents

Preface to the Second Edition

In 1959, I was a new seminary graduate heading overseas to do doctoral study in the Netherlands. I asked my presbytery to ordain me so that if an opportunity to minister overseas developed, I would be able to accept the call without having first to travel back to Nebraska to be ordained. So the Presbytery of Nebraska City ordained me as a "traveling evangelist."

As it happened, I did serve as organizing pastor of an English-speaking congregation in the Netherlands on behalf of the Dutch Reformed Church. However, I feel that I have only really entered into my vocation as a "traveling evangelist" since the initial publication of this book in March of 2006. Friends and allies began to hear about the book and invited me to come and speak at their churches, in their communities, and at universities around the country. What started out as a short trip up the coast to speak at a gay and lesbian bookstore and a few churches eventually turned into a nationwide book tour that has taken the better part of two years.

This book tour has been one of the most wonderful experiences of my life. In those two years, I spoke at 142 events in 22 different states. As you might imagine, I was invited to speak to many progressive congregations on the west coast and in the northeast. But my tour also took me to some of the most conservative states in the country—Georgia, North Carolina, South Carolina, Tennessee, Texas, Louisiana, Iowa, Nebraska, Kansas, and Missouri. Usually in these states my host pastor would pull me aside before the speech and explain, "We hope you won't be disappointed, but I don't imagine we'll have very many people tonight. People just aren't ready to talk about this topic." Then we would arrive at the event and discover a large enthusiastic crowd made up of people from throughout the community. It showed the widespread yearning people have to talk about this matter and understand it on a deeper level.

I have been moved by the courage and compassion of the local organizers who invited me in to speak. In the fall of 2007, I was scheduled to speak at Drury University in Springfield, Missouri. I had heard that Springfield was a rather conservative town. At dinner with local hosts before the event, I met Jolie Cave, a remarkable student organizer who was the vice president of Allies, the gay/straight alliance at the university. Jolie explained that the group had posted five hundred flyers advertising my speech the night before the event only to discover that most of them had been torn down and thrown into trash cans by the next morning. Allies responded by creating another flyer, this one proclaiming, "We will not be silenced; closets are for clothes, and trash cans are for ignorance," which they posted around campus along with the crumpled flyers they rescued from the trash cans.

The Drury University event took place on National Coming Out Day in an historic Baptist church where the Rev. Martin Luther King Jr. reportedly had preached. Peter Browning, the university chaplain, estimated that we might have thirty or so people in attendance. I arrived early to do some book signing and discovered the room was quickly filling as organizers dashed about to put up additional folding chairs. By the time the event started, about 125 people had crowded into the room, filling every pew and the choir loft, with still others standing in the back and sitting in the aisles. The atmosphere was electric. When Peter introduced the members of Allies and explained the courage and determination they had shown in organizing the event, they received a standing ovation. The energy just built from there. Students seemed to connect with my remarks, and afterward they asked thoughtful questions that showed a deep understanding of how their faith calls them to social justice. Seeing the courage and commitment of these students lets me know that the future of the church is in good hands.

Out on the road I have met extraordinary, faithful people dedicated to Christ. I have heard their stories, and they have touched my heart. I am now in a pastoral ministry of the kind that I haven't had since I was a pastor in the Netherlands. This ministry has three aspects. First, it is a ministry of comfort and encouragement to people who have been terribly hurt. Second, it is a ministry that supports marriage and family life. Third, and interwoven with the other purposes, it is a ministry of evangelism, in which people come to Christ and the church.

A MINISTRY OF COMFORT AND ENCOURAGEMENT

At almost every event my presentation is followed by a question-and-answer period and a book signing. Usually as I'm sitting at a table signing books, people bend down very close to me and tell me their stories.

Hearing people's stories, I have come to appreciate on a much deeper level the enormous pain that has been caused by the church's exclusionary policies.

In April of 2006, at a book signing at St. John's Presbyterian Church in Berkeley, California, an older woman came through the line to ask me to sign a book. She was exactly the sort of person you'd want for a neighbor—kind, gentle, soft spoken. She told me about her family. She had five daughters. Her middle daughter was a lesbian, who was so convinced that God didn't love her that she committed suicide. I just wanted to hold this woman and cry with her.

In North Carolina an older man told me that his gay son had shot himself twice but lived because he missed his heart. That son is now a successful businessman, living with a partner. He was just ordained an elder in a More Light Presbyterian church. This father said that he and his wife had always loved their son unconditionally, but the church had not. He told me what a thrill it was for them to lay hands on their son at his ordination.

On the book tour, I met bright church and professional leaders who had lost their jobs because someone found out they were gay. I met couples who have been together for ten, twenty, even forty years, who have raised children and cared for each other in sickness and in health, who are barred by the church and forty-seven states (at the time of this writing) from consecrating their union through marriage. I met faithful Christians who have excelled at some of the most conservative colleges and seminaries in the country yet were later shunned when it was revealed that they are lesbian, gay, bisexual, or transgender (LGBT).

In the summer of 2008, I spoke to about two-hundred LGBT evangelical Christians at the West Coast conference of Evangelicals Concerned, a group founded by Dr. Ralph Blair, a New York psychotherapist, gay man, and evangelical Christian. Blair founded this organization to meet the needs of conservative Christians who also know themselves to be gay. At the conference I became reacquainted with three former students from my teaching days at Fuller Theological Seminary. I had not known that the three men were gay. Each of them shared with me essentially the same story: when he had finally acknowledged that he was gay, people who had previously loved and admired him suddenly rejected him and refused to allow him to participate in church leadership.

These men had all participated in so-called "ex-gay" groups or therapy. They had been told by their church leaders that the Bible condemned homosexuality and that their salvation was at risk. So they had turned to organizations that promised to help them change their sexual orientation. One man had tried for three years. Another had stayed in an "ex-gay" group for ten years. They had each spent enormous time in prayer, therapy, and self-loathing. But they all finally came to realize that they had not chosen nor could they change their sexual orientation, no matter how hard they tried. When these three former students finally accepted their sexual orientation, they were able to find meaningful relationships and personal stability, and they were able to start building a healthy family life.

This book tour has shown me firsthand the enormous pain caused by the church's unjust policies. All of this suffering is completely unnecessary and preventable. As I show in this book (and as countless other scholars have shown in their work), the Bible, properly understood, does not condemn people who are LGBT, and it does not prohibit faithful same-sex relationships. The church's historical prohibitions against marriage and ordination for people who are LGBT are an anachronism— much like the church's previous policies that prohibited interracial marriage or ordaining people of African descent, women, or people who are divorced and remarried. Indeed our faith calls us to do justice, provide hospitality, and embrace equality for all God's people.

A MINISTRY OF SUPPORTING MARRIAGE AND FAMILY LIFE

Supporting people who are LGBT is also about supporting families. One of the most striking things for me is the number of families I meet that are led by same-sex couples. The 2000 United States Census counted 594,391 families led by same-sex couples.[1] Research by other organizations suggests that the actual numbers may be higher. "A 2004 analysis by the Urban Institute, a nonpartisan research organization in Washington, DC, estimated that the census figures on same-sex households may be 25 percent too low."[2]

When people know that God loves them and can accept who they are as a gift from God, it can be wonderfully healing for families. I was in Louisville, Kentucky, speaking at the national Presbyterian Women's Gathering. An elderly African American woman stopped me in the hall after my speech. She asked me to sign her book there so she would not have to walk down the stairs to the bookstore. I pulled up two chairs so we could sit for a moment. "This is relevant to me," she said as she handed me the book. "How so?" I asked. The woman sat in silence for a moment, then said, "I was so worried about my son. He seemed so confused and wild. Now that he has accepted who he is and has settled down with his partner of two years, he is happy. His partner is like another son to me."

In Fort Worth, Texas, I met a bright, well-behaved four-year-old boy and his two fathers. One father gave up his law practice to stay at home and raise the boy, while the other father works as an engineer. Over lunch, after church on Sunday, I learned from the stay-at-home dad that he and his partner had been active members of a church in Houston for ten years. The pastors knew they were gay and all seemed to be well. And it was—until they asked the church to baptize their son (born to a surrogate mother). The pastors refused. The parents asked, "Surely you will take this to the session?" An associate pastor informed them, "No, that will never happen in this church."[3]

Eventually the engineer's career moved the family to Fort Worth, where they found a new church home. The couple are very supported and valued now at St. Stephen Presbyterian Church, where their son was baptized. That night I called my wife, Sharon, and told her about this family and what they had been through. She said that earlier on that same day, at Pasadena Presbyterian Church, one of our copastors, Barbara Anderson, "baptized the two babies of a lesbian couple in the church. They were accompanied by members of their family and were supported in love by the congregation. It felt like we were all one family. It was beautiful." One couple who came for the baptism inquired afterward about becoming members of the church.

Churches like St. Stephen in Fort Worth and Pasadena Presbyterian and many other congregations I have visited give me hope. Our churches and nation are being transformed. Everywhere I go, I meet pastors, elders, and church members who truly embody Christ's love and who freely embrace all kinds of people, just as Jesus did.

I have seen firsthand that most people in the church deeply believe that everyone should be treated equally. They just have not always had the information and support they need to counteract the inaccurate things they have been told about the Bible.

A MINISTRY OF EVANGELISM

Thanks be to God, my book tour has also turned into a ministry of evangelism. After my remarks at a large conservative church, an Asian American woman and her boyfriend, both in their midtwenties, came up to me. The young woman said, "I haven't been able to give my life to Christ because of the hateful attitude toward gay people by the church." Gesturing toward her boyfriend, she said, "It has been a problem between us." I replied, "You *can* give your life to Christ. Jesus accepts gay and lesbian people whether a particular congregation does or not." She looked thoughtful for a moment and then visibly relaxed and smiled. I believe she gave her life to Christ in that moment while her boyfriend beamed.

At the Presbyterian General Assembly, shortly after the book came out, I talked with a friend and former student who is a professional fund-raiser. She keeps balance in her life by being a commissioned lay pastor of a very small church near her home in Redlands, California. She told me that a member of her church had taken my book and given it to a gay friend at work. The man read it and came back and said, "This book changed my life. My whole life, I thought God hated me. But this book is telling me that Jesus loves me." Then he paused and said, "I wonder, could I come to your church?" "Of course!" was the answer.

One of the most deeply moving aspects of speaking to diverse audiences across the country is to see the reactions on people's faces as I tell them that Jesus loves them. That should be obvious, right? Jesus loves you. It is the fundamental message of Christianity. Yet somehow in all the hate-filled rhetoric of the debate about homosexuality, the central message of Christ's redemptive ministry sometimes gets lost. As I remind people that Jesus loves them, I can see the glimmer in their eyes as they reconnect with their faith.

One story, for me, sums up the extraordinary experiences that I have had during this book tour. I was in Richmond, Virginia, teaching an adult church school class. During the discussion period, a well-dressed middle-aged woman with dark hair, sitting in the second row, shyly raised her hand. She asked if she could tell her story before she asked a question. She explained that she was a psychiatrist and a lesbian who had been with her partner for twenty-one years. She had grown up in a different faith but had stopped practicing it long ago. Her partner was raised in a rigid Southern Baptist home and had likewise turned away from her faith.

This couple decided to move from downtown Richmond out to the country for more peace and quiet. Their nearest neighbor was a young Southern Baptist minister with a small, rural church. As good neighbors do, this minister paid them a visit. He just wanted to get to know them as people. And, over time, these neighbors became friends.

Something transformative happens when we really get to know someone. We drop our categories and our preconceived notions. Peter and

Paul and Barnabas discovered it with Gentiles out in the mission field (see my discussion of Acts 15 in chapter 5). And this young Southern Baptist minister discovered it in rural Virginia. He came to realize that this lesbian couple was okay just as they were. They didn't have to change their sexual orientation. In turn, they became interested in his gospel message. The result was that this woman asked to be baptized, and she and her partner joined the little church. She had been a Christian for one year. That is evangelism. Accepting all people as children of God, as Jesus did, gives us the opportunity to share the good news of the gospel.

SHARING THE GOOD NEWS

A large part of the success of this book is due to the many committed Christians who supported its message and me. Prior to the start of the book tour, the copastors of our church, Mark Smutny and Barbara Anderson, arranged a small gathering to raise money to help get the book out to others. At that event, Barbara said, "This is about saving lives. Telling people about this book will help save lives."

I now know from personal experience that what Barbara said is true. Sharing the good news that Jesus loves people for who they are saves lives, reunites families, and brings people back into relationship with Jesus and the church. It is a privilege to be engaged in this ministry. My life has been forever transformed by the people I have met over the course of this journey.

I am grateful for the opportunity to present this second, revised and expanded edition of *Jesus, the Bible, and Homosexuality*. In the last two years the Presbyterian Church (U.S.A.) has taken several important steps toward equality for all of its members. I have revised and added new material to chapter 7 to reflect these new developments. Chapter 8 is completely new and explores three biblical stories that show how Jesus' teachings illuminate God's extravagant welcome for all who have faith. I have also added an appendix that documents the remarkable progress toward LGBT equality over the last forty years in denominations throughout the United States.

Jack Rogers
September 28, 2008

Preface to the First Edition

Why am I doing this? I am not gay. No one in my family is gay. That is why I was able to stay on the sidelines for so long. It didn't touch me personally.

I am a Christian who cares deeply about Christ's church. The church is being torn apart by controversy over whether people who are homosexual can have full rights of membership.[1] Not just my own Presbyterian Church, but all of the denominations in this nation are divided.

Our country is also being rent by this controversy. Attitudes toward people who are lesbian, gay, bisexual, and transgender—LGBT—are among the factors that have divided us into red and blue states, rural versus urban areas, midlands versus the coasts. How we choose to respond to this issue is a test of who we will become as a nation.

This is a defining issue of our time. For some it is an issue of maintaining traditions and customs that have given order to our society. For others, it is an issue of justice—all citizens should be entitled to equal rights under the law. For me, it is a moral and spiritual issue. How can the church live up to the highest ideals of Jesus Christ? How can we most faithfully act according to the central principles of the Bible? How can we most honestly and equitably share the love of God with all people?

I first dealt with this issue in the local congregation where my wife, Sharon, and I worship. Since that time I have explored it by using my training as a scholar. I have not specialized as a biblical scholar, but I have wrestled with the biblical texts that are most commonly cited regarding people who are homosexual. I have not specialized as a church historian, but I have delved deeply into the history of how we have coped with other bitterly divisive issues in the church. I am a theologian and a historian of doctrine (the beliefs of the church), especially in its creeds and confessions. Seeking guidance from the church's central traditions, I have looked afresh at these foundational documents of the church.

I am a minister and a teacher, and I had the honor to be elected the Moderator of the 213th General Assembly of the Presbyterian Church

(U.S.A.) in 2001. The Moderator is sort of an honorary head of the church for one year.[2] I had the privilege, as Moderator, of traveling all over the United States, and in several foreign countries. I met people in congregations with 15 members and congregations with 4,500 members.

I have been exposed to every kind of opinion on the issue of whether LGBT people should have equal rights in the church and in society. I have encountered people red-faced with anger who have shouted at me. I have met people who wept because they felt rejected. I have met people who just didn't want to be involved in controversy. I have known people who could not quite understand what the fuss was all about. I have come to know a great many people who are homosexual that I am now grateful to call my friends.

I want the church to be healed of this great wound in the body of Christ. My favorite seminary professor often said: "If Christ is divided, who bleeds?"[3] My attitude toward this problem has changed. For a long time I thought that we just had to wait, that time would heal the controversy. I no longer believe that. The Presbyterian Church took that attitude toward slavery until the nation and the church were finally torn in two.

I have gone through a change in my mind and heart. I have gone from being a silent spectator to actively working for change. I believe people who are homosexual should be given full rights of membership in the church and citizenship in the nation. I believe that this is the only way to heal the wounds of the church and the nation.

We in the church are not living according to the ideals of our Savior and Sovereign, Jesus Christ, when we discriminate unjustly against any group of people in our midst. To act unjustly weakens our witness to Christ in the world. I believe that we will be one holy and whole church only when all our members are treated equally. Then, together we will be able to evangelize, worship, and serve with the integrity of those who live according to Christ's teachings. To help us reach that goal is my reason for writing this book. I invite all who share the goal of healing the church to join me as I describe my journey of discovery and my change of mind and heart.

In this book each chapter represents a step in my own journey. In chapter 1, "Studying Homosexuality for the First Time," I describe how my journey began, on a task force in my local congregation to study the status of people who are lesbian or gay. Then I wanted to know how the church had dealt with other, similarly volatile, issues. In chapter 2, "A Pattern of Misusing the Bible to Justify Oppression," I review how our leading theologians, for two hundred years, preached and taught that the Bible justified the enslavement of people of African descent and the subordination of women to men.[4] In chapter 3, "A Breakthrough in Understanding the Word of God," I present the dramatic change in biblical interpretation that began in the 1930s, and I rejoice in the way that it supported movements toward equality for African Americans and liberation of women from limiting stereotypes. Chapter 4, "Interpreting the Bible in Times of Controversy," tells the story of how, in the 1980s, the Presbyterian denominations, north and south, developed guidelines for biblical interpretation. Here I walk through seven guidelines, see their support in our Reformed confessions, and consider their application to the lives of people who are gay and lesbian. In chapter 5, "What the Bible Says and Doesn't Say about Homosexuality," I study in detail the usual biblical texts that are cited to condemn homosexual behavior and the theories, imposed on these texts, that twist their meaning. Chapter 6, "Real People and Real Marriage," will enable us to move beyond stereotypes by introducing us to the powerful witness of faithful gay and lesbian Christian couples. In chapter 7, "Recommendations for the Presbyterian Church (U.S.A.)," I look back on what we have learned and discuss the appropriate action that will move us forward. In that chapter I make recommendations for what the Presbyterian Church can do to right the wrongs of our present situation and to heal the divisions in the church. I hope that people in other denominations facing these same issues will be encouraged to reflect on the parallels in their setting and plan what they will do to bring healing to their communities.

Let us begin.

Acknowledgments

ACKNOWLEDGMENTS FOR THE SECOND EDITION

This second edition of *Jesus, the Bible, and Homosexuality* would not have been possible without the steadfast love and support of my wife, Sharon; the editorial and research assistance of my son, Toby; and the skilled guidance of my editor, Stephanie Egnotovich, at Westminster John Knox Press.

David Dobson, editorial director of Westminster John Knox, first posed the idea of including the study guide in the next printing of *Jesus, the Bible, and Homosexuality*. That initiative was further developed in conversations with David Maxwell and other Westminster John Knox colleagues. I am grateful to the entire team at Westminster John Knox for their amazing support for this project since its inception.

Few people might have heard about the first edition (and hence no second edition!) were it not for the extraordinary grassroots organizing efforts of countless people across the United States who helped coordinate my book tour. I especially want to thank Pam Byers, Anitra Kitts, Tricia Dykers Koenig, Lou East, Jay McKell, Karen Turney, and Michael Adee for their tireless efforts to coordinate events and help spread the word. Harry Knox and Sharon Groves in the Religion and Faith Program at the Human Rights Campaign have been wonderful in their support for the book tour and this second edition.

Throughout the summer and into the fall, Toby conducted interviews with the leaders of many of the LGBT advocacy groups in denominations across the country that contributed to the new appendix. We would especially like to extend our thanks to Nancy Wilson and Cindi Love, Metropolitan Community Churches; Keith Kron, Office of Bisexual, Gay, Lesbian, and Transgender Concerns, Unitarian Universalist Association; Ken Pennings, Association of Welcoming and Affirming Baptists; Ruth Garwood, Coalition for LGBT Concerns, United Church of Christ; Michael Schuenemeyer, Lesbian, Gay, Bisexual, and Transgender Ministries, United Church of Christ; Susan Russell and

John Clinton Bradley, Integrity USA (Episcopal Church USA); Emily Eastwood, Lutherans Concerned North America; Amalia Vagts, Extraordinary Lutheran Ministries; Troy Plummer and Sarah Megan Howery, Reconciling Ministries Network (United Methodist); Bob Bouchard and Dave Ferguson, Kinship International (Seventh-day Adventist); and Olin Thomas and Hugo Salinas, Affirmation: Gay & Lesbian Mormons.

Roy Ritchie, the Director of Research at the Huntington Library graciously extended my use of an office to finish this new edition. Special thanks to Jeff Siker, who cast his eye as a New Testament scholar over an early draft of chapter 8 and to Alice and Bob Evans for their wise counsel on the study guide. I am thankful for the insightful questions from persons at conferences and churches with whom I shared elements of this second edition.

I dedicate this revised edition to the multitudes of people who are lesbian, gay, bisexual, or transgender and have kept their faith in God despite all that the churches have done to exclude them.

Jack Rogers
Advent 2008

ACKNOWLEDGMENTS FOR THE FIRST EDITION

I have dedicated this book to my son, Toby Rogers, himself a writer, who has been deeply invested in this project from its inception. He helped to shape and focus the stories and the argument of the entire work.

My wife, Dr. Sharon Rogers, along with her significant work in special education, for forty-eight years has always made time to encourage and support me, and for that I am grateful.

Stephanie Egnotovich, my editor with Westminster John Knox Press for the past ten years, has been patient with my delays and gracious in continuing to encourage me. I value her friendship and especially appreciate her support for this project from its beginning and through all of its various incarnations. I was helped additionally by the comments of WJK editor and friend Don McKim.

The Huntington Library in San Marino, California, has provided me with the most helpful research and writing environment possible: an office with a door; access to an incomparable collection of historical and literary works, which enabled me to research the history of institutional change regarding race, women, divorce, and now homosexuality; and beautiful gardens in which to lunch and chat and walk with other scholars.

Dean Thompson was very gracious to let me tell a part of his story while I was telling mine. I thank the many people who generously read and critiqued an earlier version of this study. Many of their insights are now imbedded in the text. Where I failed to profit from their insights, the fault is mine. Thanks go to Scott Anderson, Pam Byers, Gary Demarest, Bob Lodwick, Bill Pannell, Bear Ride, Mel White, and John Wilkinson. I am especially grateful for the continuing conversations with my Huntington lunch and walking partners, Ron White and Paul Zall, and to Henk van de Rest for providing an international perspective. Others who read a later version and commented helpfully include Bill Hopper, Ron Oglesbee, Mark Smutny, and Susan Hylen on chapter 5.

I have benefited by the opportunity afforded by the Covenant Network of Presbyterians to present portions of this study at their national and regional conferences. I have learned from the interaction with students in my classes at San Francisco Theological Seminary, Southern California, and from people in numerous congregations where this material has been discussed.

I am well aware that some will challenge my conclusions. I acknowledge that controversy on the subject of homosexuality may continue for some time. My earnest hope is that, as with the conflicts over race, women, and divorce, the church will finally admit all of its members to the full rights of membership and discover in doing so that we all will benefit and the church will be healed.

Jack Rogers
September 28, 2005

1

Studying Homosexuality for the First Time

Dean Thompson was faced with a problem.

As pastor and head of staff at the Pasadena Presbyterian Church, Dean (as he was affectionately known by his congregation) was confronted with an issue that he would rather have avoided. In the spring of 1993, a gay man, who had earlier been elected a deacon, wrote to the session,[1] the local governing body, of the Pasadena Presbyterian Church. He asked the session to initiate a program of study and, at the end of a year, formally consider designating Pasadena Presbyterian Church a More Light Church—a congregation that was willing to ordain gay, lesbian, bisexual, and transgender people to all offices in the church, despite a denominational prohibition against it.[2] The gay man's action was supported by the deacons and a number of elders.[3] Consequently, the session asked the three pastors on the staff to establish a task force to create an educational program that would sensitize the whole congregation to gay and lesbian issues.

Dean had grown up in West Virginia and earned both an MDiv and a PhD in American church history from Union Seminary in Richmond, Virginia. He served pastorates in West Virginia and in Austin, Texas, before accepting the call to Pasadena Presbyterian Church in California. A genial and humble person, he was known for loving his congregation and for preaching biblical sermons, grounded in the Reformed tradition.

Pasadena Presbyterian Church was older than the city itself. It had a history of great preachers. It had been a leading voice in the community during the civil rights struggle.

Now Dean was in a no-win position. If the task force recommended in favor of becoming a More Light Church, several more traditional families would surely leave the church. If the task force recommended against becoming a More Light Church, members who supported equal rights for people who are gay and lesbian, including openly gay members and their families, would feel alienated and possibly leave. To his credit, Dean assembled a diverse task force that included a broad representation of different people and viewpoints.

Dean knew that I was opposed to the ordination of gay and lesbian people. He asked me to be a member of the task force.

I said no.

I thought I had a perfect excuse. Although I worshiped regularly at Pasadena Presbyterian Church, as an ordained Presbyterian minister, my membership was not in the local congregation, but in the presbytery, the regional denominational governing body.

Then Dean put his request on a personal level: "If you are my friend, you will do this." I probably had many reasons for resistance, but they all came down to my not wanting to be involved in studying the issue of ordaining gay and lesbian people to church office. It just was not a problem that I wanted to take on. Reluctantly, I acceded to Dean's request and agreed to serve.

The three pastors on the church staff appointed a task force of fifteen members who, among them, covered the whole range of opinions. It included the gay man who had requested the task force and the mother of a lesbian young woman who had grown up in the congregation. One more-conservative couple on the task force left the church when we began to look at more than what they considered the only biblical perspective. A retired missionary also on the task force said he would stand in the church door to bar a lesbian evangelist, Janie Spahr, from entering the building.

After nearly a year of study, the task force presented a twelve-week adult education course at Pasadena Presbyterian Church. More than one hundred people attended each class meeting. We devoted three sessions to biblical interpretation and three to psychological and sociological perspectives. We heard from gay and lesbian members of the West Hollywood Presbyterian Church and looked at videos on different responses by family members. We spent one session discussing what was in the best interests of children. We listened to people who said that sexual orientation or behavior could be changed. We studied the denomination's form of government to see how it affected this issue. And we designed the final session with two opposing speakers, again to balance the viewpoints. We tried very hard to be balanced and fair to every perspective, but invariably some thought we had not given their view enough support.

As an educator, I thought the curriculum was excellent, but the results of the study were mixed. The congregation as a whole did seem more comfortable with the issue.[4] The session did not vote to become a More Light Church. The gay man who had initiated the process was disappointed and left the church. And for the first time in my career, I had been forced to study the issue.

During this period I did not change my Reformed theology or my method of biblical interpretation. For the first time, however, I had to apply them to the issue of homosexuality. That has led me on a journey that in many ways has been uncomfortable. In other ways it has resulted in growth and satisfaction. I want to share that journey with you. I hope it will encourage you in your own journey.

MY FORMATION AS AN AMERICAN EVANGELICAL CHRISTIAN

Let me begin by putting my own life experience in context. In 1934 my devout, Christian parents had a healthy, white, male baby. In Nebraska, at the state fair each year, there was a judging, not only of pigs and calves, of apple pies and bread-and-butter pickles, but of children. My parents entered me in a contest. I don't know what the criteria were, but I do have a silver trophy inscribed "1935, NEBR STATE FAIR, MOST PERFECT BOY." When I looked at that trophy many years later, it was a visible confirmation for me of what most white, American males experienced. We knew that in some intangible but very real way we were superior. As I grew older and became aware of an attraction to girls, I subconsciously added another element to my personal list of male superiority: I was heterosexual.

The culture of the 1940s and 1950s reinforced that stereotype of superiority. The jokes, the ways teachers related to us, the opportunities we were given—all made us know that boys were better than girls, that whites were better than coloreds, and that straights were normal and queers were not.

It took the civil rights movement of the 1960s to begin to crack the facade of white racial superiority. In the 1970s, the women's movement forced a grudging acknowledgment that women were of equal value to men. In the late 1980s and the 1990s, the first awakenings began to come for many people that gay and lesbian people were different in some respects, but of no less worth than people who were heterosexual.

During all of this time I was also an evangelical. I was baptized a Methodist. I became a Presbyterian by geography after my father was drafted into the Navy in World War II and we were forced to sell our car. There was a small neighborhood United Presbyterian church just a block and a half from our house. We began to attend there and continued after the war. I grew up in that church until I left home to attend seminary.[5]

The old United Presbyterian Church of North America (UPCNA) was a small denomination (about 250,000 members). It was conservative but not fundamentalist.[6]

The pastor under whom I joined the church was named Harold (Shorty) Irwin. I was about twelve years old and was impressed that, as a former cheerleader, he could walk on his hands. He also made us study and memorize large sections of the Bible. Those of us in his communicants class understood that we were lost in sin and that Christ had paid the penalty for our sins and that by trust in Christ we received our salvation. I believed it then, and I believe it now. As I grew older, I also sometimes attended the local Youth for Christ meetings. I went "down the aisle" several times, confirming my sense of being saved.

That small church gave me many opportunities for leadership. I was the president of our presbytery youth organization. I also had the opportunity to attend several national youth conferences. My first was at Lake Geneva, Wisconsin. There I met attractive young people and capable pastors who encouraged me in my Christian growth. One summer I won the national Bible reading contest. The speakers at these conferences were often professors from our one denominational seminary, Pittsburgh-Xenia. I was drawn to their message as I was drawn to them personally.

Those national youth conference experiences were a significant factor in my feeling called to the ministry as a sophomore in college. During Christmas break I counseled with my pastor about my sense of vocation. His advice was, "Don't go into the ministry if you can be happy doing anything else." That did it. I decided that I couldn't be happy doing anything else. The most dramatic moment for me came one evening when, after praying, I got up off my knees, walked into my parents' bedroom, and announced that God had called me into the ministry. The conviction of that calling has never left me.

Given my background, it was natural for me to head to Pittsburgh-Xenia Seminary when I graduated from the University of Nebraska. I knew that I was a conservative Christian. At seminary, I learned that in the larger Christian culture we were called evangelical.

At seminary I learned a particular Anglo-Saxon, American, Presbyterian tradition that was presented as Christian orthodoxy. This orthodoxy was defined confessionally by the Westminster Confession of Faith, and the Westminster Confession was interpreted theologically in the tradition of Charles Hodge and Benjamin B. Warfield, of nineteenth-century Princeton Seminary.[7] Practically, orthodoxy was defined as the most adequate understanding of life and reality. Our task was to defend it reasonably and to preach it using interesting illustrations and practical applications.

My view of orthodoxy was that it had come down in an unbroken line from the apostle Paul to Augustine to Calvin to the Westminster Confession to Warfield and then to my professors of theology and church history. I believed that all of them were treating Scripture in the same way. I always felt that the key to the Christian life and a better world was understanding and interpreting Scripture. The doctrine of Scripture was always my chief academic interest.

When I graduated from seminary, I wanted to go on to study for a doctorate in theology, and I had the good fortune to receive a modest scholarship for one year of study overseas. One of my seminary professors, John Gerstner, urged me instead to go to Harvard, as he had, where I would be confronted with liberal theology and become stronger by fighting against it. That didn't appeal to me. I wanted a deeper understanding of the Reformed tradition.[8] I consulted with Cary Weisiger, the senior pastor of a large church where I was interning. He suggested that I study with G. C. Berkouwer at the Free University of Amsterdam in the Netherlands. Dr. Weisiger felt that Professor Berkouwer was deeply Reformed and also fair in his assessments of others. Berkouwer was engaged in writing a series of volumes on the main topics of theology. That sounded like just what I wanted.

I identified with Abraham! One of my favorite verses in Scripture is, "And he set out, not knowing where he was going" (Heb. 11:8). Since my wife and I were going overseas, I requested ordination by my presbytery on the grounds that if I had an opportunity to serve while I was in the Netherlands, I couldn't come running back to Nebraska. So they ordained me as a traveling evangelist!

Four years in the Netherlands were transformative in our lives. I did my course work and comprehensive examinations. In our second year, my wife, Sharon, got a job teaching school for English-speaking children of Dupont engineers in Dordrecht. I became the organizing pastor of an English-speaking congregation for the Dutch Reformed Church, serving the same English-speaking community. Our first son, Matthew, was born. Then we moved to New Wilmington, Pennsylvania, so I could teach at Westminster College (one of the six UPCNA colleges).

After two years there, I took an unpaid leave of absence to finish my dissertation. Sharon and Matthew and I spent the summer in Princeton, where I made use of the Speer and Firestone libraries. Then we flew to London for six months of research at the British Museum

Library. I took twelve metal boxes, each with a thousand quote cards, back to Holland, where I could work with my doctoral professor. After another ten months of writing, I graduated in January of 1967 with a printed dissertation entitled *Scripture in the Westminster Confession* and returned to teaching at Westminster College.[9]

TEACHING AT FULLER THEOLOGICAL SEMINARY

Four years later, I received a call to teach philosophy of religion at Fuller Theological Seminary, a multidenominational, evangelical seminary in Pasadena, California. I was then engaged in translating and editing G. C. Berkouwer's two-volume work on *Holy Scripture,* so in my first quarter at Fuller I gave a seminar on Berkouwer's doctrine of Scripture.[10] My memory is that four students signed up. We had a good time and I was continuing to pursue my longtime interest in interpretation of the Bible.

As a professor of philosophical theology at Fuller I was immersed in the culture of the evangelical world. The struggle to develop an evangelicalism distinct from its formation in fundamentalism was played out at Fuller Seminary.[11] In the late 1940s, Billy Graham, Harold John Okenga, Carl F. H. Henry, and others developed a movement called evangelicalism, which was distinguished from the militant fundamentalism that separated from the mainstream churches and stood against changes in American society.

I would define an evangelical theologically as someone who accepts three propositions: (1) People can and should have a personal relationship with God through trust in Jesus Christ. (2) The Bible is the final authority for salvation and living the Christian life. (3) God's grace in Jesus Christ is such good news that everyone should hear about it. If you add something to these affirmations, you are becoming denominational or fundamentalist. If you take away one of these affirmations, you could still be a Christian, but you would not be an evangelical.

Sociologically, evangelicalism was a movement, not a church. It was a loose coalition of people within the mainstream churches, independent associations of Christians, and parachurch organizations. Fuller Seminary was founded as its intellectual center. *Christianity Today* was its magazine. Billy Graham's revivals were a source of its members.

I am an evangelical theologically and have always been so. I am not, and never have been, completely comfortable in the evangelical subculture. I am distrustful of movements. I prefer established organizations where there are clear lines of responsibility and accountability. I need to be in a congregation that is related to other congregations in a denomination with publicly known processes for handling problems. I believe in representative democracy, where there are clear procedures and checks and balances so that the majority may move forward while the minority is able to continue to advocate for its view. I am distrustful of self-appointed leaders and of informal organizations, held together by commitment to charismatic individuals. I want equitable processes for dealing with disputes, rather than some individual guru acting as arbitrator.

Too often the media lump together evangelicals and fundamentalists—leaving the general public confused as to the distinctions between these two groups. Within evangelicalism there are a right, left, and middle regarding political and cultural issues.[12] Fundamentalism is more politically monolithic and more theologically conservative than evangelicalism. Fundamentalists like Jerry Falwell know that.[13] But the confusion serves the fundamentalists' purpose by making it appear that they have a larger constituency, and thus influence, than they do.

The doctrine of inerrancy was and is a hallmark of fundamentalism.[14] For some of its proponents, inerrancy is a symbol for the authority of the Bible and simply affirms that the Bible is true. For others, inerrancy is a particular theory about the interpretation of the Bible. Inerrancy holds that the Bible gives accurate and up-to-the-minute information, not only on religious matters, but also on all things that the Bible addresses, including science and history. It encourages a literal reading of Scripture.[15]

Shortly before I joined the faculty at Fuller, the faculty had removed a clause in the seminary's statement of faith referring to the Bible as inerrant. The Fuller faculty preferred to use the word "infallibile," which had historically been used in the church to mean that the Bible accomplishes its purpose of bringing people to a saving knowledge of God and guiding them in living the Christian life.

This theological change evoked an attack on the Fuller Seminary by its former vice president, Harold Lindsell, in a book entitled *The Battle for the Bible*.[16] My evangelical credentials were apparently strong enough for President David Hubbard to ask me to edit a volume in reply to Lindsell and to write the historical chapter in it; that book was *Biblical Authority*.[17] I asked my friend and former student Don McKim to assist me in preparing the historical chapter, with the promise that later he and I would publish a major book on this topic. Following my yearlong sabbatical in 1977–78, the book that Don and I coauthored appeared in 1979 as *The Authority and Interpretation of the Bible: An Historical Approach*.[18] It engendered a cottage industry of books by people intent on retaining and rehabilitating the concept of inerrancy as the only acceptable descriptor of the Bible.[19]

Fundamentalists and those on the far right of evangelicalism were not happy with me.[20] However, Fuller Seminary was the leading institution at the center of evangelicalism, and I was a fully acceptable representative of that centrist evangelicalism. I was frequently called upon to speak at evangelical churches and conferences.

Upon returning to Fuller after my sabbatical in 1978, I discovered that many of our Presbyterian students were being pressured by their presbytery committees on preparation for ministry to transfer to a Presbyterian seminary. In response, with administration support, I created an Office of Presbyterian Ministries and became its director. We created four courses in Presbyterian distinctives and a Monday morning meeting for Presbyterian students, and I acted as liaison between the seminary and the presbyteries. I interpreted Fuller Seminary to the Presbyterians, and I interpreted the Presbyterians to Fuller Seminary.

President Hubbard supported my efforts to bring about a better relationship with the Presbyterian Church. While at Fuller I had the good fortune to serve on three national committees of the denomination, including the Task Force on Biblical Authority and Interpretation that met from 1978 to 1982 and produced official guidelines for interpreting Scripture in times of controversy. In all of these endeavors I felt privileged to be working on the issue that I cared most about: biblical interpretation. I felt a harmony between my role as a theological evangelical and my position as a Reformed theologian in the Presbyterian Church. Either as a member of a denominational committee or at the behest of Fuller Seminary, I attended the General Assembly of the Presbyterian Church almost every year.

THE CHURCH DEBATES BIBLICAL
INTERPRETATION AND HOMOSEXUALITY

In 1976, the issue of the ordination of people who are homosexual was first broached at the United Presbyterian Church in the U.S.A. (UPCUSA) General Assembly in Baltimore.[21] I was there and followed discussions in committee and the debates in plenary session. The Presbytery of New York City asked the assembly for what is called "definitive guidance," an official counsel on whether a candidate for the ministry, who was in all other respects well prepared for ministry, could be ordained if that person was a "self-affirming, practicing homosexual." The assembly responded by creating a Task Force to Study Homosexuality.

I was also present in 1978 when the task force reported. The 1978 assembly in San Diego, California, was rich with discussion of biblical interpretation. The Task Force to Study Homosexuality had submitted a 201-page study document including majority and minority recommendations.[22] It included data from psychotherapy and the empirical sciences. What captured the attention of most members of the assembly, however, was a 70-page section entitled "Homosexuality and the Bible: A Re-examination." A subsection on "How to Read the Bible? Problems and Models of Biblical Authority and Interpretation" evoked the most comment, because, for the first time in decades, Presbyterians had in hand four alternative approaches to biblical interpretation. Each was supported with theological assumptions, cited authorities, and suggested applications.

The report labeled the four models A, B, C, and D; each model had a rough correlation with an identifiable theological school of thought. Model A was the scholastic theology of the Old Princeton School of Charles and A. A. Hodge and B. B. Warfield, which dominated the northern Presbyterian Church from 1812 to 1927. Model B could be likened to the neo-orthodoxy of the 1930s through the 1960s, citing Karl Barth, Emil Brunner, Dietrich Bonhoeffer, and the Confession of 1967. Model C was a form of liberation theology, supported by Gordon Kaufman, Dorothee Soelle, Paul Lehmann, and Rosemary Radford Ruether, among others. Model D continued the liberation motif but added emphases of process theology represented by Norman Pittenger, John Cobb, David Ray Griffin, and Daniel Day Williams.[23]

Model A proposed that ordination of people who are homosexual be forbidden on grounds of the law of God. Model B came to the same conclusion but attributed it to the Spirit of Christ. Model C argued that ordination of people who are homosexual should be permitted on the basis of justice. Model D supported that view and added love as a further reason.

The Task Force majority of fourteen people found the biblical and theological grounds in Models C and D adequate to advocate for the ordination of qualified gay and lesbian people. A five-person minority reported that homosexual behavior was sinful and that ordination should be denied on grounds given in Models A and B. The minority argued that a homosexual orientation was not sinful in itself and that gay and lesbian people could therefore be members of the church, but sexually active people who are homosexual could not be ordained to office because the "practice" of homosexuality was sinful.[24]

The assembly chose, not the majority report, but the minority report of the Task Force to Study Homosexuality. At the same time, it endorsed civil rights for people who are homosexual. The assembly's pronouncement was in the form of "definitive guidance," as counsel rather than law. It acknowledged that for ministers of Word and Sacrament, ordination was the province of the presbytery, not the national church.[25]

An additional reason for the sensitivity of the assembly is that Presbyterians are the only Protestant denomination for whom the rules of government that apply to ministers of Word and Sacrament apply to deacons and elders as well. All three groups of ordained officers must answer affirmatively the same eight ordination questions.[26] Then each group takes one additional vow that applies to its specific function—service for deacons, governance for elders, and preaching, teaching, pastoral care, and governance for ministers of Word and Sacrament. Thus Presbyterian denominational rules that prohibit people who are homosexual from being ordained to church office apply more generally than rules in some other Protestant denominations, where only ministers are affected.

Studying Biblical Authority and Interpretation

A second report that came to the 1978 UPCUSA Assembly further focused attention on Scripture. In 1976 a Committee on Pluralism had been created to study sources of conflict in the church. The report concluded:

> Of all the factors that contribute to divisiveness in our denomination, the Committee found none is more pervasive or fundamental than the question of how the Scriptures are to be interpreted. In other words, the widely differing views on the ways the Old and New Testaments are accepted, interpreted, and applied were repeatedly cited to us by lay people, clergy, and theologians as the most prevalent cause of conflict in our denomination today. . . . It is our opinion that until our church examines this problem, our denomination will continue to be impeded in its mission and ministry, or we will spiral into a destructive schism.[27]

(This last statement proved to be predictive. Between 1979 and 1981 approximately sixty churches left the UPCUSA. Most of these churches claimed a "higher view" of biblical authority as their reason for leaving.)

The confluence of these two reports, on homosexuality and on Scripture, demonstrated great diversity in biblical interpretation within the United Presbyterian Church in the U.S.A. (the northern stream) and caused the assembly to set up a Task Force on Biblical Authority and Interpretation in 1978. I was privileged to be appointed a member of the task force, which reported to the UPCUSA in 1982.

The most important mandate of the task force was to present "recommended guidelines for a positive and not a restrictive use of Scripture in theological controversies."[28] A subcommittee of the task force carefully studied the UPCUSA *Book of Confessions* that at the time contained nine theological documents, from the Nicene Creed to confessions of the Protestant Reformation to twentieth-century theological statements. From these sources the subcommittee derived six guidelines for interpreting Scripture. When our report came to the General Assembly, the committee of delegates assigned to this report developed an appropriate seventh guideline. As you will see, I use these guidelines in chapter 4 of this book.

In 1979, the Presbyterian Church in the United States (PCUS, the southern stream of the Presbyterian church) set up a parallel study on "The Understanding and Use of the Bible in the Presbyterian Church in the United States."[29] The resulting 1983 PCUS report incorporated the seven UPCUSA guidelines but reorganized and expanded them into nine. Using extensive citations from the *Book of Confessions*, the report documented the sources of the guidelines. This report, "Presbyterian Understanding and Use of Holy Scripture," proved to be a helpful study document that was in harmony with the guidelines adopted by the UPCUSA in 1982.

In identifying guidelines for interpreting Scripture, both northern and southern denominations had anticipated the reunion in 1983. Their task forces on the Bible exchanged papers, sent visitors to one another's meetings, and produced reports that were intentionally in harmony. The two reports were later published in one booklet.[30]

The Developing Debate on Homosexuality

In 1993 gays and lesbians at the General Assembly pushed for greater recognition and acceptance. At one point, some thirty gay and lesbian people were given the opportunity to come to a microphone on the stage and state simply, "My name is _____. I am gay (or lesbian). I want to offer my service to the church." It appeared later that this peaceful and respectful demonstration influenced enough commissioners to prevent passage of a motion that would have put a prohibition against homosexual ordination into the *Book of Order*, thus making it church law. Instead, the assembly asked the church to study the matter for three years. The Evangelical Lutheran Church in America, the United Church of Christ, and the United Methodist Church all attempted similar study processes in the 1990s.[31]

Concerned with the apparent growing acceptance of gays and lesbians, some conservatives pushed back. A group of pastors of large, theologically conservative churches met and formed an organization that later grew into an umbrella group called The Coalition.[32] Its first public action was a letter, prepared at the General Assembly in Orlando, dated June 8, 1993. In the letter the group stated that it regretted the request to study the issue of the ordination of homosexuals but noted that the three-year study period could be an occasion to speak with "conviction and clarity" in support of the traditional position of the church. I joined nearly two hundred Presbyterian members, elders, deacons, missionaries, and ministers in signing the letter.

By 1996, less than 3 percent of Presbyterian congregations reported having engaged in a congregational study of the issue.[33] My experience suggests that the reason for this extremely low percentage is that many people think there is nothing to study, while others just feel uncomfortable talking about sex. The culture of most Americans, including church people, has taught them that homosexuality is sin. They feel no need to investigate further. Indeed, one highly placed Presbyterian official said in my presence, "My grandma told me it was wrong, and that's good enough for me."[34]

From 1993 to 1996 the Presbyterian Church made no effort to mount any official denominational study, and as a result there were no new official documents to which people might respond. Writers both progressive and conservative attempted to fill that vacuum. Pressure for a decision regarding the ordination of people who are homosexual began to build as the period of study was coming to an end. The 1996 Presbyterian General Assembly in Albuquerque received fifty-one overtures (proposals for legislative action) relating to the ordination to church office of gay and lesbian people.

New scholarly work often appears in response to changes in the ecclesiastical or cultural scene. Writing and publishing books takes a long time. In 1996, only a half dozen books by recognized scholars were available on this subject. Two of them, collections of essays by Presbyterian seminary faculty, *Biblical Ethics and Homosexuality: Lis-*

tening to Scripture, edited by Robert L. Brawley (Louisville, KY: West-minster John Knox, 1996), and *Homosexuality and Christian Community*, edited by Choon-Leong Seow (Louisville, KY: Westminster John Knox, 1996), were not published until just before the July 1996 assembly and thus had little influence on its decisions.

Since 1996, there has been a steady flow of new works, both in support of and opposed to ordination of people who are homosexual. Scholars representing a wide range of church backgrounds are probing for new approaches to interpreting the biblical tradition. These are live issues for scholars in the Episcopal Church, United Church of Christ, United Methodist Church, Evangelical Lutheran Church in America, American Baptist Church, and Roman Catholic Church, to name only some of those whose work I cite in this book.

In 1996, the Presbyterian Church (U.S.A.) tightened its prohibition on ordaining gay and lesbian people to church office by putting the prohibition into its *Book of Order*, thus taking it from "definitive guidance" to church law. The statement reads:

> Those who are called to office in the church are to lead a life in obedience to Scripture and in conformity to the historic confessional standards of the church. Among these standards is the requirement to live either in fidelity within the covenant of marriage between a man and a woman . . . or chastity in singleness. Persons refusing to repent of any self-acknowledged practice which the confessions call sin shall not be ordained and/or installed as deacons, elders, or ministers of the Word and Sacrament.[35]

Other denominations have enacted similar prohibitions in words that reflect their polity and tradition. The debate over homosexuality crosses all religious lines and is of critical interest in American culture. It is not going away anytime soon. We need to be as informed as possible in order to cope constructively with what affects all of us.

AN ISSUE FOR ALL OF US

I want to share with you some of what I have learned through studying this issue. I will naturally speak from my own context as a Presbyterian. Yet the issue of accepting lesbian, gay, bisexual, and transgender people as fully human and equal to other people in the eyes of God is not exclusively a Presbyterian issue. By 1991, more than one hundred statements on homosexuality had been published by forty-seven denominations and religious organizations.[36]

Because of our different forms of church government, the focus of concern may differ among denominations. For Presbyterians, the issue comes to focus in the question of ordination to church office as deacons, elders, or ministers of Word and Sacrament. For Episcopalians, the issue doesn't become critical until someone is elected a bishop. That emotional chasm was crossed for Episcopalians with the consecration of an openly gay man, the Rev. Gene Robinson, as a bishop in November 2003. For some Southern Baptists, the issue is avoidance of any appearance of approval, through ordination, employment, or granting civil benefits, to people who are homosexual. In every case, however, we are debating the fate of faithful Christian people who are members of our churches.

These church contexts have parallels in our social and political life as a nation. Now, in the first decade of the new century, debate over the issue of same-sex marriage has moved to center stage in politics and the public mind. On July 1, 2000, Vermont became the first state legally to recognize civil unions between same-sex couples. On June 26, 2003, the United States Supreme Court, in *Lawrence v. Texas*, overturned a Texas law that had criminalized sodomy only for people who are homosexual.[37] On November 18, 2003, the Massachusetts Supreme Judicial Court ruled that same-sex couples had a legal right to marry under the Massachusetts Constitution.[38]

Less than two months later, on January 20, 2004, President George W. Bush, in his State of the Union address, declared that the nation must "defend the sanctity of marriage."[39] On February 12, 2004, San Francisco mayor Gavin Newsom authorized city clerks to grant marriage licenses to same-sex couples. Following that, on February 24, 2004, President Bush called on Congress to pass an amendment to the federal Constitution defining marriage as between one man and one woman.[40] Republicans in Congress made such an amendment a top legislative priority.

In the elections in November 2004, voters in eleven states approved referenda defining marriage as between a man and a woman. Legislating who can be married, or who has the right to care for children, go to the hospital with a loved one, or enter into civil contracts as a couple, impacts all of us. Every American is aware of the issue of marriage between people of the same sex, and most recognize that we are all affected in some way by the struggle between maintaining the status quo and moving in a new direction.

Some fear that any change in attitude toward people who are homosexual would mean the end of Western civilization as we know it.[41] For example, James Dobson, of Focus on the Family, exclaims, "Barring a miracle, the family as it has been known for more than five millennia will crumble, presaging the fall of Western civilization itself."[42] For others, a new openness to LGBT people would fulfill our commitment as a nation to liberty and justice for all. Extending equal rights to people who are homosexual is a critical issue for our time. How we deal with it will determine, to a large degree, the kind of people, church, and nation we will become. This book is intended as a contribution to that important discussion.

How My Mind Changed

I have had a change of mind and heart. I had never really studied the issue of the status in the church of people who are homosexual. I opposed homosexuality reflexively—it was just what I thought Christians were supposed to do. However, studying this issue in depth for the first time brought me to a new understanding of the biblical texts and of God's will for our church. The process was both very serious and painful. I wasn't swayed by the culture or pressured by academic colleagues. I changed my mind initially by going back to the Bible and taking seriously its central message for our lives.

Since then, my new conviction has been reinforced from many sources. I have studied how the church changed its mind on other moral issues. I worked through how the church, guided by the Holy Spirit in understanding the Scriptures, reversed our prohibitions against ordination to leadership for African Americans, women, and divorced and remarried people. I saw a clear picture of a shift from a literalistic method of biblical interpretation to one that looks at Scripture through the lens of the redeeming life and ministry of Jesus Christ. I studied the principles of biblical interpretation found in our Reformed confessions and discovered a continuity through history to our best practices today. I have wrestled with the biblical texts usually cited in this discussion and come to a new understanding of them. I came to know many gay and lesbian people and have had my Christian life enriched by their profound witness to the gospel. I now know many people across all theological and ideological lines who are convinced that the Spirit of Christ is leading us, based on our best understanding of the Bible, to be consistent in allowing all of our baptized members eligibility for positions of leadership.[43] My desire is to reframe the discussion regarding people who are homosexual so that we can better understand one another, heal our divisions, and move forward together in our churches.

I did not arrive at my conclusions overnight. I do not expect you to do so, either. If you, as was the case for me, have not given this issue much attention, I hope this can be the occasion for you to investigate it more fully. If you feel sure that people who are homosexual, including Christians, should not have equal rights in the church and society, I urge you to walk with me through these chapters and at least to give yourself permission to consider what I am reporting, rather than to reject it before you begin. Jesus said to his disciples: "If you continue in my word, you are truly my disciples; and you will know the truth, and the truth will make you free" (John 8:31–32). Those disciples had to change their minds a lot of times as they learned from Jesus. I had to as well.

2

A Pattern of Misusing the Bible
to Justify Oppression

Homosexuality is not the first social issue with which the Presbyterian Church has wrestled that invokes high emotion. There have been many issues that, at the time, seemed to threaten the unity, indeed the very existence, of the church. Sabbath observance was one. Prohibition was another. In 1926 the Presbyterian Church in the United States of America General Assembly debated whether people using tobacco could be ordained to the Gospel ministry.[1]

Surely the most important social issues in the American experience to which the churches have responded are slavery/segregation and the role of women. Another potentially instructive issue, which I will take up in the next chapter, is the question of divorce and remarriage of Christian people. On each of these issues, at one point the church had near unanimity of opinion and then, over time and painfully, changed its mind to almost the exact opposite view. What can we learn from how the church dealt with these issues in the past?

Many people who are opposed to full rights of membership for people who are homosexual ignore these historical analogies. Others immediately assert that the condition of being black or female is quite different from what they consider to be willful behavior like "homosexual practice." These people read Scripture regarding slavery and women as manifesting both a diversity of views and as evidencing hints toward the position that the church now takes. At the same time, they read Scripture as uniformly and unremittingly negative regarding any form of homosexual practice.[2]

All of these arguments miss the point. The issue is not what we *now* think about slavery and women. The issue is, What did American Christians think about these subjects for more than two hundred years when the accepted view was completely different than what we now think? What did Christians believe about these issues when they believed what almost everyone in the general culture believed? How could most Christians for more than 200 years accept slavery and the subordination of women with not a hint that there was any other view in the Bible? Why did good, intelligent, devout Christian people not see what we now recognize as mitigating factors in the biblical record? Why did we change our minds? How did we change our minds? How does a church change its course? Potentially, at least, we can learn something relevant to our discussion of homosexuality by discovering the answers to these questions.

I used a sabbatical leave to study how the Presbyterian Church, north and south, had dealt with slavery/segregation and the role of women. To my amazement, the same pattern appeared in each case. What was that pattern? In each case, we accepted a pervasive societal prejudice and read it back into Scripture. We took certain Scriptures out of their context and claimed to read them literally, with tragic consequences for those to whom these verses were applied.

Let us begin with the ugly history of slavery and segregation and the way the Bible was used to justify such oppression. For more than 200 years, most Americans, including Christians, shared three assumptions regarding slavery and segregation. Most people believed that (1) the Bible records God's judgment against the sin of people of African descent from their first mention in Scripture; (2) people of African descent were inferior in moral character and incapable of rising to the level of full white, "Christian civilization"; and (3) people of African descent were willfully sinful, often sexually promiscuous and threatening, and they deserved punishment for their own acts.[3] We abhor such views now, but most Christians considered such views "natural" and "commonsense" in the past. Let us look at the evidence.

HOW THE BIBLE WAS USED TO JUSTIFY SLAVERY

The Curse on Ham and Canaan

Genesis 9:20–26 was the key text used to justify slavery:

> And Noah began to be a husbandman, and he planted a vineyard: And he drank of the wine, and was drunken; and he was uncovered within his tent. And Ham, the father of Canaan, saw the nakedness of his father, and told his two brethren without. . . . And Noah awoke from his wine, and knew what his younger son had done unto him. And he said, Cursed be Canaan; a servant of servants shall he be unto his brethren. And he said, Blessed be the LORD God of Shem; and Canaan shall be his servant.[4]

Although it is nowhere stated in the biblical text that Ham is the ancestor of the black race, the Western theological tradition so designated him. The curse placed on Ham was used as the justification for slavery. Since his son Canaan was mentioned, it was further assumed that the curse continued beyond Ham and was justly applied to all of Ham's supposedly dark-skinned descendants.

Since Ham's exact sin is not specified in the text, the interpretation of this text from the Jewish rabbis down through the ancient and medieval church and into nineteenth-century America incorporated many of the evils that human beings attribute to those who are a feared "Other." The hint of sexual misconduct always lurked in the background.

Augustine in the *City of God* provided a formulation that virtually became church doctrine. He argued that slavery was justified because of the sin of the person enslaved: "It is with justice, we believe, that the condition of slavery is the result of sin. And this is why we do not find the word 'slave' in any part of Scripture until righteous Noah branded the sin of his son with this name. It is a name, therefore, introduced by sin and not by nature."[5]

Stephen R. Haynes in his book *Noah's Curse* documents the application of Genesis 9:20–26 to the justification of slavery, the attribution of sexual sin, and the assignment of dark skin to Ham and his descendants from the Jewish rabbis, through the early church theologians, medieval Christendom, the Reformation, the early modern period, the Enlightenment, down into the nineteenth century.[6] I will therefore focus on these arguments as they were applied to defend American enslavement of Africans.

Prior to and, for some, even after the Civil War, the leading theologians of the Presbyterian Church were absolutely confident that Africans were cursed and deserved slavery for both their nature and their willful sin. These theologians were not evil people per se. They were among the best thinkers and church leaders of their day. The church wholeheartedly agreed with them.

James Henley Thornwell

James Henley Thornwell (1812–62) was just such a theologian. Thornwell was a pastor, a college president, and from 1855 until his death at age fifty the professor of didactic and polemical theology at Columbia Theological Seminary. He was also actively involved in the church. As a commissioner (delegate) to the Old School Presbyterian General Assembly in 1845, Thornwell wrote to his wife, "I have no doubts but that the Assembly, by a very large majority, will declare slavery not to be sinful, will assert that it is sanctioned by the word of God, that it is purely a civil relation with which the Church, as such, has no right to interfere, and that abolitionism is essentially wicked, disorganizing, and ruinous."[7]

In an 1850 sermon Thornwell painted a clear picture that Christians supported slavery and atheists opposed it: "The parties in this conflict are not merely Abolitionists and Slaveholders; they are Atheists, Social-ists, Communists, Red Republicans, Jacobins on the one side, and the friends of order and regulated freedom on the other. In one word, the world is the battleground—Christianity and atheism the combatants; and the progress of humanity the stake."[8]

When Presbyterians in the South separated from their northern counterparts in 1861, it was Thornwell who was asked to write a man-ifesto to the world justifying their actions. The resulting seventeen-page pamphlet was presented and adopted unanimously by the Presbyterian Church in the Confederate States of America, which met in Augusta, Georgia, on December 4, 1861.

In this manifesto, Thornwell used literalism in interpreting the Bible to justify slavery, and according to which, as we shall see, particular verses of Scripture take precedence over general principles, in contra-diction of Reformed principles of biblical interpretation.

Thornwell began by identifying a set of significant cultural assump-tions concerning the ordering of society: Man's "most solemn earthly interests, [are] his country and his race."[9] He also assumed that a class system was natural, biblical, and essential, writing, "If men had drawn their conclusions upon this subject only from the Bible, it would no more have entered into any human head to denounce slavery as a sin, than to denounce monarchy, aristocracy or poverty."[10]

According to Thornwell, human rights were subordinated to a hier-archical class system instituted by God. He assumed that Africans were descendants of Ham, by nature inferior to whites, and therefore assigned by God to the status of slaves. That status was deemed, there-fore, in the slaves' best interest, for God assigned each person a place in the hierarchy according to that person's competency to fulfill his/her duties. Referring to a slave, Thornwell asserted, "There are, no doubt, many rights which belong to other men—. . . to his master, for exam-ple—which are denied to him. But is he fit to possess them? . . . The truth is, the education of the human race for liberty and virtue is a vast Providential scheme, and God assigns to every man, by a wise and holy decree, the precise place he is to occupy in the great moral school of humanity."[11]

As Thornwell saw it, slavery was a good, necessary, and normal condition for Africans in America. "As long as that race, in its comparative degradation, co-exists, side by side, with the white, bondage is its normal condition. . . . Indeed, as we contemplate their condition in the Southern States, and contrast it with that of their fathers before them, and that of their brethren in the present day in their native land, we cannot but accept it as a gracious Providence that they have been brought in such numbers to our shores, and redeemed from the bondage of barbarism and sin."[12]

Thornwell next asked, "Is slavery, then a sin?" and began to lay the groundwork for his reply: "In answering this question, as a Church, let it be distinctly borne in mind that the only rule of judgment is the written word of God."[13] For Thornwell, the written word of God and his nineteenth-century "common sense" always agreed.

Thornwell then put two questions. First, do the Scriptures directly condemn slavery? His answer was no! "Slavery is no new thing. . . . It has not only existed for ages in the world, but it has existed, under every dispensation of the covenant of grace, in the Church of God."[14]

Second, do the Scriptures indirectly condemn slavery? Again his answer was no! He acknowledged the requirements of love and justice, writing, "Let us concede, for a moment, that the laws of love, and the condemnation of tyranny and oppression, seem logically to involve, as a result, the condemnation of slavery." But then he clarified the method of his newly articulated theory: "Yet, if slavery is afterwards expressly mentioned and treated as a lawful relation, it obviously follows, unless Scripture is to be interpreted as inconsistent with itself, that slavery is, by necessary implication, excepted."[15] An evil practice of ancient Near Eastern culture, recorded in the Bible, was thus allowed to overrule central teachings of Jesus.

Thornwell developed a form of biblical interpretation according to which the particulars of Scripture take precedence over the general principles: Unless something is expressly prohibited, it can be done. Nothing ought to be done unless there is a specific biblical warrant for it. Thus the presence or absence of particular verses took precedence over general principles, including the gospel of Christ.

From this hermeneutic, or method of interpretation, grew Thornwell's doctrine of the "spirituality of the church," which became a central principle of southern Presbyterianism for almost a century and was used to justify both slavery and segregation. Southern Presbyterians, following Thornwell, claimed that the Bible affirmed both slavery and segregation. Furthermore, they believed that the church should not be involved in dealing with such secular social problems. Judgments about both slavery and segregation were to be left to the conscience of individuals and regulation by the state.

Thornwell also offered a natural-law argument—what his common sense accepted he assumed to have the divine character of a natural law: "Whatever is universal is natural. We are willing that slavery should be tried by this standard."[16] Confidently he went on, "But what if the overwhelming majority of mankind have approved it? What if philosophers and statesmen have justified it, and the laws of all nations acknowledged it?"[17] On that argument, that all people recognized a law of nature justifying slavery, Thornwell rested his case.

Shortly before his death in 1862, Thornwell wrote to his wife, "Every day increases my sense of the value of the principles for which we are contending. If we fail, the hopes of the human race are put back for more than a century."[18] The human race, for Thornwell, was structured hierarchically. For him, the well-being of the "inferior classes," such as Africans, depended on the power and benevolence of the ruling classes, which in this case meant southern white men.

Robert Lewis Dabney

Robert Lewis Dabney was the premier theologian of the southern Presbyterian Church from 1865 until 1892. He became the chief public voice of the Presbyterian Church in the South after Thornwell's death. Dabney was a professor at Union Theological Seminary in Virginia. In 1861, Dabney had enlisted in the Confederate Army, where he served first as a chaplain and then as a major on the staff of a personal friend, General Thomas (Stonewall) Jackson.[19]

While the war was still in progress, Dabney published the first volume of *A Defense of Virginia*, which contained a one-hundred-page defense of slavery based on his interpretation of the Bible. The second volume followed in 1867. Dabney's views remained, if anything, stronger following the South's defeat.

In his two volumes, Dabney set forth a genetic argument for the inferiority of Africans, arguing that blacks and whites were different and unequal species. That implied for him that blacks were less capable than whites in most aspects of life: "But while we believe that 'God made of one blood all nations of men to dwell under the whole heavens,' we know that the African has become, according to a well-known law of natural history, by the manifold influences of the ages, a different, fixed *species* of the race, separated from the white man by traits, bodily, mental and moral almost as rigid and permanent as those of *genus*."[20]

Granting social equality to blacks, according to Dabney, was unthinkable. He believed that the North's goal was to dilute the "pure racial heritage" of the South by promoting intermarriage of blacks and whites: "Hence the offspring of an amalgamation must be a hybrid race, stamped with all the feebleness of the hybrid. And this apparently is the destiny which our conquerors have in view. If indeed they can mix the blood of the heroes of Manassas with this vile stream from the fens of Africa."[21]

Dabney brought a sexual component into the picture by alluding to "the indecent and unnatural sin of Ham." Although he did not specify what that sin might be, he did view slavery as God's "punishment of and remedy for . . . the peculiar moral degradation of a part of the race."[22]

After the Civil War, some prominent white southern pastors argued for the full equality of African Americans in the church, including ordination to the ministry. In 1867, some Presbyterian pastors in Virginia chose a moment when Dabney was absent from a meeting of the Synod to propose: "Resolved . . . that ordination to the work of the Gospel ministry is to be given to all those called of God to and qualified for that work without respect of persons."[23]

Action on the motion was delayed, and the next day Dabney was given the opportunity to speak. He saw the situation in apocalyptic terms, calling it "a moment of life and death for the church."[24] He argued passionately against ordination to the ministry for African Americans: "Every hope of the existence of Church, and of State, and of civilization itself hangs upon our arduous effort to defeat the doctrine of negro suffrage."[25]

Dabney appealed to the deep-seated fears of his white male audience: "He must be 'innocent' indeed, who does not see whither all this tends, as it is designed by our oppressors to terminate. It is (shall I pronounce the abhorred word?) to *amalgamation!*"[26] Dabney raised the specter that if African Americans were ordained, it might mean "this Negro of yours, reviewing and censuring the records of white sessions, and sitting to judge appeals brought before you by white parties, possibly by white ladies!"[27] He continued to press the possibility of a physical mixing of the races. "Do you tell me that after you have admitted this Negro thus to your debates, your votes, your pulpits, your sick and dying beds, your weddings and funerals, you will still exclude him from your parlours and tables? . . . I tell you, Sir, this doctrine, if it does not mean nothing, or if it does not mean Yankee hypocrisy, means ultimately, *amalgamation*."[28]

Dabney's speech made it clear that he was not simply reacting to the consequences of American slavery. Rather, he was proclaiming a doctrine of white racial superiority. He argued his point by appealing to what he viewed as the racial inferiority of Mexicans compared to their pure-blooded Castilian conquerors: "We have before our eyes in Mexico, the proof and illustration of the satanic wisdom of their [Yankee] plan. There we saw a splendid colonial empire, first blighted by abolition; then a frantic spirit of leveling, declaring the equality of the coloured races with the Spaniard; and last, the mixture of the Castilian blood—the grandest of all the Gothic—resulting in the mongrel rabble which is now the shame and plague of that wretched land."[29]

The motion to open ordination to all who were called of God and qualified for the work was defeated. With his speech, Dabney turned southern Presbyterian attitudes away from the possibility of racial integration to developing a system of segregated institutions for persons of color.[30]

In 1888, twenty-three years after emancipation, Dabney was still using these arguments. In an article entitled "Anti-Biblical Theories of Rights" he defended slavery. Dabney announced, "The radical social theory asserts, 'All men are born free and equal.'"[31] Dabney contended, "The honest student, then, of the New Testament can make nothing less of its teachings on this point than that domestic slavery, as defined in God's word and practiced in the manner enjoined in the Epistles, is still a lawful relation under the new dispensation as well as the old."[32]

Dabney then grounded his argument in the ancient story of Ham and Canaan: "In Genesis ix. 25–27, Ham the son of Noah, is guilty of an unfilial crime. His posterity are condemned with him and share the penalty to this day. In Ex. xx. 5, God declares that he will visit the iniquity of the fathers upon the children to the third and fourth generations."[33]

For Dabney, and the southern church, the bottom-line reason for the enslavement of people of African descent was the belief that their foreparents willfully chose to sin—and that this sinful condition and its penalties were passed on to their posterity for all time. Dabney believed that African Americans, as a "degraded race," continued to behave sinfully in the present.

To Dabney, racial purity was the ultimate value, and racial segregation was essential to protect the purity of the white race. The loss of the Civil War had already meant the loss of "the honor, the hospitality, the integrity, everything which constituted Southern character." What had to be maintained at all cost was the superiority of the white race, exemplified in the "ruling class" of white Southerners.[34]

The same arguments used to justify slavery were also used to justify the subordination of women to men.

HOW THE BIBLE WAS USED TO OPPRESS WOMEN

In the previous section, we saw vivid illustrations of how leading Christian theologians applied three nonbiblical assumptions to people of African descent. These same assumptions were also applied, by men, to women for more than two hundred years. Men argued that (1) the Bible records God's judgment against the sin of women from their first mention in Scripture (the curse on Eve); (2) women are inferior in moral character and incapable of rising to the level of full white, male Christian civilization (because women were seen as emotional and not rational); and (3) women are willfully sinful, often sexually promiscuous and threatening, and deserve punishment for their own acts (women tempt men).[35]

The Curse on Eve

The biblical text used to support this distorted view of women is in Genesis 3:1–16 (selected verses):

[1]Now the serpent was more subtle than any beast of the field which the LORD God had made. And he said unto the woman, Yea, hath God said, Ye shall not eat of every tree of the garden? . . . [6]And when the woman saw that the tree *was* . . . pleasant to the eyes, and a tree to be desired to make *one* wise, she took of the fruit thereof, and did eat, and gave also unto her husband with her; and he did eat. . . . [13]And the LORD God said unto the woman, What *is* this *that* thou hast done? And the woman said, The serpent beguiled me, and I did eat. . . . [16]Unto the woman he [God] said, I will greatly multiply thy sorrow and thy conception; in sorrow thou shalt bring forth children; and thy desire *shall be* to thy husband, and he shall rule over thee. (KJV, 1611)

The early church theologian Tertullian in the third century identified Eve as the origin of sin in a manner that has been repeated endlessly: *"You* are the Devil's gateway. *You* are the unsealer of that forbidden tree. *You* are the first deserter of the divine Law. *You* are she who persuaded him whom the Devil was not valiant enough to attack. *You* destroyed so easily God's image of man. On account of *your* desert, that is death, even the Son of God had to die."[36]

Traditional Christian culture had long portrayed woman as a sexual temptress. She was thought to have little control over her primal sexual urges. Men were constantly warned to avoid women lest they be seduced and brought down by them.[37]

In the nineteenth century, women were spoken of more gently but nonetheless kept carefully segregated from any place of power. America was shifting from an agrarian to an industrial society. As men left farms for factories, the role of women changed. Now they were not colaborers in the fields, but were given a separate sphere from men, the home, with care of children the foremost priority. In the Victorian era in America, as Betty DeBerg notes, "a relatively quick turn-around was accomplished . . . when women were transformed from sensual temptresses to 'passive partners with little sexual appetite.'"[38] The argument still was that men were rational and women were emotional and therefore unfit for positions of leadership in the public sphere.

Even after the formation in 1789 of the first Presbyterian General Assembly in America, two decades passed before women were even mentioned in the official documents of the Presbyterian Church. The first recognition came for their work in voluntary organizations for missions, benevolence, and reform. In 1811 the General Assembly made its first formal acknowledgment of the positive role of women in the church: "It has pleased God to excite pious women to combine in association for the purpose of aiding, by their voluntary contribution (to the church). . . . Benevolence is always attractive, but when dressed in female form possesses peculiar charms. . . . We hope the spirit which has animated the worthy women of whom we speak will spread [to] animate other bosoms."[39] In that same year, a Presbyterian minister, Matthew La Rue Perrine, supported the concept of women joining together in their own organizations, but in a typically patronizing manner: "Who will not delight in the sweet and heavenly work of honouring the weaker vessels, and of endeavouring to make them ornamental and useful in the house of God?"[40]

Ornamental Womanhood

From 1825 to 1855, three leading theologians of the Old School Presbyterian Church attempted to counsel pastors and church members on the role of women. Princeton Seminary professors Charles Hodge, Archibald Alexander, and Samuel Miller wrote on "ornamental womanhood" in the *Biblical Repertory and Princeton Review*, advising that women's activities should be limited to piety, sobriety, and righteousness in the wedded and maternal state, and that no female should attempt to assume any authority. The Princeton Association of Gentlemen, including the three noted above, probably got their concept of "ornamental womanhood" from a 1692 treatise of New England minister Cotton Mather, who wrote a manual for women entitled *Ornaments for the Daughters of Zion, of the Character and Happiness of a Vertuous Woman*. "Ornaments" were the essential qualities that should clothe the female character. Women should express their piety in private. The public realm was for men only. The "female sex" was to complement the male role by its radiant but silent presence.[41]

We need especially to note the impact of Charles Hodge (1797–1878), the leading figure among these "gentlemen," and a seminal influence in shaping Presbyterian attitudes toward women. Hodge was on the faculty of Princeton Seminary for fifty-eight years. He trained three thousand seminarians, more than any other American in the nineteenth century. Every year from 1835 to 1867, with one exception, Hodge wrote an influential review of the actions of the General Assembly. His three-volume *Systematic Theology*, published in 1872, remained the standard text at Princeton and was used in many American seminaries into the 1930s and some places as late as 1960.[42]

We should not be surprised to discover that Hodge, in company with most men of his day, opposed public education, abolitionism, and women's suffrage. Hodge's attitude toward women centered in his understanding of marriage and family values. As he wrote, "Marriage is a divine institution ordained by God for His glory and the happiness of men." While a husband in the marriage ceremony had to promise to be "faithful and loving," the woman had in addition to promise to be "obedient."

Hodge, in a book review, used the analogy of the necessary subordination of women to defend slavery:

If women are to be emancipated from subjection to the law which God has imposed upon them; . . . if, in studied insult to the authority of God, we are to renounce, in the marriage contract, all claim to obedience, we shall soon have a country over which the genius of Mary Wollstonecraft would delight to preside, but from which all order and all virtue would speedily be banished. . . . There is no deformity of human character from which we turn with deeper loathing than from a woman forgetful of her nature and clamorous for the vocations and rights of men.[43]

There were parallels in the southern Presbyterian Church (PCUS). Theologian Robert L. Dabney of the PCUS in 1888 developed a rationale for denying women leadership in the church. He argued that God's curse on Eve was applicable to women for all time, claiming, "'The woman was first in the transgression,' for which God laid upon Eve two penalties (Gen. iii.16), subordination to her husband and the sorrows peculiar to motherhood. The New Testament declares (I Tim. ii.11 to end) that it is right her daughters shall continue to endure these penalties to the end of the world. (See also I Peter, iii. 1–6.)"[44] Dabney was repeating here the interpretative tradition established by the rabbis and handed down through the ancient and medieval church into nineteenth-century America. At the same time he relied on the general cultural acceptance of the notion that women were cursed by "Eve's transgression." Dabney denounced women's rights, declaring, "Another hostile banner is already unfurled, and has gathered its millions of unbelievers for a new attack on God's Word."[45]

In 1891 the PCUS General Assembly denied women the right to speak, lead in prayer, and participate in public discussions in mixed assemblies. It did however affirm the propriety of women holding meetings among themselves, "for mutual edification and comfort by pious conversation and prayer."[46] The notion that women might organize themselves into larger, for example, presbyterial, groups for service was denounced by PCUS ministers and characterized as "unscriptural, un-Presbyterian, unwomanly." The declaration caused one PCUS woman to declare that the men could see "the cloven hoof of woman's suffrage under our petticoats."[47]

The PCUS General Assembly in 1916 adopted a resolution that prohibited women to "publicly expound God's Word" from the pulpit or to be ordained or licensed, reaffirming actions taken by previous General Assemblies. However, this 1916 resolution omitted any reference to women's right to speak in "promiscuous assemblies," by which they meant those with men as well as women in attendance, and recommended that "other services of women be left to the discretion of the sessions and the enlightened consciences of our Christian women themselves." Sixty-one commissioners immediately protested that the resolution went too far and might allow women to speak in the local congregation's prayer meeting, which the protestors believed would be a reversal of the position of the PCUS without scriptural warrant. The assembly answered sharply: "The Scriptures may have their authority discredited not merely by a violation of their precepts, but also by any attempt on the part of ecclesiastical courts to bind the consciences of God's people on matters of doubtful interpretation."[48] Thus early in the twentieth century, a PCUS assembly recognized that there was doubt about the correctness of the traditional interpretation of Scripture that limited women's rights in the church. However, most of the church's male ministers continued to maintain the rightness of racial segregation and the suppression of women's rights to full participation in society.

HOW CHURCH AND SOCIETY GOT IT WRONG

How could learned men like Thornwell, Dabney, and Hodge ignore basic principles of the Bible such as "Love your neighbor as yourself," and "Do unto others as you would have them do unto you"? And why were their theological arguments accepted so uncritically by others? What were the intellectual sources that allowed people to view customs of the ancient Near East as directly applicable to nineteenth-century America? How could certain theologians and pastors be so confident that they understood the Scriptures, when we now believe that they were so wrong? What were the primary philosophical and theological resources of early America that directed people to think in ways that we now can hardly comprehend?

The answers to these questions can be found by examining the influence of Scottish Common Sense philosophy and the Scholastic theology of Francis Turretin.

The dominant theological tradition in nineteenth-century America was fully developed at Princeton Seminary with its founding in 1812 and practiced until the 1940s. Archibald Alexander established the curriculum at Princeton Seminary in 1812. He recommended Scottish Common Sense philosophy as the method of biblical interpretation. He chose as the textbook in theology, not Calvin, nor any of the writers of the Westminster Confession, but the *Loci* (Topics) of the late-seventeenth-century Swiss scholastic Francis Turretin. Let us briefly examine each of these influential intellectual influences in turn.

Scottish Common Sense Philosophy

Common Sense philosophy was developed in Scotland by Thomas Reid (1710–96). It came to the College of New Jersey (which became Princeton University) when the Scot John Witherspoon became president in 1768. It was the pervasive American philosophical view when American colleges and universities were being formed, and so had a greater degree of influence than it might have had in another time or in other circumstances.[49]

According to Scottish Common Sense philosophy, people should accept what was the common sense of all humankind—that we know the reality of the world exactly as it is. Everyone can be a scientist by simple observation of the "facts" of nature. Charles Hodge, as an ardent follower of Common Sense, asserted that "the Bible is to the theologian what nature is to the man of science. It is his storehouse of facts."[50] A word in a book was to Hodge a fact, in just the same way as an object was in nature.

Furthermore, all people, in all places and at all times, think alike, at least those of the "better classes" do. Everyone can know, for example, exactly what the apostle Paul was thinking without any knowledge of ancient languages or cultures. Scottish Common Sense accepted no problems of interpretation. The truth is obvious.[51]

This essentially democratic and egalitarian philosophy fit the American mind-set. Thomas Jefferson in Paris in 1789 met a disciple of Reid's philosophy named Dugald Stewart. Enthralled, he declared Stewart one of the greatest of thinkers. The first words that Jefferson wrote in the Declaration of Independence could have come straight from Scottish Common Sense: "We hold these truths to be *self-evident* [emphasis added]."[52] The truth is obvious.

At age sixteen the bookish and precocious James Henley Thornwell, who would later support slavery by theological argument, had come across a copy of Dugald Stewart's *Elements of the Philosophy of the Human Mind*. Thornwell later said that he "felt that his fortune was now made." His biographer, Benjamin Palmer, called Scottish Common Sense philosophy "the pivot upon which his whole intellectual history subsequently hinged."[53]

Thornwell, as a Common Sense thinker, had what was, for his time, a "modern" method of proving things to be true. He employed two sets of "facts," arguing that we must "accept the facts of revelation as we accept the facts of nature."[54] Both of Thornwell's sets of facts were fit together in a rational system built in large part on the commonsense assumptions of nineteenth-century southern, white, American culture.

This rationalistic and literalistic use of Scripture allowed Thornwell to defend slavery. Since the Bible did not explicitly condemn it, and since it was practiced universally, it could be assumed to be legitimate.[55] Texts could be taken from their ancient Near Eastern cultural setting and used as universal laws in nineteenth-century America.

Francis Turretin

Francis Turretin was professor of theology in Geneva more than one hundred years after Calvin and a decade after the Westminster Confession of Faith was written in England. Turretin's theology provided a framework into which the "facts" of the Bible could be fitted. Charles Hodge declared, "So the Bible contains the truths which the theologian has to collect, authenticate, arrange, and exhibit in their internal relation to one another."[56] Scottish Common Sense philosophy enabled the theologian confidently to understand the "natural" meaning of the "facts" he observed in nature or read in the Bible. Turretin's theology provided the framework in which these "facts" could be properly arranged.

By emphasizing "facts" over faith and using natural law to organize those "facts," Turretin and his followers created a method that allowed social prejudice to receive biblical sanction. If slavery was mentioned in the Bible and if slavery had occurred throughout history, they therefore assumed that slavery must be supported by the Bible and sanctioned by God.

Whatever theory of interpretation people use powerfully affects how they understand Scripture. Common Sense philosophy and Turretin's theology allowed seemingly good, intelligent, devout people to ignore the basic principles and lessons of Scripture and to brutalize other human beings by enslaving them. The combination of Common Sense and Turretin enabled people to use the Bible to claim divine justification for common cultural prejudices.

The theologians at Princeton and their graduates, who were spread all over nineteenth-century America, had what for them was a method of certain knowledge. Ascertain the "facts" in nature and Scripture by Scottish Common Sense philosophy, and arrange them in Turretin's theological system. Southern theologians adopted the same philosophical and theological methods as their northern counterparts. Many persisted in their antiabolitionist and proslavery views even after the end of the Civil War.

ABOLITIONISM AND THE WHOLE BIBLE

While Thornwell, Dabney, and Hodge confidently proclaimed that the Bible mandated such things as slavery, racial hierarchy, and oppression of women, other groups of Americans read the Bible and came away with a different view. For example, Christian abolitionists saw slavery as a "stain on the character of American Christianity."[57]

Abolitionists appealed to the Bible as a whole and gave priority to its central themes, especially that Jesus was the central figure in Scripture and that he always displayed love, which required remedying injustice for those who were oppressed.[58] John Rankin, a leading Presbyterian abolitionist, summarized this argument: "The whole Bible is opposed to slavery. The sacred volume is one grand scheme of benevolence. Beams of love and mercy emanate from every page, while the voice of justice denounces the oppressor, and speaks to his awful doom."[59]

Christian abolitionists had been influenced by the Great Awakening, an evangelical revival that swept across the country in the opening decades of the nineteenth century. Individuals were called on to repent of their personal sins and to work for the moral improvement of the community.

Abolitionists were also influenced by postmillennialism, the idea that Christ would return to earth and reign after an ideal, moral society had been established.[60] This idea offered a powerful incentive to Christian abolitionists to rid the world of the unchristian blot on society of African enslavement in America. By working to end slavery, abolitionists were preparing the way for Christ's return to earth.

Enslaved Africans, although not formally educated, knew that the Bible, properly understood, did not sanction oppression. Abolitionists within the larger denominations, following the principle "no fellowship with slavery," often withdrew to form new antislavery churches.[61] Among these were the Wesleyan and Free Methodist churches and several black denominations such as the African Methodist Episcopal and

African Methodist Episcopal Zion. Some smaller denominations like the Quakers, the United Brethren, and the Covenanters had been consistently antislavery.

Yet other abolitionists grew tired of the mainstream churches' failure to condemn slavery. For example, a leading New England abolitionist, William Lloyd Garrison, was deeply disappointed when his own pastor, Lyman Beecher, refused to endorse immediate emancipation of the slaves, calling the idea "commendable, but misguided."[62] Garrison and some of his followers reacted by rejecting the authority of the clergy and the divine inspiration of the Bible.[63]

We now know, of course, that the Christian abolitionists got it right. Their method of biblical interpretation looked at the Bible as a whole and gave priority to its central themes, especially that Jesus was the central figure in Scripture and the one we should seek to emulate. Their method of biblical interpretation anticipated the adoption a century later of a Christ-centered method of biblical interpretation by the "Christian mainstream."

CONCLUSION

When we study the church's historical positions on race and the role of women, a clear pattern emerges: In each case, leaders in the church claimed that (1) the Bible records God's judgment against the sin of people of African descent and women from their first mention in Scripture; (2) people of African descent and women are somehow inferior in moral character and incapable of rising to the level of full white male, "Christian civilization"; and (3) people of African descent and women are willfully sinful, often sexually promiscuous and threatening, and deserve punishment for their own acts.

How did they get it so wrong? They followed Scottish Common Sense philosophy and the theology of Francis Turretin, rather than putting their trust in the teachings of Jesus Christ.

What is instructive about these examples is that a similar pattern is emerging today regarding people who are homosexual. Those who oppose homosexuality claim that (1) the Bible records God's judgment against the sin of homosexuality from its first mention in Scripture; (2) people who are homosexual are somehow inferior in moral character and incapable of rising to the level of full heterosexual "Christian civilization"; and (3) people who are homosexual are willfully sinful, often sexually promiscuous and threatening, and deserve punishment for their own acts.

The church is once again repeating the mistakes of the past. And, as I will show in subsequent chapters, the reason why many people fail to apply Jesus' gospel to the issue of homosexuality is that they are once again using a "commonsense" method of biblical interpretation and are following the lead of fundamentalist theologians whose methods are similar to those of Turretin.

We are thankful that most Christians no longer believe in racial and gender hierarchy. Why? What changed our minds? How was the church able to change? In the next chapter we will review the way in which a new, Christ-centered approach to biblical interpretation carried forth the best insights of the dissenting abolitionists and expanded and applied them. This christological approach, which used the whole Bible, with Jesus as its central character and interpreter, enabled the church to change its mind and heart on issues of race and women. Let us examine this new approach.

3

A Breakthrough in Understanding the Word of God

HOW THE CHURCH CHANGED ITS MIND

How was the church able to change its mind on racial segregation and women's rights? White men in the mainstream churches had great power to claim that their experience was normative for all. After all, they held all the positions of power in church and in state. They interpreted reality according to their experience of being in a privileged position in society. That gave them the freedom to label others as inferior. Through their complete domination of society, they were able to pass off their biases as "common sense."

By the middle of the nineteenth century, the mainstream U.S. Protestant consensus on interpretation of the Bible fragmented.[1] Two events were crucial. One was the Civil War, in which Christians were divided north and south on biblical interpretation regarding slavery. The other was the publication of Darwin's *The Origin of Species* in 1859. Responses to Darwin's theory of evolution tended to separate people within the mainstream Protestant churches into two camps.

Those who came to be called modernists felt obliged to embrace the new science. They believed that the human race was moving toward God, Scripture represented the evolving experience of humankind, and creeds were only a human attempt to express religious experience.

In contrast, others, who came to be called fundamentalists, believed that God had created the world once and for all in a certain way, the Bible contained God's literal words as recorded by humans, and creeds represented a systematic presentation of doctrinal truths.[2]

Modernists and fundamentalists in these churches fought each other for decades over the meaning of Scripture. Modernists denied the authenticity of certain parts of the Bible, while fundamentalists insisted that the entire Bible, in the original manuscripts, was inerrant. By this, fundamentalists meant that God was the author of Scripture, and therefore whatever the Bible said could be applied directly to present-day circumstances, overriding science if science conflicted with their own views of what was considered biblical. Modernists, in frustration, appealed to the scientific method of observation and experimentation as having greater authority for modern people.

The two dueling parties came to a stalemate in what was called the fundamentalist-modernist controversy of the early twentieth century. Fundamentalists in the Presbyterian Church had developed, and persuaded the denomination to adopt, a list of five "essential and necessary doctrines" that all candidates for ministry had to accept: (1) the inerrancy of Scripture, (2) Jesus' virgin birth, (3) his vicarious substitutionary atonement on the cross, (4) his bodily resurrection, and (5) the power of Jesus' mighty miracles.[3] Presbyterian General Assemblies in 1910, 1916, and 1923 made acceptance of the fundamentalists' five "essential and necessary doctrines" mandatory for all candidates for ordination to the ministry.

The decades-long fundamentalist-modernist conflict in the Presbyterian Church came to a crisis point at the General Assembly in 1925, when it appeared that the church might split. In response, the Moderator, Charles Erdman, left the chair[4] and moved that a special commission be formed to discern the "causes of unrest" in the church. The leading spokespersons for the two competing parties both seconded the motion.

In 1927, this powerful commission proposed that no one, including the General Assembly, could create a short list of essential doctrines and demand adherence to them. The church's doctrine, the committee said, was to be found in its confessional statements, at that time the Westminster Confession of Faith and the Larger and Shorter Catechisms. If a person had a "scruple," or disagreement, it was up to the regional governing body, the presbytery, to adjudicate that conflict through the judicial process.[5]

The 1927 General Assembly overwhelmingly accepted the report of its commission. Affirmation of the five "essentials," including the inerrancy of the Bible, was no longer required for ordination.[6] However, the General Assembly never declared that the "essentials" were wrong and inconsistent with the Reformed tradition. Thus, an ambiguity resulted that has allowed some people ever since to appeal to these "fundamentals" as if they were authoritative and had only been bypassed by a decision on church government.

The opposite is actually true. The church at that time had a strong theological center. For example, in 1924 a large group of pastors signed a document called the Auburn Affirmation.[7] These influential church leaders included people of various persuasions regarding the "essentials." However, they all opposed the imposition of the five "essential and necessary doctrines" as church law. The signers of the Auburn Affirmation said they were able to distinguish between the "facts" of the Christian faith, to which they all adhered, and the "theories" embodied in the "essentials," about which they could disagree.[8]

Theology Guides Biblical Interpretation

Just as the fundamentalist-modernist controversy was concluding in the 1930s, a fresh theological breeze blew in from Europe. This theological movement broke the stalemate of the fundamentalist-modernist controversy and enabled the church to move forward in a renewed commitment to Christ.

The movement was variously called Neo-Calvinism, Neo-Protestantism, and Neo-Reformation theology.[9] The most familiar and most often used name was neo-orthodoxy. It was "neo" because it was a *new* approach that was not dependent on either fundamentalism or its modernist opponents. It was "orthodox" in that it turned people's attention to Jesus Christ as revealed in Scripture and depended on the work of the Holy Spirit to make the biblical message alive through preaching. Neo-orthodoxy focused on the traditional doctrines of the Christian faith, but looked at them afresh in the light of current scholarship.

The names of Swiss neo-orthodox theologians Karl Barth and Emil Brunner became common in American theological schools in the 1940s and 1950s.[10] These Neo-Reformation theologians encouraged people to study the sources of the Protestant movement, especially Calvin and Luther. Reading Reformation theologians, and the contemporary theologians who had been influenced by them, produced a new kind of theology that had reverence for the Bible and used all the tools of contemporary scholarship to understand it.

World War I, which had involved some of the most "civilized" countries in Europe, dashed the existing liberal optimism about human nature. Human effort, it appeared, was not bringing in God's kingdom, nor was human reason proving adequate to know God. Neo-orthodoxy's defining insight, taken from the Danish philosopher Søren Kierkegaard, was that people and God are known by personal encounter, not by rational analysis.[11] The revelation of God comes *not* in an inspired book, but in the person of Jesus Christ, who is God incarnate.[12] The Bible is a witness to Christ. Thus, this approach to biblical interpretation was called "christological." In illustration of this, a print of Mattheus Grünewald's Isenheim altarpiece from Colmar, France, hung over Barth's desk in Basel, Switzerland. In it, John the Baptist, symbolizing the role of the Bible, stands pointing a long, bony finger at Christ on the cross. Because the Bible, like John the Baptist, points away from itself to Christ, the issue of possible mistakes in the Bible was irrelevant to Barth. According to him, by the action of the Holy Spirit, through preaching, the Bible *becomes* the word of God to people of faith.

Neither modernism nor fundamentalism survived World War II intact. In World War II, modern science was again used to produce weapons that killed millions. Fascism in Europe demonstrated the danger of a rigid worldview that did not allow for diversity of opinions. People in Europe and America were ready for new ways to think about and experience God. Theologians in the mainstream churches welcomed the message of neo-orthodoxy. People were able to focus on Christ, to whom Scripture pointed, and at the same time were encouraged to use all the tools of scholarship to interpret the Bible.

Neo-orthodoxy offered a new approach to theology and biblical studies.[13] In biblical studies this shift in thinking was called the "biblical theology movement."[14] The difference between neo-orthodoxy and "biblical theology" was primarily in the academic disciplines practiced by their adherents. Neo-orthodoxy was the name applied to the views of systematic theologians and historians of doctrine. Scholars who studied the text of the Old Testament and/or the New Testament were part of the biblical theology movement.[15] The biblical scholars shared with the theologians both a concentration on the divine self-disclosure and a recognition of the very human element involved in recording historical events. Both stressed the uniqueness of biblical religion against the ancient Near Eastern background. They were open to all of the scientific biblical scholarship, while also insisting on one overarching theology proclaimed in the Bible.[16]

Biblical scholars influenced by neo-orthodoxy no longer debated reliable authority versus human authorship, as had been the case in the fundamentalist-modernist controversy. They did not view the Bible as a collection of inerrant facts, but as a very human document that reliably recorded a very real encounter of real people with a real God.[17] As biblical scholar Eugene March noted, "It seems clear in retrospect that the main concern among biblical theologians of the '40s and '50s was to declare the validity of biblical authority in such a way as to steer clear of the mistakes of both Liberalism and Fundamentalism."[18] Common Sense philosophy and the rationalism of Turretin, which had dominated theology in the preceding era, were now replaced by a more Christ-centered method of biblical interpretation.[19]

Some fundamentalists reacted strongly against the rise of a new theological perspective. In 1940, a Charlotte, North Carolina, businessman named Tom Glasgow attacked E. T. Thompson, a professor at Union Theological Seminary, for failing to maintain what Glasgow considered the traditional interpretation of the faith. Glasgow believed that the theology of Charles Hodge and B. B. Warfield, professors at Princeton in the nineteenth and early twentieth centuries, should remain normative for the church. Regarding the inspiration of the Bible, Glasgow agreed with the Old Princeton position that the Bible was "an oracular Book, as the Word of God, in such a sense that whatever it says, God says."[20]

Since Glasgow refused to press formal charges of heresy in the church courts, Thompson was given no opportunity to defend himself; so Thompson asked his presbytery to examine him. The presbytery did so and found Thompson not guilty of the charges alleged against him. This judgment was precedent-setting in that it specifically denied that a theological professor had to accept the interpretation of the confessions made by his predecessors.[21] This decision marked the beginning of a gradual sea change in the southern Presbyterian Church in its attitude toward both biblical inerrancy and the Old Princeton interpretation of the Westminster Confession.

SOCIAL CHANGE

The influence of neo-orthodoxy and the biblical theology movement enabled the church to take a fresh look at oppressive social institutions. Theologians, and the pastors whom they had taught, no longer were bound by Turretin's theology or Scottish Common Sense philosophy. Instead of proof-texting, that is, taking particular verses out of their context and treating them as universal laws, they looked at the totality of the Bible in its cultural context. They began with Jesus Christ. Each passage of the Bible was viewed through the lens of Jesus' redemptive life and ministry. From that starting point, and stimulated by changes in American society, church leaders began to rethink controversial social issues.

A New Look at Race

Social and cultural events soon provided an occasion for the new biblical understandings of social issues to be put into practice. When, on May 17, 1954, the United States Supreme Court, in *Brown versus Board of Education,* ordered desegregation of the public schools, the southern Presbyterian Church (PCUS) was ready. On May 27, its General Assembly affirmed the principle of the Supreme Court's decision and urged all members to support those charged with implementing it.[22] The assembly further adopted the recommendation of its Council of Christian Relations "that the General Assembly affirm that enforced segregation of the races is discrimination which is out of harmony with Christian theology and ethics." The assembly urged the church at all governing body levels, from the local session to the General Assembly, to be open to people of all races.[23]

The PCUS was the first major church body in the United States to embrace the Supreme Court decision. Many believed that the PCUS General Assembly was ready to condemn racial segregation even if the court had not spoken.[24]

Then, in 1956, a PCUS report on the biblical justification for the equality of women also clearly rejected the biblical justification of slavery. The committee, in its final statement on the principles of biblical interpretation, wrote:

> Coming closer to our own day, we no longer argue that human slavery is justified by the Bible, and in accord with God's will. Some of our grandfathers did so argue, declaring that slavery was God's permanent institution. Through the illumination of the Holy Spirit, we have come to a different understanding on this subject. We see that the Bible passages they quoted were not kept by them in the larger context of the Bible as a whole.[25]

This statement was a direct repudiation of Thornwell's 1861 theory that the particular text should have priority over the general principle. New methods of biblical interpretation focused on the Bible as a whole. The statement understood the Bible's central themes to be salvation and service, with the life and ministry of Christ as the central interpretive principle.

A New Look at the Role of Women

One of the best illustrations of the application of the new principles of biblical and confessional interpretation is found in the 1956 PCUS report on the status of women. Women had been ordained as elders since 1930 in the northern Presbyterian Church, and as ministers since 1956. In that year, their southern cousins were still struggling with ordination of women to office in the church. A committee dealing with the status of women developed an approach based on the denomination's confessional stance. They believed that a solution could be found in accord with the Westminster Confession of Faith's principle that "the infallible rule of interpretation of Scripture, is the Scripture itself; and therefore, when there is a question about the true and full sense of any scripture (which is not manifold, but one), it may be searched and known by other places that speak more clearly."[26]

The committee applied this principle by saying, "We find it clearly and unmistakably stated in Scripture that God endowed at least some women for leadership among His [sic] people in Bible days. Therefore, we conclude that what God has done and has promised to do (Acts 2:17) may be done in our own day."[27]

Thus, Presbyterians in the 1950s reached back to the 1640s and drew from the Westminster Confession a principle that enabled them to apply the gospel to a new situation. Empowered with this more expansive understanding of God's will, southern Presbyterians made ordination to all offices of the church available to women and in 1965 ordained their first woman minister of Word and Sacrament.

A New Look at Divorce and Remarriage

The PCUSA and the PCUS reflected the ambivalence of both church members and ministers by, beginning in 1926, alternately (1) attempting to rigidify church law by prohibiting any divorce and then (2) expanding the exception clauses that allowed for divorce and remarriage. Over the next thirty years, the Presbyterian churches cautiously felt their way toward a new understanding of the meaning of marriage, which involved applying the new christological interpretation of Scripture that had taken hold after World War II.

Today's more pastoral attitude toward divorce and remarriage began when the Presbytery of Dubuque in 1929 reacted against the attempt of the previous General Assembly to eliminate all exceptions and forbid divorce in every instance. The Dubuque overture asserted that a strict legalism would "not solve the problem, but may cause hardship and injustice."[28]

In 1930 the PCUSA General Assembly received a thorough study of divorce and remarriage in the church. The Commission on Marriage, Divorce, and Remarriage took a spiritual, rather than legalistic, approach to both Scripture and the confessions. Jesus' attitude toward divorce, expressed in Matthew 19:3–13 and Mark 10:2–12, was presented as an ideal toward which young people should strive, for it embodied "the meaning and values of marriage."[29]

The commission's report did not ask for change in the existing standards, which recognized only two grounds for divorce—adultery or irremediable desertion—and allowed remarriage after divorce only for the innocent party in either case. It did, however, offer an expanded, spiritual understanding and application of the Westminster Confession and Catechisms: "Beyond the fact that the marriage relation is terminated by death, is the further fact that it may be destroyed by either party to the agreement proving unfaithful to the vows taken."[30] The commission concluded: "Anything that kills love and deals death to the spirit of the union is infidelity," citing the biblical phrase, "The letter killeth; but the spirit giveth life."[31] With this interpretation, the report introduced the concept of a moral equivalent of death to justify divorce.

Some twenty years later, after World War II, in 1952, the report of a Special Committee on Proposed Changes in the Confession of Faith stated that "remarriage after a divorce granted on grounds explicitly stated in Scripture or implicit in the gospel of Christ may be sanctioned in keeping with his redemptive gospel."[32] This provision called for revisions to the Westminster Confession of Faith, which were approved by the presbyteries and adopted by the PCUSA General Assembly in 1953. The changes allowed divorce and remarriage on these theological grounds.

During the same period the southern stream was engaged in a parallel struggle. In a 1929 attempt by a PCUS committee to eliminate "desertion" as a ground for divorce, the concept of moral equivalency was introduced. Dr. Charles E. Diehl, then president of Southwestern

College in Memphis, argued, "We recognize the violation of the Seventh Commandment *or its moral equivalent* [emphasis added] as the only ground for divorce," and he suggested that desertion, "and perhaps some other causes, constitute what may be termed 'moral equivalent.'"[33]

In the aftermath of World War II, in 1945, the PCUS had received an overture asking the church to conduct a careful study of church laws on grounds for divorce and the procedure for remarriage.[34] In 1950, the Council of Christian Relations submitted its initial report on "Divorce and Remarriage." The report commented on biblical interpretation in a way that reflected the new PCUS approach, taken since World War II: "Any attempt to build a Christian doctrine of marriage and divorce on a few isolated 'proof-texts' will always fail for at least two reasons: (a) the usual proof-texts are open to more than one interpretation, and (b) they fail to give due weight to the implications of Jesus' total teaching with respect to man's [*sic*] personal responsibilities and social relationships."[35]

The report further noted that "infidelity can be spiritual as well as physical and it manifests itself in many forms. It is therefore unrealistic to hold that divorce is permissible only when marriage has been broken by one of two forms of infidelity, both of which are physical acts."[36] It concluded, "Wherever free Protestant churches are studying this problem today in the light of Jesus' total teachings on human relations, the trend is unmistakably away from a strictly legalistic approach to one more finely and fundamentally spiritual."[37]

The PCUS Council of Christian Relations reported to the 1952 assembly that limiting grounds for remarriage after divorce to adultery and desertion "may be doing grave injustice to a multitude of injured people who are victims of forces they could not control." In a spirit of honesty it observed that "in practice they [PCUS ministers] are ignoring the letter of our Church's law in order, as they see it, to be true to the spirit and total teachings of our Lord, to the practical realities of life and to the demands of Christian justice."[38]

In 1959, after fourteen years of debate within the church, the PCUS amended the Westminster Confession of Faith regarding divorce. The presbyteries overwhelmingly approved new wording that, although hedged with qualifiers and footnoted with numerous Scripture references,[39] was similar to the PCUSA revised section of the Westminster Confession: "The remarriage of divorced persons may be sanctioned by the Church in keeping with the redemptive Gospel of Christ, when sufficient penitence for sin and failure is evident, and a firm purpose of and endeavor after Christian marriage is manifested."[40]

In the 1950s, both branches of American Presbyterianism took the remarkable step of revising the Westminster Confession of Faith on divorce and remarriage. In both cases, Presbyterians had shifted their emphasis from a public norm to the good of the people involved. The primary purpose of marriage was no longer the benefit of society but the benefit of the people entering the marriage covenant.[41]

The Presbyterian denominations had turned away from what they considered a legalistic approach to marriage and divorce based on a literal interpretation of biblical and confessional texts. Now they cited the spirit and totality of Jesus' teaching as mandating a pastoral approach that allowed exceptions to previous rules. This was solidified by changes made in the Confession of Faith.

How is this relevant to granting equality to gay and lesbian members of our churches? Jesus' words that divorce is equivalent to adultery are among the clearest statements on a moral issue in Scripture. The Westminster Confession was clear as well, although it did set a precedent for allowing exceptions in the case of adultery or desertion. If we were to take literally Jesus' teaching on divorce, we would still not be accepting divorced and remarried people as office bearers in the church. Yet church law now asks that we take literally less clear statements regarding homosexual behavior. It is a double standard: current church law permits a pastoral approach concerning marriage and divorce for people who are heterosexual and mandates a legalistic approach toward people who are homosexual.

We can learn from the way in which the Presbyterian churches, north and south, slowly shifted from legalistic proof-texting to looking at Scripture through the lens of Jesus' life and ministry. Jesus did not set forth immutable laws to break people. Rather, he set forth an ideal toward which we all should strive—lifelong faithfulness in married relationships. That ideal could apply to gay or lesbian couples as well as to heterosexual couples.[42]

A Personal Note

In 1952–53, I was a sophomore at the University of Nebraska. Debate was my principal extracurricular activity. That year the debate coaches suggested that I also try competition in oratory. As a young Christian I was very concerned with divorce and decided to work on that topic for my oration. As a member of the United Presbyterian Church of North America, I was unaware of the fierce debate concerning divorce and remarriage going on at that time in the PCUSA and PCUS denominations. To get experience that I could draw on, I attended divorce court on the day before Christmas 1952. I expected to see some fiery emotional outbursts. Instead, I was struck with how quickly and easily divorce could take place. As I said in the oration, "I was startled to realize that a partnership which was supposed to last for life, had been terminated while a choir was singing three verses of a Christmas hymn."[43]

I took a very hard line on divorce in that oration. I asserted, "To protect people against themselves, we must make the laws so strict that divorce is almost impossible. . . . For those couples who no longer wished to live together, but whose circumstances were not exceptional, there would be legal separation."[44]

I see things differently now. The northern and southern Presbyterian denominations learned something in the 1950s. I have learned the same lessons since. Jesus' statements in Matthew 19 and Mark 10 are not an inflexible law intended to separate sinners from the righteous. Instead, Jesus is showing us an ideal that offers hope to all of us. I count many divorced people and remarried Christian couples as my friends. I thank God for who they are and for the wholeness they have experienced. It is helpful and humbling to realize that I can change my mind on something about which I was once so sure.

Consolidating the Theological Consensus in a Confession

The theological consensus of neo-orthodoxy and the biblical theology movement in the 1940s, 1950s, and 1960s enabled the Presbyterian denominations for the first time in two hundred years to reject discrimination against African Americans and women and to deal more personally and pastorally with divorced and remarried people. The churches then moved to consolidate that consensus on biblical interpretation by embodying it in a confession of faith.

The process, for Presbyterians in the North, began in 1956, when the Presbytery of Amarillo (PCUSA) overtured the General Assembly, asking that the Westminster Shorter Catechism be rewritten in contemporary language. An assembly-appointed committee, after a year of reflection, proposed an alternative: That a committee be named to draft "a brief contemporary statement of faith to be included in the Constitution after the union is consummated in 1958." (This 1958 union was of the Presbyterian Church in the U.S.A. [PCUSA] and the United Presbyterian Church of North America [UPCNA]. The resulting church was named the United Presbyterian Church in the United States of America [UPCUSA].)

The rationale for this new statement of faith was that "it should bring to all members of our Church some sense of participation in the thrilling revival of theology." That "thrilling revival" was, of course, the neo-orthodox and biblical theology movement consensus that had begun to develop in the 1940s and 1950s.[45]

In 1958 the uniting General Assembly named nine men to a Committee on a Brief Contemporary Statement of Faith. Edward A. Dowey Jr. of Princeton Theological Seminary was appointed the chair. Over the next four years, eleven members, including one woman, ruling elder Mrs. E. Harris Harbison, were added to the committee as some of the original members dropped out.[46] Most of the members of the committee had been shaped by the return to Reformation roots fostered by the neo-orthodox revival of the '40s and '50s.

For chairman Dowey and most of the committee, as for Barth, what mattered was revelation in the person, Jesus Christ. Neo-orthodoxy, they believed, would rescue the Scriptures from the Old Princeton doctrine of the inerrancy of the Bible.

In 1966 a revision committee was appointed at the General Assembly, which had the power to amend the new confession of faith submitted in 1965. A compromise was reached between those on the original drafting committee, who wanted to speak only of Jesus Christ as the Word of God, and those on the revision committee, who insisted on also speaking of Scripture as the Word of God. The final draft on Scripture in the resulting Confession of 1967 reads, "The one sufficient revelation of God is Jesus Christ, the Word of God incarnate, to whom the Holy Spirit bears unique and authoritative witness through the Holy Scriptures, which are received and obeyed as the word of God written." A capital *W* was used when Christ was referred to as the Word of God, a lowercase *w* for word of God in reference to Scripture.[47] The compromise held, and the Confession was adopted.

The Social Effects of the Confession of 1967

In the Confession of 1967 a christological interpretation of Scripture was the basis of a commitment to racial reconciliation. The authors of the Confession of 1967 believed that God's reconciling work in Jesus Christ was the heart of the gospel in any age and that the church of that generation was especially called to the ministry of reconciliation.[48] Referring to racial discrimination, the Confession of 1967 said, "God has created the people of the earth to be one universal family. In his reconciling love, he overcomes the barriers between brothers [sic] and breaks down every form of discrimination based on racial or ethnic difference, real or imaginary. . . . Therefore, the church labors for the abolition of all racial discrimination and ministers to those injured by it."[49]

This new christological hermeneutic also took root in the South. In 1976 the PCUS General Assembly adopted "A Declaration of Faith" that said, "When we encounter apparent tensions and conflicts in what Scripture teaches us to believe and do, the final appeal must be to the authority of Christ."[50] On race, the declaration said, "The antagonisms between races, nations and neighbors, . . . are manifestations of our sin against God."[51] A christological interpretation of Scripture finally overcame the Presbyterian Church's silence on the sin of slavery and racial segregation.

Theological Backlash: Women's Ordination

By 1965, women in the Presbyterian Church, both north and south, had been admitted to all of the offices of the church—deacon, elder, and minister of Word and Sacrament. Yet pockets of resistance to women's leadership remained. When the United Presbyterian Church of North America united with the Presbyterian Church in the U.S.A. in 1958, one very large issue was never publicly discussed and was left unresolved: The UPCNA did not ordain women as either elders or ministers.

This unresolved issue erupted in the 1970s in a celebrated case involving Walter Wynn Kenyon, a senior at Pittsburgh Seminary. Kenyon was one of a group of students who were staunch followers of Professor John H. Gerstner Jr., who taught a form of Calvinism that was an extension of the Old Princeton theology of Charles Hodge and B. B. Warfield. One of the convictions of this group was that the Bible "clearly teaches women should be subordinate ('silent') in the official teaching and ruling ministry of the Christian Church."[52]

Gerstner's followers, including Kenyon, contended that the matter of women's ordination was a nonessential detail of the Presbyterian system of doctrine and governance. Therefore they felt free, in the language of the Adopting Act of 1729, to "scruple" against, or disagree with, this point and yet be ministers in good standing in the denomination.[53] In that spirit, Kenyon made clear to the Candidates and Credentials Committee of Pittsburgh Presbytery that he believed that the Bible forbade the ordination of women.

The Candidates and Credentials Committee recommended against ordaining Kenyon because he could not affirmatively answer question five (of the eight) ordination questions: "Do you endorse our Church's government, and will you honor its discipline? Will you be a friend among your comrades in ministry, working with them, subject to the ordering of God's word and Spirit?"[54]

Kenyon, Gerstner, and several colleagues wrote a pamphlet explaining and defending their position:

> Our purpose is simply to demonstrate what we believe to be the real issue: Biblical authority. . . . The Scriptures consistently teach that in the church and in the home women are placed in a subordinate position. No one can read the Bible and not see authority "writ large" therein. Everywhere we meet a chain of command. . . . Everyone who loves and fears God should acknowledge that the Word of God authoritatively establishes authority—male authority—in the church.[55]

The presbytery overruled its committee and recommended ordination for Kenyon. That decision was appealed to the synod, which then reversed the presbytery and recommended that Kenyon not be ordained. In turn, the synod's ruling was appealed to the Permanent Judicial Commission (PJC) of the General Assembly, which upheld the synod's decision not to ordain Kenyon.

In its 1974 decision, the Permanent Judicial Commission in the Kenyon Case cited the Confession of 1967. The PJC decision stated that the equality of women and men is an essential of Presbyterian theological beliefs: "The question of the importance of our belief in the equality of all people before God is thus essential to the disposition of this case. It is evident from our Church's confessional standards that the Church believes the Spirit of God has led us into new understandings of this equality before God."[56]

This decision, affirming the equality of women and men in church leadership, was based on the insight of the Confession of 1967 concerning the equality of people of all races. The PJC quoted the Confession of 1967: "Congregations, individuals, or groups of Christians who exclude, dominate, or patronize their fellowmen [sic], however subtly, resist the Spirit of God and bring contempt on the faith which they profess."[57] The PJC followed that citation by declaring, "The

UPCUSA, in obedience to Jesus Christ, under the authority of Scripture (and guided by its confessions) has now developed its understanding of the equality of all people (both male and female) before God."[58] Here we see the method of biblical interpretation that took hold in the 1940s and was embodied in the Confession of 1967 enabling the church to reject the older literalist method of interpreting Scripture.

A Brief Statement of Faith on Women

In 1991 the equality of women and men was given explicit confessional status. The Articles of Agreement that governed the 1983 reunion of the PCUS with the UPCUSA mandated that the reuniting assembly of PC(USA) instruct its Moderator to appoint a committee "representing diversities of points of view and groups within the reunited Church to prepare a Brief Statement of the Reformed Faith for possible inclusion in *The Book of Confessions*."[59]

This committee was unique in the history of Reformed creedal formation in two ways. First, the group was chosen specifically for its diversity and then expected to write a document evoking unity. Second, it was the first time that a significant number of women were members of a committee engaged in preparing a Reformed confessional document.

Most importantly, for the first time in Reformed creedal history, women were declared equal to men and were affirmed to be called to all of the ministries of the church. In the PC(USA) *Book of Confessions*, A Brief Statement of Faith made explicit the equality of all people: "In sovereign love God created the world good and makes everyone equally in God's image, male and female, of every race and people, to live as one community."[60] A Brief Statement of Faith also provided clear confessional warrant for the ordination of women, declaring that the Spirit "calls women and men to all the ministries of the Church."[61]

For some, the confession's most startling innovation was its use of feminine as well as masculine language to refer to God: "Loving us still, God makes us heirs with Christ of the covenant. Like a mother who will not forsake her nursing child, like a father who runs to welcome the prodigal home, God is faithful still."[62] The statements comparing God to a mother and a father are taken directly from the biblical text; mother is from Isaiah 49:15–16, father from Luke 15:11–32.

This use of metaphorical language also sharply contrasts with a naive literalism in the use of biblical language. The writers of A Brief Statement of Faith knew that God is neither male nor female. They acknowledged that we use human illustrations to point beyond ourselves to the reality of a personal God whose love exceeds that of our best human examples.[63]

LEARNING FROM OUR THEOLOGICAL, SOCIAL, AND CONFESSIONAL PAST

Guided by neo-orthodoxy in the 1940s and '50s, the church began to deal responsibly with social issues. Under the influence of a Christ-centered understanding of Scripture, the church spoke out against racial segregation, ordained women, and allowed divorced and remarried people to have full rights of church membership.

Now, however, faced with the issue of homosexuality, many churches are repeating the mistakes of the past. When churches meet a new situation where oppressed people are questioning the cultural status quo, many people instinctively become defensive and retreat. To justify their inability to cope with cultural change, they turn to the Bible and proof-text, that is, they take verses out of the context of the whole and make universal laws of them. Instead of reading the Bible through the lens of Jesus' life and ministry, many have again tried to make the Bible a law book, which they then apply selectively, only to those with whom they disagree.

This need not be the case. When Christians read the Bible through the lens of Jesus' gracious life and ministry, they will be able to see lesbian, gay, bisexual, and transgender people as their sisters and brothers, faced with all the usual human problems, and loved equally by God.

The method of biblical interpretation that neo-orthodoxy introduced in the 1940s was rooted in the methods of biblical interpretation used by the sixteenth-century Protestant Reformers. When Barth, Brunner, and others encouraged American Presbyterians to read Calvin and Luther, scholars began to discover a heritage that had been obscured by the nineteenth-century Princeton theology. Reid's Common Sense philosophy and Turretin's theological system both came after the sixteenth-century Reformers and the development of the Westminster Confession of Faith. So, what was new in the 1940s led theologians and biblical scholars back to an earlier Reformation heritage.

In the early 1980s Presbyterians reaffirmed that heritage and used the principles of biblical interpretation found in the Reformed confessions to formulate principles, or guidelines, of biblical interpretation for use in theological controversies. These guidelines, if followed, will be extremely useful in dealing with the controversy over whether homosexual members of the church are permitted the full rights of membership.

In the next chapter we will examine these guidelines, their confessional origins, and their application to people who are homosexual. Upholding our best principles and practices in interpreting the Bible will help us to move forward together as a community of faith.

4

Interpreting the Bible in Times of Controversy

Presbyterians have a very orthodox official position on the authority and interpretation of the Bible![1]

In 1982 and 1983 both the northern and southern Presbyterian churches adopted guidelines for the interpretation of Scripture. The reports of the two denominations were self-consciously harmonious because, at root, they were both based on study of the Reformed confessions. They were published together by the reunited PC(USA) in 1992 with the comment, "The two papers were written in response to the need for a common basis in a diverse church for understanding and using Scripture."[2]

These principles of biblical interpretation are not exclusive to Presbyterians. They are essentially the same principles that are used by most mainstream Christian denominations today. They come from our common heritage in the Protestant Reformation.

Moving beyond Neo-orthodoxy

By the time the Confession of 1967 was adopted by the United Presbyterian Church, the era of neo-orthodoxy was nearing an end. By 1970 it was clear that there were new and important issues that Karl Barth and the other neo-orthodox scholars had not addressed: cultural pluralism; feminism; the rising consciousness of the two-thirds world; the reassertion of science, especially the social sciences.

Neo-orthodoxy had opened a new understanding of Scripture that was both Christ-centered and open to scholarly study of the texts. However, the distinctive element of neo-orthodoxy, which said that only Christ was the Word of God and that Scripture was only a witness to Christ, no longer seemed helpful.

Following the Reformed confessions, the guidelines adopted in the 1980s affirmed that while Jesus Christ is the living Word, the Bible was appropriately called the written Word of God.[3] Scholarly attention turned to giving the most careful and prayerful attention to the written Word in order to discover God's saving message in Christ.

By paying the closest attention to these human words in their historical and cultural context, the UPCUSA report in 1982 noted, we are helped to understand the divine message that speaks to our human condition, rather than only to a particular historical situation in the ancient Near East.[4] That report concluded, "Openness to the Holy Spirit's leading, as well as the tools of scholarship, implemented in faith and love, must be operative to yield the application of the message, especially in areas of controversy."[5]

Ironically, while the guidelines were intended to be used in times of controversy, by the time the denominational reports were finally published in 1992, in the debate over homosexuality people were already entrenched in positions that looked all too much like those of the bad, old fundamentalist-modernist conflict. Indeed, some people still seemed to want to replay that unhelpful fight.

Using these guidelines will not guarantee that we will all immediately agree. However, we can at least be sure that we are talking about the same thing and that we are looking at all we can learn from the Bible, not just one narrow slice of it. With that common understanding, we may find a common way forward. That is my prayer.

SEVEN GUIDELINES FOR INTERPRETATION

In the discussion that follows I first present each guideline. Then I cite its origins in the Reformed confessions. Finally, I discuss the interpretive principles involved and how each guideline might help us in our current debate concerning homosexuality. I use the 1982 UPCUSA guidelines, because they are a bit simpler and I am more familiar with them. I also incorporate insights from the 1983 PCUS document and its helpful confessional citations.

Let us go to these recommended guidelines for "a positive and not a restrictive use of Scripture in matters of controversy."[6]

Guideline 1. "Recognize that Jesus Christ, the Redeemer, is the center of Scripture. The redemptive activity of God is central

to the entire Scripture. The Old Testament themes of the covenant and the messiah testify to this activity. In the center of the New Testament is Jesus Christ: the Word made flesh, the fulfillment of Israel's messianic hope, and the promise of the Kingdom. It is to Christ that the church witnesses. When interpreting Scripture, keeping Christ in the center aids in evaluating the significance of the problems and controversies that always persist in the vigorous, historical life of the church."[7]

Confessional Origin

As the following statements show, our Reformed heritage affirms that Christ is the central interpretative principle of Scripture:

Calvin, in his commentary on John 12:48: *"In our reading of Scripture we shall hold simply to that which speaks clearly and definitely to our conscience and makes us feel that it leads us to Christ."*[8]

The Geneva Confession of 1541, concerning how we have the *"right knowledge of God,"* the knowledge that tells us God loves us and desires to be our Father and Savior: *"By his Word, in which he declares his mercy to us in Christ, and assures us of His love toward us."*[9]

The Synod of Bern (1528): *"But where something is brought before us by our pastors or by others which brings us closer to Christ, . . . we will gladly accept it and will not limit the course of the Holy Spirit."*[10]

The Scots Confession (1560): *"When controversy arises about the right understanding of any passage or sentence of Scripture, or for the reformation of any abuse within the Kirk of God, we ought not so much to ask what men have said or done before us, as what the Holy Ghost uniformly speaks within the body of the Scriptures and what Christ Jesus himself did and commanded."*[11]

The Theological Declaration of Barmen, written in Germany against Nazi interference in the church (1934): *"Jesus Christ, as he is attested for us in Holy Scripture, is the one Word of God which we have to hear and which we have to trust and obey in life and in death."*[12]

The Confession of 1967: *"The Bible is to be interpreted in light of its witness to God's work of reconciliation in Christ."*[13]

A Declaration of Faith, adopted by the General Assembly of the PCUS in 1976, but not approved by the three-fourths of the presbyteries required for it to be included in the *Book of Confessions*; nonetheless it is widely used in the denomination: *"Jesus Christ stands at the center of the biblical record."*[14]

Commentary

The Bible is about God and what God is doing in the world. Jesus is central to that story. For Christians, Jesus is the Christ, the Messiah, the incarnation of God in our world.

This message is at the heart of what the church believes and what I believe. Some years ago, I was preaching on the classical text about biblical inspiration in 2 Timothy 3:16–17: "All scripture is inspired by God and is useful . . . so that everyone who belongs to God may be proficient, equipped for every good work." As I was preaching, I became increasingly aware of three boys, about ten years old, sitting in a front pew on my right, with no parental supervision. They weren't being bad, but they were pretty wiggly. So, suddenly I stopped and addressed the boys: "Boys, I can tell you everything the Bible is about in the next ten seconds. Why don't you time me?" This is what I said: "God made a good world. We messed it and ourselves up. God came in Jesus to put us and it back together again." One of those ten-year-old boys stood right up in church and said, "Nine seconds!" At least I had his attention for nine seconds.

The Bible is a story, and its central character is Jesus Christ. Thus the Bible is in some ways like a novel or a play. Its plot is creation, fall, and redemption—the outline of the Christian story.

Approaching the Bible through the lens of Jesus' life and ministry is not an easy task. It would be much simpler to live according to the black-and-white Hebrew laws of the Old Testament. But Jesus was not a legalist. In order to follow Jesus, we are called upon to show love for God, our neighbors, and even our enemies. Jesus showed love even for the outcasts of society. It is demanding and humbling to try to follow his example.

Can you imagine Jesus turning away someone who is despised, discriminated against, and distraught to the point of attempting suicide? I cannot. Yet some in the church have done just that to Christians who are homosexual.[15] When we keep our focus on Jesus, we will be able to come to a deeper understanding of the gospel. Then we need to pray for grace to see everyone in this discussion of homosexuality as our sister and brother in Christ.

Guideline 2. "Let the focus be on the plain text of Scripture, to the grammatical and historical context, rather than to allegory or subjective fantasy."

Confessional Origin

John Calvin: *"There are many statements in Scripture the meaning of which depends upon their context."*[16]

The Second Helvetic Confession (1566): *"But we hold that interpretation of the Scripture to be orthodox and genuine which is gleaned . . . (from the nature of the language in which they were written, likewise according to the circumstances in which they were set down)."*[17]

The Confession of 1967: *"The Scriptures, given under the guidance of the Holy Spirit, are nevertheless the words of men, conditioned by the language, thought forms, and literary fashions of the places and times at which they were written. They reflect views of life, history, and the cosmos which were then current. The church, therefore, has an obligation to approach the Scriptures with literary and historical understanding."*[18]

A Declaration of Faith (1976): *"God has chosen to address his inspired Word to us through diverse and varied human writings. Therefore we use the best available methods to understand them in their historical and cultural settings and the literary forms in which they are cast."*[19]

Commentary

This guideline warns against reading into Scripture what we want it to say. In medieval times, allegorism was a popular method that allowed one to find as many as seven levels of meaning in a text behind its plain meaning. Just as we must avoid a surface literalism, so we must avoid this sort of subjectivism that brings our biases to the text. We must, instead, take seriously the text as it is given to us and seek to understand it fully in its context.

The 1983 PCUS study indicates that to do justice to the plain text we must

1. define the appropriate literary units (passages, paragraphs, pericopes, etc.),
2. recognize the cultural conditioning of the language, and

3. understand the social and historical circumstances of the writing.

That means, for example, "Epic poetry is not historical chronicle; symbolic stories are not science; and admonition to a particular person or community is not general law."[20] Our Reformed confessions confirm these principles.

The "plain text" is "plain" only in its context. That means that it always requires responsible interpretation. Regarding homosexuality, we do well to heed the warning given in the PCUS "Guidelines": "While a particular text may name a subject with which we are also concerned in the present, the assumption should not be immediately made that the contemporary subject is the same as that addressed in the biblical text or that the circumstances and conditions of the biblical writer and modern interpreter are similar."[21]

For example, it seems wise to ask whether biblical statements that condemn idolatrous and immoral sexual activity can appropriately be applied to the sexual relationships of contemporary Christian gay and lesbian people who are neither idolatrous nor immoral. Is it right to take verses that condemn the worship of other gods and use them against Christian people who are worshiping the one true God whom Jesus called us to worship?

New Testament scholar Richard Hays notes that there is not "an exact equivalent for 'homosexual' in either Greek or Hebrew."[22] The Bible, in its original Hebrew and Greek, has no concept like our present understanding of a person with a homosexual orientation. Indeed, the concept of an ongoing sexual attraction to people of one's own sex did not exist in European or American language until the late nineteenth century.[23]

To be faithful to the "plain text" of Scripture, we must be very careful to understand the meaning of the text in its original context. Then we must be equally careful to discern if it is appropriate to apply that text in a quite different, contemporary context.

Guideline 3. "Depend on the guidance of the Holy Spirit in interpreting and applying God's message."

Confessional Origin

The Westminster Confession: *"We acknowledge the inward illumination of the Spirit of God to be necessary for the saving understanding of such things as are revealed in the Word."*[24]

The Westminster Confession: *"The Supreme Judge, by which all controversies of religion are to be determined, and all decrees of councils, opinions of ancient writers, doctrines of men, and private spirits, are to be examined, and in whose sentence we are to rest, can be no other but the Holy Spirit speaking in the Scripture."*[25]

The Confession of 1967: *"God's word is spoken to his church today where the Scriptures are faithfully preached and attentively read in dependence on the illumination of the Holy Spirit and with readiness to receive their truth and direction."*[26]

Commentary

Calvin promised that the "inner testimony of the Holy Spirit," which persuades us of the authority of Scripture, also assists us in interpreting Scripture. How? Not by giving us new information, but rather by giving a receptive attitude. With this attitude we can see, in the plain text, the essential message that God wants us to receive.

The Holy Spirit sometimes provides us with a new understanding of Scripture. The PCUS approach to biblical interpretation insists that "the confessions understand well that the church's traditional interpretation of Scripture is fallible and subject always to revision and correction."[27] The Holy Spirit has continually inspired change in the Christian church. The Spirit leads us into new beliefs and behaviors. This ability to change has enabled the church to cope with the changing world and to reach out to new people with the message of God's love in Christ. The early disciples in Jerusalem heard and accepted the reports of Peter and Paul that the Holy Spirit had descended on Gentiles (Acts 10 and 15), an idea that was previously unthinkable. Much of the Judaism in which they had been raised was based on the need to be separate from Gentiles, but the apostles and elders in Jerusalem changed their minds, and the church expanded.[28]

Christians in early America read their Bibles as saying that they should obey kings. But by the time of the American Revolution, people no longer took that admonition literally. Similarly, Christian people for centuries assumed that their Bibles condoned slavery and the subordination of women to men. Yet, over time and often reluctantly, people came to follow the Holy Spirit's leading to accept people of African origin and women as full and equal members of the church.

It seems that the Holy Spirit is once again working to change our church—making us restless, challenging us to give up our culturally conditioned prejudices against people of homosexual orientation. As we come to know faithful, obedient Christian disciples whose sexual orientation is different from that of the heterosexual majority, we discover that they have been blessed by the Holy Spirit even as heterosexual people have been. Under the guidance of the Holy Spirit, a change in our attitudes and actions can be a faithful response to God's leading.

> **Guideline 4. "Be guided by the doctrinal consensus of the church, which is the rule of faith."**

Confessional Origin

The Heidelberg Catechism, Question and Answer 22: Q. *"What, then, must a Christian believe? A. All that is promised us in the gospel, a summary of which is taught us in the articles of the Apostles' Creed, our universally acknowledged confession of faith."*[29]

Most of the Reformation-era confessions, and even Calvin's *Institutes*, are elaborations on the Apostles' Creed, the Ten Commandments, and the Lord's Prayer, as is the Presbyterian adult Study Catechism approved in 1998 by the General Assembly for use in congregations.

The Second Helvetic Confession, confirming the importance of referring to the doctrinal consensus of the church: *"The apostle Peter has said that the Holy Scriptures are not of private interpretation (II Pet. 1:20), and thus we do not allow all possible interpretations."*[30]

The 1983 PCUS report, "Presbyterian Understanding and Use of Holy Scripture," stating that the Scriptures are always to be interpreted by and in the community of the church, the body of Christ: *"Since the guidance of the Holy Spirit is promised to individual Christians for the sake of building up and equipping the community of Christians for its mission in the world, the church's consensus is likely to be more accurate than the opinions of individual persons."*[31]

Commentary

The "rule of faith" refers to the doctrinal consensus of the church developed over time. When you read the affirmations of faith in the creeds, confessions, and catechisms of the church, such as those in the Presbyterian *Book of Confessions*, you cannot help but notice the amazing continuity of the essentials of the Christian message. There naturally are differences among the documents because of the different historical and cultural contexts in which they were developed, yet they all basically tell the same story. That is because each of them is reflecting a faithful response to the same biblical story. Thus we are given a solid footing on which to stand as we adapt the "old, old story" to new and changing circumstances.

At first glance, it might appear that the consensus of the church has been against the full acceptance of people who are homosexual. We must remember, however, that until very recently it was the practice of the Western church to deny full rights of membership to people of color and to women. Past practice is not necessarily a recommendation for future faithfulness. We must continue to distinguish between the culturally conditioned practices of the church and the essential teachings of the church found in its creedal statements, which are the "rule of faith."

The Reformed confessions, properly translated, say nothing about homosexuality.[32] In fact, they say very little about sexuality itself. The Nicene and the Apostles' creeds make no mention of sexuality. A Brief Statement of Faith, 1991, makes no mention, and the same is true of the Scots Confession. The Barmen Declaration of 1934 makes no mention of sexual relations. The Heidelberg Catechism says that we should *"live chaste and disciplined lives, whether in holy wedlock or in single life."*[33] The Second Helvetic Confession speaks of those *"who have the gift of celibacy from heaven,"* but notes that *"if the gift be taken away,"* they should feel free to marry. It speaks at length about marriage and condemns polygamy. At the same time, it rebukes those who condemn second marriages.[34] The Westminster Confession outlaws divorce, but it allows exceptions for the *"innocent party"* in cases of adultery or desertion. The Westminster Larger Catechism, in chronicling the sins forbidden in the prohibition of adultery, broadens the list to include *"all unclean imaginations, thoughts, purposes, and affections."*[35] In listing the duties required by the Seventh Commandment, it includes *"conjugal love and cohabitation."*[36]

The original draft of the Confession of 1967 focused on three global problems: racial discrimination; enslaving poverty in a world of abundance; and the need for peace, justice, and freedom among nations.[37] The revision committee added a fourth issue: anarchy in sexual relationships,[38] citing human beings' *"perennial confusion about the meaning of sex"* and stressing that this confusion *"has been aggravated in our day."* It then notes seemingly opposite pressures, such as *"new means of birth control"* and *"world overpopulation."*[39]

Our creedal "rule of faith" makes clear that opinions about homo-sexuality are not essential matters of faith.

> **Guideline 5. "Let all interpretations be in accord with the rule of love, the two-fold commandment to love God and to love our neighbor."**

Confessional Origin

The Scots Confession: *"We dare not receive or admit any interpretation which is contrary to any principal point of our faith, or to any other plain text of Scripture, or to the rule of love."*[40]

The Second Helvetic Confession: *"We hold that interpretation of the Scripture to be orthodox and genuine which . . . agree[s] with the rule of faith and love, and contributes much to the glory of God and man's salvation."*[41]

Commentary

When we interpret Scripture in a way that is hurtful to people, we can be sure that we are not glorifying God. "You will know them by their fruits" was Jesus' criterion for judging false prophets (Matt. 7:16). Whether our interpretations of Scripture result in love for God and neighbor is a practical test of whether our interpretation is correct.

Treating everyone by the same just and loving standard would seem to be a criterion for the application of our interpretations of Scripture. The PCUS report in 1983 notes, "No interpretation of Scripture is correct that leads to or supports contempt for any individual or group of persons either within or outside of the church." Further, it states, "Any interpretation of Scripture is wrong that separates or sets in opposition love for God and love for fellow human being."[42]

Walter Wink, professor of New Testament at Auburn Seminary, states:

> The crux of the matter, it seems to me, is simply that the Bible has no sexual ethic. Instead, it exhibits a variety of sexual mores, some of which changed over the thousand-year span of biblical history. Mores are unreflective customs accepted by a given community. Many of the practices that the Bible prohibits, we allow, and many that it allows, we prohibit. The Bible knows only a love ethic, which

is constantly being brought to bear on whatever sexual mores are dominant in any given country, or culture, or period.[43]

> **Guideline 6. "Remember that interpretation of the Bible requires earnest study in order to establish the best text and to interpret the influence of the historical and cultural context in which the divine message has come."**

Confessional Origin

The Westminster Confession of Faith, in chapter 1 on Scripture, subsection 7, on what we know by experience: *"All things in Scripture are not alike plain in themselves, nor alike clear unto all; yet those things which are necessary to be known, believed, and observed, for salvation, are so clearly propounded and opened in some place of Scripture or other, that not only the learned, but the unlearned, in a due use of the ordinary means, may attain unto a sufficient understanding of them."*[44]

The most important notion above is that only beliefs having to do with salvation are both essential and clear.

Subsection 8 announces that in "controversies of religion" we are to study Greek and Hebrew and, by extension, the historical and cultural context of the passages in question.[45]

In saying that we require earnest study, especially regarding controversies of religion, we imply that our ideas and/or our behavior could be wrong. The Westminster Confession: *"All synods and councils since the apostles' times, whether general or particular, may err, and many have erred; therefore they are not to be made the rule of faith or practice, but to be used as a help in both."*[46]

The Scots Confession, preface: *"We protest that if any man will note in this confession of ours any article or sentence repugnant to God's holy word, that it would please him of his gentleness and for Christian charity's sake to admonish us of the same in writing."*[47]

Commentary

Establishing the "best text" means doing the arduous work of comparing ancient manuscripts of the biblical material in order to establish a

Bible that is as close to the original as possible. At the time of the Protestant Reformation much scholarly work remained to be done to compile a basic text on which all scholars could agree. Today scholars have compared such a large number of manuscripts that they feel fairly certain that they are very close to what the original text must have been, and thus are working with a generally authentic biblical text.[48]

When we move to the question of interpretation, again we have a strong consensus on the central message of the Bible. Scripture has a clear central saving message of creation, fall, and redemption in Christ. Sometimes Christians have had difficulty differentiating the surrounding cultural milieu from that central saving message. Describing these two different aspects of biblical literature is a task for biblical scholarship. We need to use the ministry of those who are experts in ancient languages, cultures, and philosophies to understand nuances of ancient Middle Eastern thought and practice that we encounter in the Bible.

God's message did not come to us in a fax from heaven. God dealt with real people who lived in particular cultures, and those cultures shaped the ways in which people understood and applied their understandings of God's word to them. Practices that we now rightly reject, including polygamy and slavery, were taken for granted in ancient cultures. Scholarly study can help us discern the difference between, on the one hand, something that is there in Scripture just because it was an accepted part of the culture and, on the other hand, the new and normative message from God.

For example, the assumption of male gender superiority is a significant aspect of the historical and cultural context of the biblical passages that seem to discuss homosexuality. Old Testament scholar Martti Nissinen has concluded from his cross-cultural research that "ancient Near Eastern sources in general are concerned with gender roles and their corresponding sexual practices, not with expressing a particular sexual orientation."[49] Thus, generally in the ancient Near East, sexual contact between two men was condemned as a confusion of gender roles. The cultural emphasis on male gender superiority also appears in Old Testament narratives and laws. Old Testament scholar Phyllis Bird concludes, "In the final analysis it [prohibition of homosexual behavior] is a matter of gender identity and roles, not sexuality."[50] The same attitude is present in the New Testament, reflecting its Greek and Roman cultural context. New Testament scholar Victor Paul Furnish states that Romans 1:26–27 presupposes "that same-sex intercourse compromises what patriarchal societies regard as the properly dominant role of males over females."[51]

When we are engaged in controversy, we need to be patient and tolerant with each other until we better understand the contexts from which the controversial passages have come.

Guideline 7. "Seek to interpret a particular passage of the Bible in light of all the Bible."

Confessional Origin

The Second Helvetic Confession: *"We hold that interpretation of Scripture to be orthodox and genuine which is gleaned from the Scriptures themselves . . . and expounded in the light of like and unlike passages and of many and clearer passages."*[52]

The Westminster Confession: *"The infallible rule of interpretation of Scripture, is the Scripture itself; and therefore, when there is a question about the true and full sense of any scripture (which is not manifold, but one), it may be searched and known by other places that speak more clearly."*[53]

Commentary

In this final guideline we return to where we began. This guideline affirms that there is a central unifying theme in Scripture—creation, fall, and redemption in Jesus Christ. Scripture is not simply an assortment of quotable sayings. It is a story about a real person. It has a saving purpose. We need to interpret the parts by the whole, the complex by the simple, the peripheral by the central.

If we interpret every particular passage in the light of the whole Bible, with its overarching theme of creation, fall, and redemption in Jesus Christ, we will be helped to put the discussion of homosexuality into proper perspective. This guideline echoes the first when it says "keeping Christ in the center aids in evaluating the significance of the problems and controversies that always persist in the vigorous, historical life of the church."[54] When we recognize that all of us, of whatever sexual orientation, are created by God, that we are all fallen sinners, and that we can all be redeemed by the life, death, and resurrection of Jesus Christ, homosexuality will no longer be a divisive issue. Peace and progress will again characterize the church when we stop making exceptions to our fundamental principles and we restore the full rights of membership to all our members.[55]

CONCLUSION

Each of these seven guidelines for biblical interpretation is drawn from our Reformed confessional heritage and has been adopted by the church for use in dealing with controversial issues. They are very similar to the principles of interpretation used in other mainstream denominations. I list them again to reinforce their unity of purpose and approach:

1. Recognize that Jesus Christ, the Redeemer, is the center of Scripture. The redemptive activity of God is central to the entire Scripture. The Old Testament themes of the covenant and the messiah testify to this activity. In the center of the New Testament is Jesus Christ: the Word made flesh, the fulfillment of Israel's messianic hope, and the promise of the kingdom. It is to Christ that the church witnesses. When interpreting Scripture, keeping Christ in the center aids in evaluating the significance of the problems and controversies that always persist in the vigorous, historical life of the church.

2. Let the focus be on the plain text of Scripture, to the grammatical and historical context, rather than to allegory or subjective fantasy.

3. Depend on the guidance of the Holy Spirit in interpreting and applying God's message.

4. Be guided by the doctrinal consensus of the church, which is the rule of faith.

5. Let all interpretations be in accord with the rule of love, the two-fold commandment to love God and to love our neighbor.

6. Remember that interpretation of the Bible requires earnest study in order to establish the best text and to interpret the influence of the historical and cultural context in which the divine message has come.

7. Seek to interpret a particular passage of the Bible in light of all the Bible.

Interpreting the Bible according to these guidelines from our Reformed heritage provides a more accurate understanding of Scripture that brings us into a closer relationship to God and one another.

In the next chapter, I will examine the handful of texts that are usually used to condemn faithful Christian people who are homosexual. I will be guided by these Reformed rules for interpreting the Bible in times of controversy. Let us see what we discover.

5

What the Bible Says and Doesn't Say about Homosexuality

The Bible is a drama of a good God who created a good world. A tragic fall into sin by the world's people alienated them from God. But God would not leave these people alone. God came into the world in the person of Jesus Christ, whose life, teaching, death, and resurrection overcame alienation and renewed the relationship between God and God's people.

Why do I remind you of what you know so well? The reason is that this perspective is often absent from the current debate about homosexuality in the church. That debate focuses on, at most, eight texts: Genesis 19:1–29; Judges 19:1–30; Leviticus 18:1–30; Leviticus 20:1–27; 1 Corinthians 6:9–17; 1 Timothy 1:3–13; Jude 1–25; and Romans 1. Together they cover a maximum of twelve pages in the Bible. None of these texts is about Jesus, nor do they include any of his words.

New Testament scholar Richard Hays, who teaches at Duke University Divinity School, says, "The Bible hardly ever discusses homosexual behavior. There are perhaps half a dozen references to it in all of scripture. In terms of emphasis, it is a minor concern, in contrast, for example, to economic injustice."[1] Nonetheless, in the debate on homosexuality these texts are often taken out of their linguistic, historical, and cultural context and used to condemn a whole group of people. Only Romans 1 deals with some of the central themes of the Bible. Often those who use Romans 1 to condemn homosexuality insert nonbiblical theories to justify their position in ways that subvert the central message of the text.

Most Christians have been told at one time or another that the Bible condemns all homosexual relationships. That view is simply incorrect. For hundreds of years the Bible has been used inappropriately to oppress people who are homosexual. The eight passages I noted above are pulled out of their biblical context to justify that oppression. However, as we will see, when we apply the best methods of biblical interpretation, as derived from the Reformed confessions and adopted by the church (as discussed in the last chapter), a very different picture emerges. Let us look at those eight passages, using the guidelines for biblical interpretation presented in the last chapter.

THE FIRST SEVEN TEXTS

Sodom and Gomorrah: Genesis 19:1–29
The Rape of the Levite's Concubine: Judges 19:1–30

The Old Testament stories most often cited as opposing homosexuality are (1) God's judgment on the men of Sodom and Gomorrah in Genesis 19:1–29 and (2) the parallel story of the rape of the Levite's concubine in Judges 19:1–30. These texts take us into an ancient Near Eastern world whose values are very different than ours. The central idea in these passages is the sacred obligation of hospitality for travelers (and the ways in which sinful people often violated this sacred obligation). In a desert country, to remain outside at night, exposed to the elements, could mean death.[2]

In both stories, a host invites traveling men into his house. Later an angry mob of townspeople surround the house and demand that the host turn his guests over to them. Foreigners are clearly not welcome, and the implication is that they may be raped or killed.[3] Daniel Helminiak, professor of psychology at the State University of West Georgia, points out that in the ancient world homosexual rape was a traditional way for victors to accentuate the subjection of captive enemies and foes. In that culture, the most humiliating experience for a man was to be treated like a woman, and raping a man was the most violent such treatment.[4] As Dale B. Martin, professor of religion at Duke University, says, "To be penetrated was to be inferior because women were inferior."[5] It is an expression of the "ancient horror of the feminine."[6]

In each of the stories, the host attempts to placate the threatening gangs by offering women of his household for the mob to abuse instead of his male guests. Notice the cultural emphasis on the superiority of men over women. As Old Testament scholar Martti Nissinen of the University of Helsinki notes, the critical issue in the ancient Near East was not sexuality but gender, and it was important that the superior position of men over women be maintained.[7] In that culture, the hosts felt that it was more important to protect male visitors in their house than to protect women, even their own daughters or common-law wife! The hosts do not seem to think of the attackers as primarily homosexual, or they would not offer women for them to abuse.

The best available scholarship shows that these texts have nothing to do with homosexuality as such. C.-L. Seow, professor of Old Testament at Princeton Theological Seminary, points out that the sin of Sodom is mentioned several times elsewhere in the Bible, but never in connection with homosexual acts.[8] In Old Testament references to Sodom, the sins of the city are variously described as greed, injustice, inhospitality, excess wealth, indifference to the poor, and general wickedness.[9] In the New Testament, when Jesus referred to the sin of Sodom, as recorded in Luke 10:12 and Matthew 10:15, he was passing judgment on cities that refused hospitality to his traveling disciples.[10] A focus on the supposed homosexual aspect of the Sodom story comes only later, in nonbiblical literature, influenced by Greek philosophy, and also in the Muslim Qur'an.[11]

The Old Testament Laws: Leviticus 18 and 20

Leviticus includes a collection of laws known as the Holiness Code, so named because the dominant idea in Leviticus is God's command: "You shall be holy, for I the LORD your God am holy" (Lev. 19:2). Two texts in this collection of laws are cited by those opposed to homosexuality as explicit prohibitions against homosexuality: Leviticus 18:22 and 20:13.

The Israelites had been slaves in Egypt; they had wandered in the desert, subject to attacks from other tribes, starvation, and infectious diseases. They needed cohesiveness, cleanliness, and order in every aspect of their lives. They wanted to keep pure their manner of worshiping God, who had brought them to this land. They were struggling for their own identity. Failure to form a tight-knit community could threaten their long-term survival. They needed a code for living.

In response, they developed a Holiness Code to define their religious, civic, and cultural identity. The Holiness Code's function was to achieve the "holy purity" they sought. Its underlying theme was that they must be separate, different from the Egyptians, from whom they had escaped, and unmixed with the Canaanites, into whose land they had now come. How were they to achieve holy purity?

First, Israel's worship practices had to be different from those of the tribes or nations around them. To be like the Canaanites would make them impure, or "defiled." Phyllis Bird, professor of Old Testament at Garrett-Evangelical Seminary, notes: "Israel is enjoined not to follow the practices of the Canaanites who preceded them in the land. . . . The previous inhabitants, through their 'defiling' actions, caused the land to become defiled so that God punished the land, making it vomit out its inhabitants."[12] In contrast, Israel was to be faithful to God, so that they would prosper on this land.

Second, they could not mix with any other kind of people or adopt alien customs if they were to remain pure. Practically, this meant no intermarriage with non-Israelites. However, the Israelites generalized this aspect of the code to mean no mixing of any kind. Thus the Holiness Code forbids such things as sowing a field "with two kinds of seed" and wearing a garment "made of two different materials" (Lev. 19:19).[13]

Third, male gender superiority had to be maintained. We find in Leviticus that actions undermining male gender superiority incur the death penalty. A child who cursed his parents could be put to death, for such an act threatened the social order in a patriarchal society. Adultery was similarly punishable by death, because it was an unlawful use of a woman, who was a man's property, and therefore jeopardized lines of ownership and inheritance. Engaging in homosexual acts was punishable by death, because a man took a passive role and was penetrated, which was the role assigned to a woman.[14] Victor Paul Furnish, professor of New Testament at Perkins School of Theology, Southern Methodist University, points out that a man penetrated was thus impure.[15] By, in effect, mixing genders, he had crossed a cultural boundary, and that could not be tolerated.[16]

It is against this background that Nissinen, Bird, and others interpret the statement, "You shall not lie with a male as with a woman; it is an abomination" (Lev. 18:22; cf. 20:13).[17] The Hebrew word *toevah*, translated as "abomination," refers here to something that makes a person ritually unclean, such as having intercourse with a woman while she is menstruating.[18] Ritual purity was considered necessary to distinguish the Israelites from their pagan neighbors.

Jesus was concerned with purity of heart. In Matthew 15 he said to a crowd, "Listen and understand: it is not what goes into the mouth that defiles a person, but it is what comes out of the mouth that defiles" (Matt. 15:10–11). Later he explained to his disciples: "What comes out of the mouth proceeds from the heart, and this is what defiles. For out of the heart come evil intentions, murder, adultery, fornication, theft, false witness, slander. These are what defile a person, but to eat with unwashed hands does not defile" (Matt. 15:18–20).

When we see Jesus as the fulfillment of the law (Matt. 5:17), we understand that our challenge is not meticulously to maintain culturally conditioned laws, but rather, with Jesus, to love God and love our neighbor (Matt. 22:36–40). When these texts in Leviticus are taken out of their historical and cultural context and applied to faithful, God-worshiping Christians who are homosexual, it does violence to them.

They are being condemned for failing to conform to an ancient culturally conditioned code that is not applicable to them or their circumstances. Even Louisville Presbyterian Seminary New Testament
professor Marion Soards, who opposes homosexuality on other
grounds, agrees that "it is impossible to declare the necessary relevance
of these verses for our world today."[19]

New Testament Vice Lists: 1 Corinthians 6:9; 1 Timothy 1:10

Opponents of equal rights for people who are homosexual also cite a
pair of New Testament texts—1 Corinthians 6:9–17 and 1 Timothy
1:3–13—as informing us about homosexuality. What makes these passages distinct is that, in their original Greek, they contain two words,
arsenokoites and *malakos*, that some scholars argue refer to male homosexual activity.[20] As a result, a disproportionate amount of scholarly
attention has been given to these texts and these two words. But to give
attention to these two words is to embark on a journey of linguistic
technicality. Brian Blount, then professor of New Testament at Princeton Theological Seminary, notes that the meaning of these words is not
at all clear, and their reference to homosexuality as such has been challenged.[21] Martti Nissinen observes that both words appear in lists of
vices that seem to reflect general concerns of Hellenistic Jews about the
deplorable state of Greek society.[22]

Arsenokoites and *malakos* both occur in 1 Corinthians 6:9, and
arsenokoites recurs in 1 Timothy 1:10. Because the words occur in lists
with no context, it is difficult to know exactly what they mean. Com-
pounding the situation, Nissinen notes that Paul, in the list he cites, is
using *arsenokoites* for the first time ever either in Greek or Jewish literature, thus making it very difficult to interpret.[23]

The debate over the meaning of these words illumines the various
methods that scholars use to define terms. Dale Martin disagrees with
those who read the two words, *arsen* (male) and *koites* (bed), as one and
thereby create a new term for men who have sex with men.[24] Martin
objects that "this approach is linguistically invalid," using as an illustration that the English word "understand" has nothing to do with either
standing or being under. He articulates an important principle: "The only
reliable way to define a word is to analyze its use in as many different contexts as possible."[25] Martin concludes, after analyzing Greek writings both
secular and Christian, that *arsenokoites* probably refers to "some kind of
economic exploitation, probably by sexual means: rape or sex by eco-

nomic coercion, prostitution, pimping, or something of the sort."[26] He further asserts that "no one should be allowed to get away with claiming that 'of course' the term refers to 'men who have sex with other men.'"[27]

The term *malakos* is somewhat easier to understand because it is a common word. It literally means "soft" and often connotes effeminacy, which in that culture was treated as a moral failing. Nissinen observes that, in the patriarchal culture of the time, lack of self-control and yielding to pleasures were both considered signs of effeminacy.[28] Contemporary scholars would rightly be embarrassed to invoke effeminacy as a moral category today. Unfortunately, however, as Martin laments, translating biblical terms on the assumption that all homosexual behavior is sinful is not yet embarrassing.[29]

In 1 Timothy 1:10, which many scholars date later than Paul's work, *arsenokoitēs* appears in a list of vices.[30] The NRSV translates it with the ambiguous word "sodomites." Victor Furnish notes that the word "sodomite" is not used in the Hebrew text of the Old Testament, not even to mean "a resident of Sodom." It was introduced in English in a half dozen Old Testament passages in the King James Version of the Bible in 1611. Nor does the word appear in the Greek text of the New Testament.[31] In 1 Timothy 1:10, "the fact that *arsenokoitai* [the plural of *arsenokoitēs,* which the NRSV translates as "sodomites"] is followed by slave traders, a group who exploited others, adds weight to Martin's evidence for *arsenokoitai* as sexual exploiters of some sort, since the vices in the lists were often grouped according to their similarity to other vices in the list."[32]

Nissinen argues, "The modern concept of 'homosexuality' should by no means be read into Paul's text, nor can we assume that Paul's words in I Corinthians 6:9 'condemn all homosexual relations' in all times and places and ways. The meanings of the word are too vague to justify this claim, and Paul's words should not be used for generalizations that go beyond his experience and world."[33] Many scholars, such as Marion Soards, believe that "only indirectly may we derive information regarding homosexuality from this material."[34] Once again, careful attention to the linguistic, historical, and cultural context has led to a richer and more nuanced understanding of the plain text.

Jude 5–7

The Letter of Jude consists of only one chapter, which runs just over one page and comes right before the book of Revelation. Very few writers pay much attention to this brief and obscure book. Yet New Testament scholar Thomas E. Schmidt, who is director of the Westminster Center in Santa Barbara, California, claims that the book of Jude makes reference to homosexuality.[35]

The Letter of Jude is the only book of the Bible that relates the sin of Sodom and Gomorrah to "sexual immorality." Schmidt, however, makes the broad claim that "the first Christians undoubtedly connected the sin of Sodom to the sin of same-sex relations."[36] The situation is, however, much more complex.

In Genesis 6:1–4 angels ("sons of God") are described as coming down to earth to have sex with human women ("daughters of humans").[37] When Jude 6 refers to "angels who did not keep their own position," it is believed by most scholars that he is referring to events in Genesis 6:1–4. In Genesis 19:1–29 Lot's guests are also described as angels.

Jude 7 draws a parallel between the "unnatural lust" of angels who wanted to have sex with human women (Gen. 6:1–4) and the men of Sodom who wanted to have sex with (male) angels (Gen. 19:1–29).[38] Jude writes that for their transgressions the Lord has kept the angels "in eternal chains in deepest darkness for the judgment of the great day" (v. 6). Likewise, the men of Sodom suffered "a punishment of eternal fire" (v. 7).

As one can see, in Jude there is a lot of discussion about sex between humans and angels (angels with human women, and human men with male angels) that is labeled as "sexual immorality" and "unnatural lust." But for Schmidt, or anyone else, to make the leap that this text somehow condemns present-day Christians who are homosexual strikes me as bizarre. In studying the seven texts that are often cited in opposition to homosexuality, we discover a significant body of scholarship that concludes that these texts have no direct application to faithful, God-loving, twenty-first-century Christians who are homosexual. What is more, this scholarly consensus includes many people who have traditionally opposed equal rights for people who are homosexual, such as scholars Richard Hays and Marion Soards. That leaves just one text, Romans 1.

ROMANS 1

The conflict over the meaning of biblical texts becomes acute when we look at Romans 1. Some conservative scholars who dismiss the relevance of the seven previously discussed texts to the issue of homosexuality argue that Romans 1 is a theological statement that has direct application for our time. I believe, however, that a close and careful look at the text, using the best methods of biblical interpretation, will reveal that Paul is making a statement about idolatry, not sexuality per se, and that Paul's writings also reflect many of the cultural assumptions of his time.

Paul's thesis statement for his letter to the Romans comes in Romans 1, verse 16: "For I am not ashamed of the gospel; it is the power of God for salvation to everyone who has faith, to the Jew first and also to the Greek." The very next sentence states that thesis in another way: "The one who is righteous will live by faith" (Rom. 1:17). No one is excluded from the possibility of receiving God's salvation. The gospel that Paul is proclaiming in Romans does not center on the issue of sexuality. It focuses on the universality of sin and the free grace of salvation through the life, death, and resurrection of Jesus Christ. That is the essence of the Christian message.

Idolatry, Not Sexuality

In Romans 1:18–32, Paul is writing about idolatry, that is, worshiping, giving our ultimate allegiance to anything in the creation instead of God, the Creator.[39] Paul is writing from Corinth, a bustling seaport town that was "notorious for vice of all kinds." Apparently, in the Roman Empire a common name for a prostitute was "a Corinthian girl."[40] Paul writes of people worshiping "images resembling a mortal human being or birds or four-footed animals or reptiles" (v. 23)—instead of God. Paul concluded that because the Corinthians engaged in idolatry, "God gave them up to degrading passions" (v. 26).

It seems as though Paul is setting up his Jewish readers. It is easy at this point in the text for them, and for us, to feel self-righteous. Jews didn't worship images of birds or animals or reptiles. Those were typical Gentile sins. But then Paul lowers the boom on his readers by listing other sins that proceed from idolatry—covetousness, malice, envy, strife, deceit, craftiness, gossip, slander. Idolaters could become haughty, boastful, rebellious toward parents, foolish, faithless, heartless, ruthless. Now Paul is talking to all of us, speaking to those sins of attitude to which we sometimes succumb when we turn our ultimate allegiance away from the true God.

Paul makes this point again, in Romans 2:1. We are without excuse, especially when we judge others. Why? Because in God's sight we are all given to idolatry. Paul is driving home the point that is at the heart of Reformation theology: no one is righteous before God. Paul has been criticizing those idolatrous Corinthian Gentiles. Now he is saying to his Jewish colleagues, and to us, No one is righteous. We are all sinners. That is Paul's point in Romans 1.

Cultural Norms, Not a Theology of Creation

What does Paul mean by "natural" and "unnatural" in Romans 1:26–27? In the original Greek, the words are *physis,* "nature," and *para physin*, "against nature."[41]

For Paul, "unnatural" is a synonym for "unconventional."[42] It means something surprisingly out of the ordinary. The most significant evidence that "natural" meant "conventional" is that God acted "contrary to nature" (Rom. 11:13–24). That is, God did something very unusual by pruning the Gentiles from a wild olive tree, where they grew in their natural state, and grafting them into the cultivated olive tree of God's people (Rom. 11:24). Since it cannot be that God sinned, to say that God did what is "contrary to nature" or "against nature" (v. 24) means that God did something surprising and out of the ordinary.[43]

Paul is not talking in Romans 1:26–27 about a violation of the order of creation. In Paul's vocabulary, *physis* (nature) is not a synonym for *ktisis* (creation). In speaking about what is "natural," Paul is merely accepting the conventional view of people and how they ought to behave in first-century Hellenistic-Jewish culture.[44]

Male Gender Dominance

The theme of male gender dominance appears again and again in the texts that many claim deal with homosexuality, including Romans 1. Both the Hebrew and the Greek cultures were patriarchal. Men were, and intended to remain, dominant over women. Paul assumes the conventions of these cultures that he is addressing. He uses terms familiar in the Greek-speaking synagogues such as "impurity" (1:24) and "shameless" (1:27), which are part of the Jewish language of purity. And he is equally familiar with terms that are rooted in Greek Stoic philosophy, such as "lusts" (1:24) and "passions" (1:26), which denote erotic passion and uncontrolled desire.[45]

In Romans 1:26, Paul writes: "Their women exchanged natural intercourse for unnatural." As Nissinen notes, the phrase "their women" is a clear indication of a gender role structure.[46] But, he contends, "Paul's understanding of the naturalness of men's and women's gender roles is not a matter of genital formation and their functional purpose, which today is considered by many the main criterion for the natural and unnatural."[47] Rather, in the culture Paul is addressing, a man and a woman each had a designated place and role in society, which could not be exchanged. For example, Paul in 1 Corinthians 11:3–16 outlines a strict hierarchical ladder of God-Christ-man-woman. Strict gender role differences are set out, manifested by different hairstyles. Paul asks, "Does not nature itself teach you that if a man wears long hair, it is degrading to him, but if a woman has long hair, it is her glory?" (1 Cor. 11:14). In that culture, to violate these roles would be a matter of shame before God.[48]

For Paul, transgressions of gender role boundaries cause "impurity," a violation of the Jewish purity code (Rom. 1:24).[49] Nissinen explains that it is women taking the man's active role in sex that was seen as "unnatural."[50] The text does not say that women had sex with other women. They could have been condemned for taking the dominant position in heterosexual intercourse, or for engaging in nonprocreative sexual acts with male partners.[51] The issue is gender dominance, and in that culture women were to be passive and not active in sexual matters.

Control and Moderation in All Things

In Hebrew culture and in Stoic philosophy (which was influential in the Roman Empire, particularly in Greece, during Paul's time), control and moderation in all things were highly valued, especially regarding emotion and sexuality. Going to excess—whether eating too much, sleeping too much, or giving in to excessive passion of any kind—was viewed as a moral failing.[52] The goal was to make correct "use" of all things. The "natural use" of sex was to be very controlled, avoiding passion.[53] Paul in Romans 1:26–27 would be rightly understood to be talking not about wrongly oriented desires, but about inordinate desires—going to excess, losing control.[54] Idolaters fail to give God glory and gratitude. God then allows them to lose control in erotic passion, which brings them dishonor.[55]

The Plain Text

Those who are opposed to equal rights for Christian gay and lesbian people make several serious errors in interpreting Romans 1: (1) they lose sight of the fact that this passage is primarily about idolatry, (2) they overlook Paul's point that we are all sinners, (3) they miss the cultural subtext, and (4) they apply Paul's condemnation of immoral sexual activity to faithful gay and lesbian Christians who are not idolaters, who love God, and who seek to live in thankful obedience to God.

Heterosexual sex can be either moral or immoral, depending on its context. The same is true of homosexual sex. If Paul walked into a party at the Playboy Mansion today or observed college students "hooking up" at a fraternity party, he would be appalled and rightly condemn the activities going on there. But no one would conclude from that observation that Paul had ruled out all heterosexual sex as immoral. Everyone would understand that Paul was not talking about married Christian heterosexual couples who love God and seek to follow Jesus.

Paul's condemnation of immoral sexual behavior is not appropriately applied to contemporary gay or lesbian Christians who are not idolaters, who love God, and who seek to live in thankful obedience to God. I think Jeffrey Siker, professor of New Testament at Loyola Marymount University, says it best: "We know of gay and lesbian Christians who truly worship and serve the one true God and yet still affirm in positive ways their identity as gay and lesbian people. Paul apparently knew of no homosexual Christians. We do."[56]

NONBIBLICAL THEORIES IMPOSED UPON ROMANS 1

Those who oppose homosexuality claim that they are appealing to Romans 1. Upon closer examination, it is clear that many are imposing their own nonbiblical theories on the Pauline text. The most common additions to the plain text of Romans 1 are (1) appeals to natural law and (2) the assumption that Genesis somehow contains a prescription for heterosexual, monogamous marriage. These are *not* necessary to understand Paul's basic point in Romans 1 that all are sinners and are saved by grace through faith in Christ. Let us examine these theories that are imported into Romans 1, and other texts, in an attempt to justify the condemnation of all contemporary homosexuality. A number of subissues under natural law and heterosexual marriage may seem out of place in a discussion of Romans 1, but I present them here because they are assumptions that, when brought to Romans 1, distort the interpretation of Paul's message.

Natural Law

One argument made by conservative interpreters is that we can be guided by a nonbiblical standard, natural law. Natural law is composed of those unquestioned assumptions that most people in the culture accept. Ralph McInerny at the University of Notre Dame defines natural law as "the claim that there are certain judgments we have already made and could not help making."[57] The problem is that this could also be a good definition for prejudice.[58]

The unreflective appeal to nature is exemplified by a remark of fundamentalist minister Jerry Falwell. On *Meet the Press* following the November 2004 presidential election, Falwell, pushing his priorities for President Bush's second term, said, "I think it's unthinkable that we're debating what a family is, a man married to a woman. They've got that right in the barnyard." In his colorful manner of speaking, Falwell appealed to what, to him, was obvious in nature—animals have sexual relations, male with female.[59] That model of nature is an often-used appeal to natural law.

As it turns out, however, not all animals are heterosexual. Biologist Bruce Bagemihl has documented homosexual relations in 450 different species in the animal world. Same-sex behavior includes not only copulation, but also courtship and parental activities.[60] I am not arguing here that we should base our understanding of sex on animal behavior, but, rather, pointing out that those who do, citing male-female relations as universal in nature, are in error.

As we saw in chapter 2 in the discussion of Scottish Common Sense philosophy, theologians often appeal to natural law in an attempt to argue divine sanction for their cultural assumptions. A classic example of the misuse of natural law in theology is Robert Gagnon's *The Bible and Homosexual Practice: Texts and Hermeneutics*.[61] Gagnon is a professor of New Testament at Pittsburgh Theological Seminary. His book is

acclaimed by some opponents of gay and lesbian equality as the definitive biblical word on homosexuality.

The irony is that Gagnon doesn't seem to need the Bible because, he
argues, everything the Bible says about homosexuality comes initially
from the observation of nature. In fact, in the conclusion to his book,
Gagnon actually says what many heterosexual people believe: "Acceptance of biblical revelation is thus not a prerequisite for rejecting the
legitimacy of same-sex intercourse."[62] So where does he believe the
constraints against homosexual behavior are found? As it turns out,
behind all of the ancient sources, including biblical sources, according
to Gagnon, is "the simple recognition of a 'fittedness' of the sex organs,
male to female."[63] He goes on to say that the Old Testament Holiness
Code "was responding to the conviction that same-sex intercourse was
fundamentally incompatible with the creation of men and women as
anatomically complementary sexual beings."[64] He also refers to "Paul's
own reasoning, grounded in divinely-given clues in nature."[65] In each
of these statements, Gagnon gives priority to nature over revelation.

According to Gagnon, pagans, as well as Jews and Christians, find
"the material creation around human beings and the bodily design of
humans themselves, guiding us into the truth about the nature of God
and the nature of human sexuality respectively."[66]

The contemporary appeal to natural law, by Gagnon and others, has
a function similar to Scottish Common Sense philosophy in an earlier
era. Both contend that the truth is obvious. Both rely heavily on sen-
sory evidence. Both assume that no interpretation is needed. Both
therefore assert common human prejudices as self-evident truths. Giving priority to natural law opens the door to bring in all manner of
assumptions and prejudices that have nothing to do with the biblical
text. Let's take a close look at some of Gagnon's assumptions.

1. Sexual Orientation: A Choice?

Relying on his inaccurate assumptions about what is "natural," Gagnon
claims, "Certainly no one is born a homosexual."[67] Clearly there is no biblical warrant for this statement. In fact, Jesus, immediately after his teaching on divorce and his recommendation of marriage, states that some
people are born eunuchs (Matt. 19:10–12). In the NEB these people are
described as "incapable of marriage" (Matt. 19:12). In ancient time, there
no doubt were people who were incapable of heterosexual sexual activity
and thus were considered "eunuchs." Old Testament scholar Martti Nissi-

nen suggests that in our contemporary context those who are eunuchs from their mother's wombs might well include people who are homosexuals, because they simply lack sexual desire for people of the opposite sex.[68]

There is also no scientific warrant for Gagnon's claim. In a comprehensive review of the literature on the subject of sexual orientation, David G. Myers, professor of psychology at Hope College, observes that based on all the available evidence, most psychologists "view sexual orientation as neither willfully chosen nor willfully changed."[69] I will discuss this more fully in chapter 6.

2. Can People Who Are Homosexual Become Heterosexual?

Having asserted that no one is homosexual by nature, Gagnon claims that all people who are homosexual have willfully chosen that behavior and therefore can successfully change their sexual identity. Once again there is no biblical or scientific warrant for that position. When all of the studies and the testimony have been sifted, it is apparent that when people claim that lesbian and gay people can change, they are almost always referring to behavior and not orientation. In fact, when you probe beyond the assertions, Gagnon acknowledges that "therapists define *success* as management of unwanted desires, not complete elimination."[70] Thomas Schmidt, who supports traditional limits on homosexuals in the church, concludes: "As numerous books by ministry leaders show, their focus is on changed behavior, [and] they are honest about the probability of ongoing temptation."[71] Even Andrew Comiskey, a prominent "ex-gay," agrees. He uses two friends, Karen and Jim, to illustrate his point. He says of them, "Neither can choose not to have homosexual feelings anymore than heterosexuals can deny their impulse for the opposite sex."[72]

By acknowledging that "reparative" or "conversion" therapy is addressing only behavior rather than orientation, opponents of homosexuality are actually admitting that, in fact, sexual orientation is a part of someone's nature and may be just as God-given as heterosexuality. David Myers, in his review of the scientific literature on sexual orientation, concludes, "Sexual orientation is like handedness: Most people are one way, some are the other. A very few are truly ambidextrous. Regardless, the way one is endures."[73]

When people who are homosexual are able to accept their orientation, it frees them to find a loving partner of their own sex and experience the joy of companionship, just as heterosexuals do in a marriage.

The church should celebrate such unions, rather than imposing unbiblical and unscientific assumptions upon this group of people.

3. Is Homosexuality Idolatry?

Since Gagnon claims, in spite of all the evidence to the contrary, that homosexuality is a willful choice, he then proceeds to *define* same-sex intercourse *as* idolatry.[74] His definition makes sense only if you *start* with the *assumption* that homosexuality is sinful. If, on the other hand, you start with the question of whether people who are homosexual are idolatrous, you could simply speak with real Christian people who are gay and lesbian and quickly discover that in fact they love Jesus and seek to serve God. The debate would be over.

Gagnon does not deal with how real Christian gay and lesbian people express their love for each other or their love for God. He does not acknowledge the devout Christian people who are living in faithful, monogamous same-sex unions. Instead, he has created his own theoretical model of idolatrous sex and then claims that it applies to all people who are homosexual.

Moreover, Gagnon does not demonstrate that the immoral sexual relations Paul condemns are related to the love of contemporary faithful gay and lesbian Christians. He simply asserts it. The lives of Christian people who are homosexual refute Gagnon's assertions. If one takes the time to know real Christian people who are homosexual, one finds that their love is not any more lustful than that of people who are heterosexual, nor is it motivated by idolatry.

Jesus dealt with real people in the midst of their daily lives. He didn't start with culturally biased assumptions and then use them as a club to punish those who were not like him. Rather, he went to the people and helped them develop a closer relationship with God. If we start with Jesus and seek to follow him, we will then be guided to deal with real people and endeavor to help everyone know and serve God.

4. Homosexual Relationships: The Worst Sin of All?

The conclusion of Gagnon's chain of reasoning, based on his appeal to natural law, is twofold: (1) lesbian and gay sexual relations are sinful as such; and (2) they are the worst sin of all. Gagnon declares that, on the basis of observation of nature, we can know that all same-sex intercourse is the "road that leads to death: physically, morally, and spiritually."[75] He simply asserts, with no supporting evidence, that sexual relations between contemporary Christian people who are homosexual are sinful as such.

Secondly, he argues, "we all sin but not all sin is equally offensive to God and not all sin is to be treated in the same way."[76] In fact, however, that is the exact opposite of what Paul argues in Romans 1:29–32! Paul declares that *all* of the sins that he lists, not just immoral sexual relations, are worthy of death. Gagnon may choose to take a position in opposition to Paul, but he cannot claim to be biblical in doing so.

Given Gagnon's assumption that homosexual behavior will cause a person to be excluded from the kingdom of God, it seems reasonable then to conclude that, for him, a prerequisite to salvation is to imitate heterosexual behavior or be celibate. That would of course contradict Paul's view that all are sinners, that no one is saved by works, and that all can be saved by God's grace.

Homosexuality an Example of the Fallenness of Humanity?

Richard Hays, writing on New Testament sexual ethics, takes a mediating, yet conservative, position on the consequences of God's judgment in Romans. He writes, "Paul is not describing the individual life histories of pagan sinners; not every pagan has first known the true God of Israel and then chosen to turn away into idolatry. When Paul writes: 'They exchanged the truth about God for a lie,' he is giving a global account of the universal fall of humanity."[77] Hays then asserts that "Paul singles out homosexual intercourse for special attention because he regards it as providing a particularly graphic image of the way in which human fallenness distorts God's created order."[78]

One of the problems with this argument is that either humanity's fall is universal or it is not. You cannot argue that everyone is fallen (the essential Christian message) and then go on to single out particular groups of people as extra-fallen. Furthermore, like Gagnon, Hays is making huge assumptions about what God intended to create. As I have already shown, examples from the animal kingdom seem to show that God pretty clearly did intend to create homosexual animals. Furthermore, the best scientific evidence also seems to show a genetic influence on sexual orientation, as well as biological differences between homosexual and heterosexual people. This data suggests that homosexuality is indeed part of God's created order.[79]

For Hays, God's "created order" includes a prescription for heterosexual marriage as the only acceptable context for sexual intercourse.

He declares, "Marriage between man and woman is the normative form for human sexual fulfillment, and homosexuality is one among the many tragic signs that we are a broken people, alienated from God's loving purpose."[80] Again, by singling out a particular group of people, Hays is contradicting the essential Christian message that we are *all* broken people, saved through the life, death, and resurrection of Jesus Christ. Furthermore, while I too believe that monogamous marriage is the best context for human sexual fulfillment, as I will show in the following section, there is no particular scriptural warrant for monogamous *heterosexual* marriage as the norm for all people.[81]

A Model of Monogamous Heterosexual Marriage in Genesis?

Many who would like to use Romans 1 to oppose equal rights for people who are homosexual ground their position in the creation accounts in Genesis 1–2. The argument goes something like this: homosexual relations are against nature, because they are contrary to the pattern placed within creation.[82] What is that pattern? According to some, like Thomas Schmidt, it is monogamous, heterosexual, marriage.[83] However, Genesis 1–2 contains no reference to homosexuality or marriage. These chapters were not written to answer the questions that are now being put to them.

As Old Testament scholar Phyllis Bird notes, the laws and traditions that regulated sexual relations and marriage in ancient Israel *never* referred to the creation texts as models.[84] Genesis 1, she argues, actually describes how humans are like and unlike God. People are made in God's image and likeness, so they are separate from and superior to other animals. But in their sexuality, they are identified as male and female, not as husband and wife, or even man and woman. Victor Furnish further reminds us that in contrast to all of the ancient Near Eastern deities, Israel's God was regarded as *asexual*.[85] Thus in their sexuality, humankind is *like* every other created species and *unlike* God.[86]

Indeed, Furnish asserts that Genesis 2:23–25 "neither commands nor presumes a 'monogamous' relationship between man and woman and . . . it offers no comment on 'marriage' as such."[87] Moreover, Old Testament heroes of the faith certainly did *not* model monogamy, but rather followed the patterns of their culture, with multiple wives, concubines, and slaves as sexual partners. The Bible not only approves but also appears to mandate such behavior. However, as Furnish notes, the prescription to "be fruitful and multiply" cannot mean that everyone must marry and reproduce, for the creation stories "take no account whatever of the physically or mentally impaired, the celibate, the impotent—or of those who in modern times have come to be described as 'homosexual.'"[88]

This notion that a model of monogamous, heterosexual marriage is somehow contained in Genesis 1 is simply not true. It appears to be an artificial construct designed to deny the rights of marriage to those who are homosexual. As David Balch, professor of New Testament at Brite Divinity School, observes, where a theology of creation is stressed, as by those opposed to equality for gays and lesbians, "subordination and submission are usually emphasized."[89] On the other hand, where a theology of redemption, such as Paul offers in Romans 3, is stressed, "freedom, mutuality, and equality are usually emphasized."[90]

I think that the contemporary model of Christian marriage is a good one for heterosexual people: one man and one woman should marry for life and, if they choose, bear and care for children. This model is not found in Genesis, however. Moreover, it took Western society many centuries to come to it,[91] and even so, half of the heterosexual people in American society do not follow it. On the other hand, many Christian gay and lesbian people have committed themselves to one lifelong partner. Many care for children, and some that I know have adopted children with special needs. They seem to have gotten the point of the contemporary Christian model of marriage and are living it out.

Reuniting the Binary Split?

An extreme version of the notion that salvation is found only in the uniting of male and female is found in Robert Gagnon's work. He renders the Genesis story in this way:

> In Gen. 2:18–24, a binary or sexually undifferentiated human (the *adam*) is split into two sexually differentiated beings. Marriage is treated by the Yahwist as a reunion of the sexual unity of the original *adam*. One can no more dismiss the story's implicit relevance for proscriptions of same-sex intercourse than one can dismiss its pertinence for attitudes against bestiality (cf. 2:20). . . . Two males or two females in sexual union would not equal an originally binary being or sexual whole.[92]

Interestingly, in Plato's *Symposium* a similar myth of an original whole being divided is presented by an intoxicated Aristophanes. Originally there were three kinds of beings, a male, a female, and an androgynon that shared equally in the male and female. Zeus sliced these beings in half, and each searched for its counterpart in order to become whole again by having sexual relations. The beings of androgynous origin would have heterosexual desires, the male half searching to be reunited with the female half. Aristophanes observes, "Our adulterers are mostly descended from that sex, whence likewise are derived our man-courting women and adulteresses."[93] It's a curious theory, but once again, there is simply no biblical warrant for that position.

The Male-Female Relationship as the Image of God in Humanity?

The Presbyterian Confession of 1967, which was influenced by the theological method of Karl Barth (see the discussion of neo-orthodoxy in chapter 3), became a significant source in the struggle to overcome prejudice against people of color and, by analogy, women.[94] Yet in 1978 the United Presbyterian Task Force on Homosexuality noted Barth's opposition to full equality for gay and lesbian people.[95] Unfortunately, Barth, like many others, made an exception to his usual method of interpreting Scripture when it came to the issue of gender and homosexuality.

Appealing to his interpretation of natural law and the false assumption that there is a model for heterosexual marriage in Genesis, Barth wrote, "Man is directed to woman and woman to man; . . . this mutual orientation constitutes the being of each."[96] According to Barth's view, being fully human is known only in the male-female relationship, and the marriage relationship is the fullest expression of the image of God in human beings.[97]

Like others who rely on natural law, Barth was biased in favor of the male gender. According to Barth, in the marriage relationship, the husband reflects Jesus and the wife reflects the Christian community. "She is," Barth wrote, "subordinated to her husband as the whole community is to Christ."[98]

In his analysis, Barth engaged in the sort of natural theology he usually condemned by appealing to what he referred to as "a little knowledge of life."[99] By making an argument on the basis of what he considered "natural," Barth departed from the biblical text and instead inserted his own culturally conditioned opinions. As Elouise Renich Fraser, professor of theology and dean at Palmer Theological Seminary, comments: "By making marriage the epitome of co-humanity, Barth places some human relationships automatically under suspicion, excludes some human beings from the possibility of full humanity, and reinforces old stereotypes of male and female, thus failing to help his readers hear the old story with new ears."[100] Barth's firm commitment to male gender superiority causes him to reject all homosexual relationships.[101]

Today many Protestants repeat Barth's assertion that monogamous, heterosexual marriage is the exemplification of the image of God in humanity and use that to oppose full membership in the church for people who are homosexual. Barth's view has also become one basis for attempts to change people who are homosexual into people who are heterosexual. For example, "ex-gay" Andrew Comiskey echoes Barth when he claims, "God also tells us that to discover our true humanity, we must be known by the opposite sex. A fundamental part of our bearing the divine image is its heterosexual reflection. God created man in His image as 'male and female' (Gen. 1:26–27)."[102] It sounds very much as if Comiskey is saying that we have to engage in heterosexual sex in order to be fully human, which would be a breathtaking misinterpretation of Paul's message in Romans 1.

The claim that the image of God is rooted in the male-female relationship leads us away from the biblical text. When I was on the task force on homosexuality at Pasadena Presbyterian Church, one of our members, a former missionary with a PhD in New Testament, argued in favor of the Barthian view that a person was not fully human unless in a heterosexual marriage. His argument offended various committee members, including a never-married woman who was a former missionary. Our one gay member quietly said, "That sure makes it hard on Jesus."

Biblically speaking, Jesus Christ *is* the image of God (Col.1:15; 2 Cor. 4:4). But the image of God in Jesus was not a consequence of some unique human attribute, like maleness or marital status. It was rather the result of his reflecting the love of God fully in his life. We human beings reflect God's love only sporadically and partially, whereas Jesus showed us God's love consistently and wholly.

The gospel, the good news, is that all people can have a relationship with God through Jesus Christ. We reflect Christ's presence in our lives by showing love for God and each other. Thus, the image of God is not a capacity embodied only in some classes of people but denied to others. To be in God's image is possible for all—black and white, male and female, gay and straight, married and unmarried.

We need to return to a biblical understanding of God, creation, sin, salvation, and love. Those who rely instead on natural law and biased cultural assumptions twist and distort the fundamental message of the gospel.

There are around three thousand verses in the Bible that express God's concern for the poor and oppressed.[103] In contrast, there is a tiny handful of verses that some people claim condemn homosexuality. None of them, properly interpreted, refers to contemporary Christian people who are homosexual.

A RELEVANT BIBLICAL ANALOGY

The acceptance of people who are homosexual is grounded in the central message of Scripture as interpreted through the lens of Jesus' life and ministry. In addition, there are specific biblical passages that show the church changing its mind and accepting people who previously were considered unclean and unacceptable. Perhaps the most instructive is the long narrative in Acts 10–15 that records how the church opened itself to receive Gentiles on whom God's Spirit had fallen, without requiring them to behave like Jews.

That narrative culminates in Acts 15, at a gathering that is usually referred to as the Council of Jerusalem. (I sometimes ask Presbyterians to think of it as their first General Assembly.) Certain individuals from the "sect of the Pharisees" resisted the new reality and insisted that in order to be saved, it was necessary for men to be circumcised and all people to keep the law of Moses (Acts 15:5).

However, both Peter and Paul had admitted Gentiles to the church solely on the basis that the Holy Spirit had been given to these non-Jews. These Gentiles did not have to meet any of the former Jewish requirements. Indeed, Peter challenged the church leaders in Jerusalem: "Now therefore why are you putting God to the test by placing on the neck of the disciples a yoke that neither our ancestors nor we have been able to bear?" (Acts 15:10).

So the council members listened to testimony by Peter and then by Paul and Barnabas. Peter recounted a vision that came to him when he was in a trance. God gave him a new revelation, that there were no clean and unclean people in God's sight. Gentiles were not unclean as a class and thus were not to be excluded from full participation in the church. Peter said, "God, who knows the human heart, testified to them by giving them the Holy Spirit, just as he did to us; and in cleansing their hearts by faith he has made no distinction between them and us" (Acts 15:8–9). Paul and Barnabas told of signs and wonders that God had done among the Gentiles. God was doing a new thing.

After hearing the testimony of those who had been working among the Gentiles, James gave an authoritative interpretation. He gave weight to the words of Peter, "We will be saved through the grace of the Lord Jesus, just as they will" (15:11). He saw a continuity of the new reality with biblical Judaism. James interpreted the prophet Amos (9:11–12) to say that God had always purposed the conversion of the Gentiles. Now the church had experienced what God had planned.[104]

Luke Timothy Johnson, professor of New Testament at Candler School of Theology, Emory University, challenges us, "Remember please, the stakes: The Gentiles were 'by nature' unclean, and were 'by practice' polluted by idolatry. . . . The decision to let the Gentiles in 'as such' . . . came into direct conflict with the accepted interpretation of Torah and what God wanted of humans."[105] Johnson thus affirms that the question of accepting people who are homosexual as full members of the church "is analogous to the one facing earliest Christianity after Gentiles started being converted."[106] New Testament scholar Jeffrey Siker, accepting that analogy, gives his testimony: "Just as Peter's experience of Cornelius in Acts 10 led him to realize that even Gentiles were receiving God's Spirit, so my experience of various gay and lesbian Christians led me to realize that these Christians have received God's Spirit as gays and lesbians and that the reception of the Spirit has nothing to do with sexual orientation."[107]

In the next chapter we will interact, not with theoretical stereotypes, but with real people who are homosexual. These real people evidence a commitment to Jesus Christ, in spite of continuing persecution from society and the misguided policies of many Christian churches. The Christians who are homosexual whom I know show a profound love for Jesus and a deep commitment to marriage and the care of children.

Let's get to know them.

6

Real People and Real Marriage

MOVING BEYOND STEREOTYPES AND CODED LANGUAGE

Jesus dealt with real people in the midst of their daily struggles. Too often in the church today, however, our debates are filled with stereotypes, abstract theories, and caricatures of people who are homosexual. Careless use of language distorts our perception of real people. Take, for instance, the pejorative phrase "the gay lifestyle." For many people it is a code that calls up images of promiscuity, bizarre behavior in gay pride parades, and the specter of AIDS. The stereotype of the "gay lifestyle" is just not applicable to all LGBT people and certainly not to the devout, Christian, homosexual people who are faithful members of our churches and who simply desire the full rights of membership. I would certainly resent it if people spoke of the "heterosexual lifestyle" and used Howard Stern and Hugh Hefner as the models for all heterosexual men.

I have also, on more than one occasion, been told what I call "The Dirty Little Secret." A heterosexual person, during a discussion of homosexuality, will lower his voice, as if telling me a private confidence. Then he will say something like, "You know *these people* are incapable of maintaining a faithful, monogamous relationship. They are inherently promiscuous." Yet comparative studies of gay couples and heterosexual couples show virtually no difference in the stability of their relationships.[1]

A lifestyle is something that people choose. There are probably as many different lifestyles as there are people. A sexual orientation is not a lifestyle. Almost all gay and lesbian people will tell you that they did not choose their sexual orientation.[2] They just discovered that they were sexually attracted to members of their own sex, usually as early as young people begin to experience sexual attraction. It is convenient for some people who are heterosexual to embrace the theory that homosexuality is a chosen "lifestyle."[3] They can then blame people who are homosexual for being who they are and not deal with the reality of people in their midst who are created differently.[4]

As a church we deplore promiscuity among gay and lesbian people, while at the same time denying the right to marry to those who want to form stable families with the supportive recognition of the Christian community. When I was at Fuller Seminary, I counseled a Missouri-Synod Lutheran student who trusted me with the knowledge that he was gay. His theology condemned him. He had tried to change and tried to be celibate, but once in a while he just couldn't stand it, and he would go to a gay bar in search of a one-night stand. I tried to help him deal with the conflict between his sexual orientation and his conservative theology. I gave him lots of material to read. I shared different theological perspectives with him, in the hope that he could find a way to live with himself. None of it worked. He dropped out of seminary, and from time to time I would get a recommendation form as he was applying for a job, usually as a language teacher. The apostle Paul's and the Reformer Calvin's assumptions that a central reason for marriage was to provide an alternative to promiscuity should certainly apply in this kind of situation.[5] Most people who are heterosexual would not be very successful living a celibate life if that was simply assigned to them by society when they had no such calling from God.[6] The wonder is that so many lesbian and gay people have formed long-term monogamous partnerships, despite all of the barriers that society puts in their way.

CLERGY SEXUAL MISCONDUCT

It is ironic that as the church attempts to identify a biblical standard of sexual morality to apply to people who are homosexual, it has not adequately confronted the issue of clergy sexual misconduct, which is currently epidemic in the church. Priests and Protestant pastors have a tremendous amount of power and influence within their congregations and communities. Unfortunately, many have chosen to abuse that power. The Roman Catholic Church is facing an institutional crisis because of thousands of cases in which adult priests abused their power and privilege to have sex with young parishioners.[7]

The Presbyterian Church, like many Protestant denominations, is plagued by widespread sexual misconduct by pastors (primarily married men who have sexual affairs with women in their congregations).[8] The denomination has taken significant steps to make clear the unacceptability of such behavior and to speed the reporting of it. However, currently, in the Presbyterian Church, these heterosexual male pastors who have clearly violated the teaching of Scripture, their marriage vows, and their ordination vows, by having affairs with female parishioners, are usually treated as individuals, with restoration always a possibility. But in the case of homosexual people, the church makes a blanket law a priori that none of them is worthy of ordination to serve as deacon, elder, or minister of Word and Sacrament.

THE EVOLUTION OF THE PURPOSE OF MARRIAGE

The issue of ordaining people who are gay and lesbian is inextricably linked to the issue of marriage. In the Presbyterian Church, as in most Protestant denominations, candidates for ministry are expected either to be married or to remain celibate. However, because gay and lesbian people are currently barred from marriage by the church, gay and lesbian candidates for ministry are never given the option of expressing their sexuality within the bonds of marriage. Instead, they are told that they must remain celibate if they hope to be ordained. It's clearly a double standard. The only fair and equitable solution is that *all* people should be expected either to be married or to be celibate.

The church's present policy of excluding a certain class of people from the rights and benefits of marriage echoes many of the now-discredited policies of the past. The Westminster Confession of Faith, for example, which was the sole doctrinal standard of Presbyterianism for more than three hundred years, declared that a valid marriage was between Protestants only: "Such as profess the true reformed Religion, should not marry with infidels, papists or other idolaters."[9] By the 1930s, however, Presbyterians began to challenge this ban on marrying Roman Catholics, arguing that "many Roman Catholics are sincere and intelligent believers in our Lord Jesus Christ."[10] Presbyterians later amended the Westminster Confession to remove offending statements against Roman Catholics, including the statement that the pope was the antichrist.[11]

Marriage between the races followed a similar path. In 1948, the California Supreme Court became the first state high court to overturn a law barring marriage between people of different races. At that time, forty of the then-forty-eight states banned interracial marriage.[12] The notion that marriage was only for people of the same race had been a deeply ingrained bias in American society and in the churches. The California Supreme Court decision to permit interracial marriage was controversial in its time.[13] But we have changed our minds, and our laws, for the better.

Marriage has also been defined in such a way as to limit women's civil and human rights. Even in the early twentieth century, in many states women could not own property; if a married woman inherited money from her family, it became the property of her husband. Women were not allowed to vote in national elections until 1920, and opportunities in higher education were limited. The normal state for women was to marry and bear children. They were to be silent partners, leaving all public functions to their husbands.[14]

Over time the Presbyterian Church has also changed its view of the purpose of marriage. Into the 1930s the denomination defined the primary purposes of marriage as bearing children, creating a family, and supporting stability in society. Although in 1930 the Presbyterian Church allowed women to become elders, in that same year a major report on marriage to the General Assembly insisted that motherhood was the proper goal for women. The report encouraged colleges to give more attention to "the science of homemaking" and expressed concern about the use of contraceptives, since the purpose of marriage was procreation.[15] When in 1931 a committee of the Federal Council of Churches recommended that parents consider using artificial means of birth control, the southern Presbyterian Church (PCUS) in indignation withdrew from the council. The northern Presbyterian Church (PCUSA) remained a member but advised the council to "hold its peace on questions of delicacy and morality."

By 1960, however, Presbyterians had adopted the position that the primary purpose of marriage was for the mutual comfort, encouragement, and support of the persons involved. Therefore birth control was appropriate. In 1960 the larger Presbyterian denominations, north and south, issued a joint statement approving of birth control.[16]

MALE GENDER SUPERIORITY AND OPPOSITION TO SAME-SEX MARRIAGE

Recent legal efforts to limit the civil benefits of marriage to heterosexual couples are grounded in the older view that the primary purpose of marriage is procreation. In a Vermont case regarding the rights of homosexual couples, for example, the Vermont assistant attorney general, Eve

Jacobs-Carnahan, defended limiting the right of marriage to hetero-sexual couples by arguing that the purpose of marriage was biological procreation.[17]

In March 2000, Californians approved Proposition 22, the "Defense of Marriage Act," which stipulated that "only marriage between a man and a woman is valid or recognized in California." The groups that pushed hardest for passage of the California act were the Mormon Church and the Roman Catholic Church. The Mormon Church was alleged to have contributed 40 percent of the funds toward marriage-limitation initiatives in other states in the 1990s.[18] Both the Mormons and the Roman Catholics still deny women full participation in the life of their churches. The primary purpose of marriage for them is still for women to bear and care for children, while men exercise public leader-ship. They have a vested interest in defining marriage in such a way as to maintain their limited and limiting vision.[19]

As we have discussed, there is a strong link between opposition to equality between men and women and opposition to homosexuality.[20] Many religious conservatives view a patriarchal family structure as the key to the health of the church and the nation.[21] In this view, patri-archy, patriotism, and Christianity are woven together into one flag, which is flown over all discussions of homosexuality. Homosexuality and women's equality are both seen as threats to the model of male dominance and by extension are seen as threats to the church and the nation. Arguing that the central purpose of marriage is procreation serves the interests of those who believe in the value of a patriarchal family structure, because it assigns women a limited and subordinate role and it bars gay and lesbian people from marriage.[22]

Jerry Falwell, in his best-selling book *Listen America!* warned that changes in gender roles and the acceptance of gay and lesbian people were two sides of the same coin. Falwell proclaimed, "We would not be having the present moral crisis regarding the homosexual movement if men and women accepted their proper roles as designated by God. . . . In the Christian home the father is responsible to exercise spiritual control and to be the head over his wife and children. . . . In the Christian home, the woman is to be submissive. . . . Homosexuality is Satan's diabolical attack upon the family, God's order in Creation."[23]

In 2003, Glenn Stanton, director of social research and cultural affairs at Focus on the Family, warned that if gay and lesbian people were allowed to marry, "the terms 'husband' and 'wife' would become merely words with no meaning. Gender would become nothing."[24] It is essential to the conservative "defense of marriage" that husbands have a superior role to wives. If two people of the same sex were allowed to marry, it would ratify the transformation of marriage that has been going on over the past thirty years, as people have developed more egalitarian ideas of their roles in marriage relationships.

James Dobson, founder of Focus on the Family (and its political arm, Focus on the Family Action), is perhaps the most vocal advocate of the strict-father model of male dominance as the ideal for the family, the church, and the nation.[25] *U.S. News & World Report* called Dobson "the best-known leader among America's 50 million-strong evangelical Christians."[26] The two most important political issues for Dobson and his followers are opposition to abortion and opposition to marriage of gay and lesbian people (notice how these two priorities serve to reinforce traditional gender roles). "You have to decide the things that matter most," he declares; ". . . if that makes us sound extreme, I'll take it."[27]

Dobson has announced, "We're involved in what is known as a culture war that is aimed right straight at the institution of the family."[28] Who is responsible for this attack on the family? Listen to statements from Dobson's Focus on the Family: "For more than 40 years, the homosexual activist movement has sought to implement a master plan that has had as its centerpiece the utter destruction of the family."[29] "They don't just want marriage. They want to destroy marriage and the family as we know it."[30] "Traditional marriage between one man and one woman cannot co-exist with homosexual marriage. It will destroy the family."[31] If you look closely at Dobson's statements, his real aim is to fight against any change in gender roles in society. Same-sex marriage, feminism, and any sort of evolution in the perceived purpose of marriage are all seen as threats to traditional heterosexual male dominance of family and society.

A striking illustration of how important male gender superiority is to Dobson came in 1997, when Dobson ran advertisements in Christian magazines questioning the trustworthiness of a proposed "gender-inclusive" translation of the popular New International Version (NIV) of the New Testament; the proposed translation would have substituted gender-neutral words, such as "people," for gender-specific words, such as "mankind." In a March 29, 1997, cover story, conservative *World* magazine's Susan Olasky had reported that NIV translators were conspiring to produce an edition of the Bible that would represent a "feminist seduction" of the evangelical church by changing pronouns and gender references.[32] In *World,* Dobson attacked the members of the NIV translation committee: "The Committee on Bible Translation (CBT) and executives of Zondervan Publishing House are editing the inspired words of God himself, . . . degenderizing the biblical text and inserting words that are not represented in the source documents."[33] He proclaimed, "Frankly, I find it breath-taking that the CBT or any other group would feel justified in editing the utterances of the Holy One of Israel."

Dobson invited eleven men—four involved in translating or publishing the NIV, and seven critics of inclusive language—to a meeting about the translation. They included leaders of the Council on Biblical Manhood and Womanhood, a group that proclaims male headship, plus representatives of denominations opposed to the ordination of women. The group produced thirteen "Guidelines for Translation of Gender-Related Language in Scripture," which among other things demanded that the term "man" be used as a designation for the human race or human beings.[34] As a result of the criticism, the International Bible Society and Zondervan Publishing Company announced that they would scrap the proposed NIV translation.[35]

Many conservative Christian scholars looked askance at the "translation guidelines" developed by the ad hoc group that Dobson had convened. They deplored the confusion of issues regarding the accuracy of translation with attempts to maintain a traditional cultural position of male dominance.[36] A woman New Testament scholar at Gordon-Conwell Theological Seminary, Aída Besançon Spencer, wrote, "Indeed, the guidelines represent an attempt by one gender, men, to hold on to power even when that means thwarting the accuracy of the biblical text and the good news it proclaims."[37] An editorial in the magazine *Christianity Today* asked if evangelicals were entering a new phase of "fundamentalist political correctness."[38]

When the views of Dobson's ad hoc committee on translation guidelines were criticized by other conservative Christian scholars as "linguistically and hermeneutically naïve and inaccurate," Dobson admitted, "I am not a biblical scholar [and] I don't have the academic qualifications to debate [these issues]."[39] He nonetheless continued to assert his cultural biases, as if they were biblically accurate, in the name of preserving his vision of the ideal American family.

It is important to note that in his work Dobson isn't defending families, marriage, or the Bible. He is defending male privilege and power. Dobson has said, "God designed man to be the aggressor, provider, and leader in his family. Somehow that is tied to his sex drive."[40]

Dobson's approach denies the full expression of gifts that God has bestowed on both women and men. As a church, when we include the views and experiences of people of color, women, persons with disabilities, the young, the elderly, and people who are homosexual, we are all wonderfully enriched.

Opposition to Science

Despite having a PhD from the University of Southern California in child development, Dobson rejects reputable scientific studies and the judgments of professional scientific associations in order to defend his view of the male-dominant model of marriage, family, and society.[41] His positions are regularly contradicted by professional scientific and medical associations. For example, Dobson and the few conservative Christian organizations that he relies on[42] insist that homosexuality is a mental disorder.[43] However, in 1973 the American Psychiatric Association voted to no longer consider homosexuality a mental disorder, and the American Psychological Association took a similar action in 1975.[44]

Nor is homosexuality considered a psychiatric disorder. For a mental condition to be described as a psychiatric disorder, it should either regularly cause emotional distress or regularly be associated with clinically significant impairment of social functioning.[45] In 1994, the American Psychiatric Association and the American Psychological Association stated: "The research on homosexuality is very clear. Homosexuality is neither mental illness nor moral depravity. It is simply the way a minority of our population expresses human love and sexuality. Study after study documents the mental health of gay men and lesbians. Studies of judgment, stability, reliability, and social and vocational adaptiveness all show that gay men and lesbians function every bit as well as heterosexuals."[46]

Dobson and his colleagues make the charge that "homosexuality is a gender identity disorder."[47] "Homosexuality is a masculine inferiority"—the result of having an overemotionally involved mother and a withdrawn, nonexpressive father.[48] Dobson's assertion is simply not true. In 1981, researchers from the Kinsey Institute published the results of a comprehensive study on sexual preference among women and men. They conducted lengthy interviews with nearly a thousand homosexual people and five hundred heterosexual people. "The investigators assessed nearly every imaginable psychological cause of homosexuality—parental relationships, childhood sexual experiences, peer relationships, dating experiences. Their findings: Apart from homosexuals'

somewhat greater nonconformity, the reported backgrounds of homosexuals and heterosexuals were similar. Homosexuals were no more
likely to have been smothered by maternal love, neglected by their
father, or sexually abused."[49] The American Psychoanalytic Association, in its position statement on the treatment of homosexual patients
(1997), indicates that Dobson's attitudes may create problems rather
than curing them: "Same-gender sexual orientation cannot be assumed
to represent a deficit in personality development or the expression of
psychopathology. As with any societal prejudice, anti-homosexual bias
negatively affects mental health, contributing to an enduring sense of
stigma and pervasive self-criticism in people of same-gender sexual orientation through the internalization of such prejudice."[50]

Dobson's views on homosexuality in relation to marriage and family
life are refuted by recent statements of the American Anthropological
Association, the world's largest organization of people who study culture. In its 2004 "Statement on Marriage and the Family," the association declared,

> The results of more than a century of anthropological research on
> households, kinship relationships, and families, across cultures and
> through time, provide no support whatsoever for the view that
> either civilization or viable social orders depend upon marriage as an
> exclusively heterosexual institution. Rather, anthropological
> research supports the conclusion that a vast array of family types,
> including families built upon same-sex partnerships, can contribute
> to stable and humane societies. The Executive Board of the Ameri-
> can Anthropological Association strongly opposes a constitutional
> amendment limiting marriage to heterosexual couples.[51]

The American Association for Marriage and Family Therapy annual
conference in September 2004 stated, "We see no evidence that same-
sex couples or family units vary significantly from heterosexual couples
or family units in terms of aspirations, hopes and goals, or in outcomes
for children."[52]

Joseph Nicolosi, president of the National Association for Research
and Therapy of Homosexuality, a frequent speaker at Dobson-sponsored
conferences, articulated the Freudian position that homosexuality is
caused by poor parenting and could be prevented or cured.[53] Nicolosi
said: "We advise parents to use clear and consistent messages: 'We do
not accept your effeminacy. You are a boy. God made you a boy. Being
a boy is special.' When parents do this, especially fathers, they can turn

their boys around."[54] "Focus on the Family is promoting the truth that homosexuality is preventable and treatable; . . . individuals don't have to be gay."[55]

Countering this position, the American Academy of Pediatrics states: "Therapy directed specifically at changing sexual orientation is contraindicated, since it can provoke guilt and anxiety while having little or no potential for achieving changes in orientation."[56] Also opposing the stance of Focus on the Family, and critical of the assumption that people who are homosexual should and can change their sexual orientation, are the American Psychiatric Association, the American Medical Association, the American Psychological Association, the American Counseling Association, and the National Association of Social Workers.[57] Together these organizations represent more than 477,000 health and mental health professionals. Collectively they have come to the conclusion that "homosexuality is not a mental disorder and thus there is no need for a 'cure.'"[58]

Dobson and his colleagues paint the very worst picture of people who are homosexual. They compare people who are homosexual to prostitutes, pedophiles, adulterers, and people who prefer animals sexually.[59] They claim that it is not possible for a homosexual to be a totally healthy person.[60] They assert that promiscuity is the defining feature of male homosexuality.[61] None of these claims can be demonstrated by objective research. Real Christian gay and lesbian people living in faithful, committed relationships bear no resemblances to Dobson's caricatures.

In a statement reminiscent of Charles Hodge's opposition to evolution in the nineteenth century, James Dobson has said, "Science can be a wonderful instrument of good as long as it respects the bounds of moral principles."[62] Hodge claimed that science was to be ignored when it departed from the Scottish Common Sense philosophy that he espoused. Similarly, Dobson rejects all scientific studies that do not conform to the fundamentalist worldview that he espouses.[63]

Violent Rhetoric

The opposition to homosexuality by religious fundamentalists is not just a matter of differing ideas. The tone of fundamentalist opposition is often crude and violent. Focus on the Family says, "The homosexual agenda is a beast. [It] wants our kids. . . . And the only thing that's standing between them and that agenda . . . are those of us who believe in the Judeo-Christian values of this country."[64]

In 2004 televangelist Jimmy Swaggart announced to his audience, "I've never seen a man in my life I wanted to marry. . . . And I'm gonna be blunt and plain, if one ever looks at me like that, I'm going to kill him and tell God he died. . . . In case anybody doesn't know, God calls it an abomination."[65]

Amazingly, in the midst of such violent rhetoric and ongoing physical violence against gays and lesbians, such as the murder of Matthew Shepard, conservative advocacy groups such as the National Religious Broadcasters association (an umbrella group of some 1,600 Christian radio and TV broadcasters) and the politically influential Family Research Council have actually mobilized to *oppose* passage of any hate-crime legislation that includes protections for gay and lesbian people.[66]

In response to such violent attitudes, Coretta Scott King has said, "Homophobia is like racism and anti-Semitism and other forms of bigotry in that it seeks to dehumanize a large group of people, to deny their humanity, their dignity and personhood."[67]

I find great wisdom in the reasoned view of the late evangelical ethicist Lewis B. Smedes, who asked: "What danger to straight people is posed by homosexuals? Some say that they are a threat to the family, but none tell us how. Some fear that they might abuse our children, but no facts have ever been adduced to show that they are any more likely to do so than heterosexual people are. Do homosexuals threaten to invade our homes, steal our property, rape our daughters? What we know is that homosexual men are murdered by heterosexual people just for being gay; what we also know is that there is no record of a heterosexual being murdered for not being gay. Why, then, I wonder, in a world of violence, starving children, cruel tyrannies, and natural disasters, are Christian people so steamed up about the harmless and often beneficent presence of gays and lesbians among us?"[68]

The Irony in the Debate over Marriage

Newsweek in spring 2004 was honest about the current state of marriage in America: "If marriage is in trouble, don't blame gays. Straights changed the rules."[69] Let us take a realistic look, for a moment, at the state of marriage in the United States. In the last one hundred years, the United States has gone from being the most marrying society in the world to the one with the most divorces and single-parent families.[70] Among all the industrialized nations, the United States has the highest rate of teenage pregnancy and teenage childbirth, despite having the highest rate of teenage abortions.[71] An estimated one-third of American children live without their biological father present.[72]

In the United States, "8.1% of coupled households are made up of unmarried, heterosexual partners."[73] A Barna poll in 2001 found that cohabitation—living with a member of the opposite sex without marriage—has been practiced at some time by 33 percent of all adults and 25 percent of born-again Christians.[74] While some view living together as a sort of trial marriage, 40 percent of those cohabiting do not marry.[75] We live in an era of family disruption that leads sociologists to talk of an "emerging culture of 'serial marriage' and 'nonmarriage.'"[76]

None of these alarming trends has been caused by people who are homosexual who want to marry.[77] None will be solved by denying same-sex couples the right to marry. In a culture of "nonmarriage," it is ironic that we are spending great amounts of money and energy in trying to prevent people from marrying who want to do so in a way that would contribute to the stability of society.

The legal rights conferred by marriage are vast. U.S. Representative Henry J. Hyde, as chairperson of the House Committee on the Judiciary, asked the General Accounting Office (GAO) "to identify federal laws in which benefits, rights and privileges are contingent on marital status." The response of the GAO, in a letter of January 31, 1997, ran to seventy-five pages. Married heterosexual couples living in the United States are entitled to 1,049 federal rights, benefits, and privileges. Depending on the state in which a couple lives, there may be as many as 400 additional legal benefits. Most of these legal and economic benefits cannot be privately contracted for or arranged. Lesbian and gay couples, especially those with children, understandably wish to be able to provide in these myriad ways for their families.[78]

Perhaps the greatest irony in the marriage debate is that self-described born-again Christians, a segment of the population that is often vocal about supporting bans on same-sex marriage, seem to exhibit greater problems with their own marriages. Evangelical pollster George Barna found that during the 1990s born-again Christians had higher divorce rates than non-Christians.[79] Professor Brad Wilcox, a Christian sociologist who specializes in family issues, notes that "compared with the rest of the population, conservative Protestants are *more* likely to divorce." He also points out that divorce rates are higher in the southern United States, where conservative Protestants make up a higher percentage of the population.[80] The states of Kentucky, Mississippi, and Arkansas, which voted overwhelmingly for constitutional amendments to ban same-sex marriage in 2004, had three of the highest divorce rates in the United States. In contrast, the state with the lowest divorce rate is Massachusetts, a state whose Supreme Court has ruled in favor of gay marriage.[81] There is clearly a disconnect between the problems facing heterosexual marriages in the United States and the conservatives' proposed solution of banning same-sex marriage.

The allegation that allowing gay and lesbian people to marry will destroy heterosexual marriage is nonsense! It is simply a diversion from dealing with the real problems of heterosexual marriage. We have heard this kind of inflated rhetoric before from respected church people. If blacks were allowed to vote, it would be the end of "civilization itself" (Robert Lewis Dabney, 1867).[82] If women were not kept subordinate to men, we would soon have a country "from which all order and all virtue would speedily be banished" (Charles Hodge, 1838).[83] These men were the leading theologians of their day. They were quite sincere in their concern. They were also dead wrong.

The current effort to prevent people who are gay or lesbian from getting married is a diversion that makes Christian people feel they are doing something to defend marriage, but it does absolutely nothing to address the real problems of marriage in the United States.

REAL MARRIAGE FOR REAL PEOPLE

On February 28, 2004, I received an award from the Lazarus Project, a ministry of reconciliation between gay and straight people in southern California. As I was preparing my speech for the awards dinner, the national battle lines in the fight over same-sex marriage shifted dramatically. On February 10, San Francisco mayor Gavin Newsom ordered the County Clerk to end discrimination against same-sex couples in issuing marriage licenses. Two days later, the county began to issue marriage licenses to same-sex couples. Over the next several weeks, more than four thousand gay and lesbian couples were married.[84]

Two impressions struck me as I looked at the newspaper pictures of people waiting for marriage licenses in San Francisco. The first was how happy they looked. This was not a political protest; it was evidence of love and the joy that marriage brings. The second was how many had children with them. These were people who loved and cared for children and wanted the respect and benefits that come with marriage for the good of their children.[85]

The events of that period in San Francisco gave the lie to stereotypes of gay and lesbian people. These were people who are just like those of us who are heterosexual and who want to live stable, faithful lives, to which they were willing to be publicly committed. There was nothing broken about them; they did not need to be fixed. We just need to quit slamming the door in their face.

Yet that is what the president of the United States was trying to do. As same-sex marriages were being performed in San Francisco, George W. Bush announced, "If we are to prevent the meaning of marriage from being changed forever, our nation must enact a constitutional amendment to protect marriage in America."[86] In 217 years of American history, there have only been seventeen amendments to the Constitution. They fall into two categories: to expand civil rights and to fix problems in the structure of government. The only one that didn't fit in one of these two categories was prohibition of "intoxicating liquors," and we all know how that one turned out![87] "No amendment has ever chiseled exclusion and discrimination *into* the U.S. Constitution. Yet that is what an amendment banning gay marriage proposes to do."[88]

MY EXPERIENCE OF GAY AND LESBIAN COUPLES

It seems to me that all human beings, gay and straight, deserve the opportunity to have the companionship of another person with whom they have formed a covenant of lifelong, loving commitment. When I was Moderator of the General Assembly in 2001–2002, my wife, Sharon, and I were invited to the lovely home of Doug and Dennis for dinner and an evening of conversation with gay and lesbian couples and their friends. We met two elderly gentlemen, Dick and Jim, who at that time had been together for forty-seven years. One of them told me that he lived every day of his life in fear that they would be "outed" and that he would lose his job. Yet they persisted in caring for one another. Many of the couples there had been together twenty years or more, and all of them ten years or more.[89] I remember a heterosexual friend telling me that in her circle of friends anyone who had stayed married for more than five years was an exceptional case. The people I met at Doug and Dennis's house were just ordinary, faithful Christians who displayed a profound commitment to each other.

I know many lesbian couples and gay couples who manifest remarkable faithfulness in their commitment to a single partner, despite all of the roadblocks that society and the church put in their way. Just a few days before I wrote this, I spoke with a lesbian couple, Cheryl and Debbie, after church. One was carrying an eight-week-old baby in her arms, and the other was carrying the child's car seat. They looked like every set of new parents—radiant and happy. Despite conservative claims to the contrary, studies show no discernable difference in good adjustment between children raised by a male-female couple and those raised by a same-sex couple.[90] Indeed, a few weeks after Cheryl and Debbie adopted their daughter, the agency called and asked if they would take a little boy—and they did.

I also know a gay couple, Tim and Dan, who have adopted two special-needs children—children often least desired by adoptive couples. They were foster parents for many years, caring for many special-needs children and hoping each time that they would be allowed to adopt them. Finally they were given permission and have even changed jobs and relocated to a community where they felt their children would be accepted and could get the best education.

I had the privilege of being with a gay couple, Neil and John, who had just been married in San Francisco during that brief window of opportunity opened by Mayor Newsom. Their story of several attempts to be at the right place and right time to get a license was hilarious and deeply touching. They love each other and wanted to make public and celebrate their commitment to each other.

I know several friends who tried not to be homosexual, who entered into heterosexual relationships, married, and had children. Then, at some point, they could no longer deny who they really were and went through the painful process of separation and divorce. Finding someone whom they could love and support has freed them to be the person God intended for them to be. How much pain could have been avoided if these people had been allowed, in the beginning, to marry someone with whom they were really compatible!

I also think of several former missionaries that I know who are gay. One broke his engagement on his wedding day and remained single.

Another has remained faithfully married to his wife for a lifetime while acknowledging that he is a gay man. Yet another was married to a woman briefly and then lived for years feeling that he could never know love. Originally a Presbyterian, he came to know the founder of the Metropolitan Community Church, Troy Perry, a former pastor in the Church of God,[91] and helped Perry develop a curriculum for the denomination's Bible School. In that process he met and fell in love with a man who loved him; and they have been together for over twenty years, as responsible members of their community. These gay men made different choices and have different histories. But this is the same: they are faithful Christians whose primary desire is to serve God and live responsibly as the people God created them to be.

A while back I attended a public discussion where four different aspects of the issue of homosexuality were being discussed, each with a pro and a con speaker. Hal Schell, a Presbyterian who often represented the position that gays could change their behavior to heterosexuality, spoke against accepting "unrepentant" homosexuals into church leadership. He presented the case, which some conservatives would like to claim as normative, that childhood abuse (physical and sexual) had caused him to live a life of promiscuous gay sex. A former Fuller Seminary colleague, Mel White, was the other speaker on the topic of experience. Mel genuinely empathized with Hal's experience: "No one should be treated like that."

However, Mel's life experience was just the opposite. He had a loving family, was successful at everything he attempted in school. The only difference was that, as Mel put it, at football games while the other guys were looking at the cheerleaders, he was attracted to the quarterback. Mel's autobiography, *Stranger at the Gate,* is the poignant story of a deeply religious, theologically conservative, highly successful minister, writer, and filmmaker who struggled all his life with the reality that he was gay and finally admitted it to himself and his family.[92] He now heads Soulforce, a movement modeled on the nonviolent resistance of Gandhi and Martin Luther King Jr., whose purpose is to stop the spiritual violence against God's lesbian, gay, bisexual, and transgender children by telling the truth about them to the churches.[93]

I am not claiming that people who are homosexual are perfect. In my experience, they are just human beings with the normal hopes and fears, struggles and challenges of others in the population. However, given the ugly and baseless allegations that are made about people who are homosexual as a class, it is important to point out that these stereotypes are just not true.

A WIDENESS IN GOD'S MERCY

During my year as Moderator, Sharon and I also had the privilege of visiting the Netherlands, where we had lived for five years during the 1960s while I worked on my doctorate and Sharon taught school. I was a graduate student at the Free University, related to the Reformed Churches in the Netherlands, and was the organizing pastor of an English-speaking congregation that was related to the older Netherlands Reformed Church. At the time, these two Dutch Calvinist denominations did not get along, but now, by God's grace, they have merged with the small Evangelical Lutheran Church, to form the Protestant Church in the Netherlands. I had the privilege of addressing the Trio-Synode, the gathering of all three denominations as they prepared for merger.

All three of these denominations already ordain gay and lesbian people to church office. Sexual orientation is just not an issue for them. In the Netherlands, where the Reformed tradition is woven into the fabric of society, gay and lesbian people can also be married.[94]

The late Lewis Smedes, my former colleague at Fuller Seminary, did his doctorate at the Free University in Amsterdam ten years before me. We had both imbibed deeply of Dutch Calvinism. In 1999 Lew, recalling a line from an old hymn, "There's a wideness in God's mercy like the wideness of the sea," argued that the church should accept people who are homosexual as full members. His last line was, "I think I know my own heart well enough to believe that if [God's] mercy is wide enough for me, it is wide enough for them."[95]

The Lazarus Project takes its name from Jesus' call to the dead Lazarus to "come out" of his tomb. Those who have "come out" as gay and lesbian people are simply asking the church to let all Christians come in. When we realize how gracious God has been to us, we cannot deny God's grace to others.

The church should be first and not last in offering this welcome. The Bible tells us so. In the book of Revelation, the risen Christ is represented as saying: "Look, I have set before you an open door, which no one is able to shut" (Rev. 3:8). Jesus has opened a door through which every one of us can enter into God's realm.

There are gay and lesbian people in most of our churches. When they can be full and equal members, we will all be blessed. The possibility that we can fully include all of our members in the life of the church is within reach. It requires only that we be true to the fundamental teachings of the Christian faith. In chapter 7, I suggest how we can do this in the Presbyterian Church and how it will resolve our present conflict.

7

Recommendations for the Presbyterian Church (U.S.A.)

It seems to me that the church and every person within the church is faced with a choice: to witness to an ancient Near Eastern cultural bias of male gender superiority, or to witness to Jesus Christ and his redemptive life and ministry. The best methods of biblical interpretation, from the Reformation on down through today, urge us to reject narrow historical and cultural bias and instead to follow Jesus' example. The purpose of the Bible is not to weld us forever to an ancient culture. The purpose of the Bible is to tell us the story of Jesus' life, death, and resurrection.

Those who choose to witness to ancient cultural bias will always be able to find certain passages, take them out of context, and turn them into church laws that benefit them and discriminate against those whom they dislike. Those who choose to follow Jesus will see Jesus as the center of the biblical story and interpret each passage in light of his ministry. Using this Christ-centered approach enriches our understanding of the gospel and brings us into a closer relationship with God and our fellow human beings.

HEALING THE CHURCH

If you believe, as I do, that homosexuality is not a sin and is not prohibited by the Bible, then the next question becomes, How do we heal the church of this injustice that has divided us? Clearly, policies, bylaws, and church constitutions, in some cases, will need to be amended.

But it seems to me that the first step is for all of us in the church to apologize, institutionally, collectively, and personally. By condemning people who are gay and lesbian and barring them from marriage and holding office in the church, we have caused an enormous amount of unnecessary suffering, while distorting Jesus' message of love. If we reach out to our lesbian, gay, bisexual, and transgender sisters and brothers and show that we truly understand that we have caused them pain, it will speed the healing process—for everyone.

There are precedents for denominational apologies. In 1995, for example, on the occasion of its 150th anniversary, the Southern Baptist Convention (SBC) officially apologized for "condoning" racism. The SBC resolution in part stated, "We apologize to all African Americans for condoning and/or perpetuating individual and systemic racism in our lifetime, and we genuinely repent of racism of which we have been guilty, whether consciously or unconsciously." Gary Frost, a black pastor who is a SBC second vice president, formally accepted the apology. He said, "We pray that the genuineness of your repentance will be reflected in your attitudes and in your actions."[1]

In 2001, Presbyterians asked the forgiveness of African Americans for slavery and segregation. The 213th General Assembly said, "We acknowledge, however, our church's common complicity in the institution of slavery and its oppressive inequities that linger to this day."[2] Two hundred thirteen years is a long time to wait for an apology. Think of how much good it would have done for our church and our nation to apologize immediately after emancipation—to immediately begin the hard emotional task of healing our churches and communities.

How long will we wait before we apologize for the sin of homophobia, "the irrational fear of and contempt for homosexual persons"?[3] If we believe the church has committed an injustice, we can drag our feet and engage in begrudging half measures for decades. Or we can turn and face our mistakes, deal constructively with them now, and move forward together again as one church family. What often makes official apologies, like the recent Southern Baptist and the Presbyterian apologies, seem hollow is that they are offered by people who themselves did not commit the original offense to people who did not suffer from the original discrimination. How much more appropriate and effective would be an apology offered now to people who are homosexual, by people who, even passively and unintentionally, have been participants in their oppression.

An apology, personally and collectively, would be a good first step. But progress requires more than words. We need to demonstrate the depth of our understanding of Christ's message through action. We need to give people who are LGBT full and equal rights within the church and work for their rights within the broader society. That means marriage, ordination, and every other right necessary to bring people who are homosexual into full equality with people who are heterosexual. As full and equal human beings, they deserve full participation under church and civil law. It is that simple. No three-fifths compromise. No separate but equal.

The trajectory of Christian history is in the direction of ever-greater openness and inclusiveness. We rejoice now in the leadership in our churches of people of color, women, and divorced and remarried people. The time will come when having gay, lesbian, bisexual, and transgender people in Christian leadership will be just as routine.

Each denomination can work out its own repentance in the way that is most appropriate and effective for it. In what follows, I point to the barriers that my denomination, the Presbyterian Church (U.S.A.), has created over the past thirty years, and to the recent actions that have begun to remove those barriers.

SOURCES OF AUTHORITY AND GUIDANCE

In most Christian denominations, the Bible is the primary source of authority and guidance. Many denominations also have subordinate standards, that is, statements of faith, written at particular times and places to expound and interpret the meaning of Scripture for a particular people. These officially adopted documents articulate a church's "understanding of the meaning and implications of the one basic confession of the lordship of Christ."[4] These statements of faith are in various settings called creeds, confessions, symbols, formulas, definitions, declarations of faith, statements of belief, and articles of faith.[5] Roman Catholics, Eastern Orthodox, Lutherans, and Presbyterians have statements adopted by ecclesiastical bodies as official expressions of their faith. Some churches, such as Anglican, Episcopal, and Methodist, have documents to which they look for guidance that have a slightly lower official status. Even so-called "free" churches, like Baptists, which claim that they follow only the Bible, often have semiauthoritative statements that can be very influential in guiding beliefs and behaviors.[6]

These subordinate standards can be very helpful in providing clarifying summaries of the main teachings of Scripture. They can also, however, create problems when they take particular teachings out of context and make them church law. In most cases, it is the policies and procedures in these subordinate standards that will need to be amended in order to grant equal rights in the church to people who are homosexual.

The Presbyterian Constitution

Presbyterians have two subordinate standards that together form their *Constitution*: The *Book of Confessions* and the *Book of Order*. The *Book of Confessions* contains eleven theological documents. Two are ancient creeds: The Nicene Creed and the Apostles' Creed. Three date from the sixteenth-century Reformation: the Scots Confession of 1560, the Heidelberg Catechism of 1563, and the Second Helvetic Confession, published in 1566. Three come from the seventeenth-century Puritan Reformation in England: the Westminster Confession of Faith, the Shorter Catechism, and the Larger Catechism. The final three are twentieth-century documents: the Theological Declaration of Barmen (1934), the Confession of 1967, and A Brief Statement of Faith—Presbyterian Church (U.S.A.), adopted in 1991.

The *Book of Order* spells out the way in which the Christian faith, expressed in Scripture and summarized in the *Book of Confessions*, is to be applied in the ongoing life of the Presbyterian Church. It consists of three parts: the Form of Government, the Directory for Worship, and the Rules of Discipline.

American Presbyterians prize their *Constitution*, which, in rudimentary form, came into being at approximately the same time as the United States Constitution. Since the Presbyterian *Constitution* functions to interpret and apply Scripture, any flaws in it assume critical importance. At the same time, we acknowledge that human beings who create the *Constitution* can make mistakes. The Westminster Confession of Faith acknowledges the fragile character of human decisions: "All synods or councils since the apostles' times, whether general or particular, may err, and many have erred; therefore they are not to be made the rule of faith or practice, but to be used as a help in both."[7]

Unfortunately, American Presbyterians in recent decades have erred in using and amending their *Constitution* in ways that violate its essential values. As I discuss below, we have *unintentionally* accepted a flaw in the *Book of Confessions* by adopting a recent translation of the Heidelberg Catechism that adds a phrase condemning people who are homosexual—a phrase that is not in the original document. What is worse, the church has *intentionally* incorporated a flaw in the *Book of Order* by voting to amend it to take away from people who are homosexual the right to hold ordained office in the church.[8]

These two flawed statements in the Presbyterian *Constitution* distort its general principles. Our history demonstrates that when an exception is made to fundamental principles, it turns out to be a mistake that must later be rescinded. The flaws in both the *Book of Confessions* and the *Book of Order* need to be removed in order for the church to uphold its best principles and practices.

Principles in the *Book of Confessions*

In its confessional statements, the church declares to its members and the world "who and what it is, what it believes, what it resolves to do."[9] The confessions "summarize the essence of Christian tradition."[10]

Although changing anything in the *Book of Confessions* requires a more exacting process than changing rules for government, worship, or discipline in the *Book of Order*, the confessions *can* be changed. The church is "reformed," rooted in the biblical and ecclesiastical tradition, and "always reforming," or being reformed, changed, "according to the Word of God and the call of the Spirit."

The content of the *Book of Confessions* is summarized in chapter 2 of the *Book of Order*, so we have an idea of the broad and enduring themes Presbyterians share with other Christians. First, we share with the universal Christian church "the mystery of the triune God and of the incarnation of the eternal Word of God in Jesus Christ."[11] Second, we are thankful inheritors of the Protestant Reformation, with its watchwords of "grace alone, faith alone, Scripture alone."[12] Third, we acknowledge some emphases of the particular Reformed family to which we belong: God's sovereignty; election of people for salvation and service; covenant life marked by order according to the Word of God; stewardship of God's creation; recognition of the sin of idolatry; seeking justice and living in obedience to the Word of God.[13] None of these doctrines is the exclusive property of Presbyterians. Note that in chapter 2 of the *Book of Order* they are stated as broad themes of Christian consensus, not as the particular opinions of one party in the church.

The confessions, like the Bible, should be interpreted by taking into account their linguistic, historical, and cultural contexts. That means that we are not bound by particular ideas in the confessions that reflect the prejudices and limitations of a given culture or time.[14] A few examples will clarify what I mean:

1. The Westminster Larger Catechism evidences an ethic that supports a rigid class system in which there are "superiors" and "inferiors."[15] In contrast, A Brief Statement of Faith, adopted in 1991,

recognizes that God "makes everyone equally in God's image, male and female, of every race and people, to live as one community."[16]

2. In 1930s Germany, the German Christian Movement accepted the Nazi party's demand that Jews, homosexuals, and the disabled be excluded from the church and society. In response, the Confessing Church rose up and in 1934 developed the Barmen Declaration, which declares as its first principle that "Jesus Christ, as he is attested for us in Holy Scripture, is the one Word of God which we have to hear and which we have to trust and obey in life and in death."[17] Therefore it concludes, "The church's commission, upon which its freedom is founded, consists in delivering the message of the free grace of God to *all* people in Christ's stead."[18]

3. The Confession of 1967, modeled on the Barmen Declaration, calls for reconciliation and the abolition of racial segregation. It states as a fundamental principle, "Congregations, individuals, or groups of Christians who exclude, dominate, or patronize their fellowmen [*sic*], however subtly, resist the Spirit of God and bring contempt on the faith which they profess."[19]

As we can see, the trajectory of the confessions, as the trajectory of the church, is clearly in the direction of acceptance and inclusion of all people, based on the love of God in Jesus Christ. Therefore, to use an inauthentic statement in the *Book of Confessions* to exclude thousands of people, despite their faithful commitment to Jesus Christ, is to misrepresent the content and misunderstand the function of this invaluable part of our Presbyterian *Constitution*.

A Flaw in the *Book of Confessions*

As I explained in chapter 4, the Reformed confessions, properly understood, do not condemn homosexuality. In fact, the Reformed confessions say very little about sexuality itself. Yet many Presbyterians mistakenly believe that the confessions contain a clear prohibition against homosexuality. So where does that mistaken belief come from?

In January of 2001, I was preparing to teach a class on the Reformed confessions at San Francisco Theological Seminary's Southern California campus. One of my favorite confessional texts is the Heidelberg Catechism. It was written and published in 1563 to insure a Reformed, rather than Lutheran, understanding of the Christian faith in the palatinate (like a small state) of Heidelberg, in what is now Germany.

The elector, or governor, Frederick III, had entrusted the writing of the catechism to two young men: Zacharius Ursinus, who at twenty-seven was the head of the College of Wisdom, the local theological seminary; and Caspar Olevianus, who at age twenty-six was the senior pastor of the Holy Ghost Church, the cathedral church in Heidelberg.

In my teaching, I try to relate the doctrines of the confessions to current issues in our denomination. The Presbyterian Church had been struggling with the issue of the ordination of people who are gay or lesbian since 1976, and we appeared ready to do pitched battle over this issue again at the 2001 General Assembly. With that in mind, I was especially interested in Question and Answer 87 in the Heidelberg Catechism [emphasis added]:

> Q.   87. Can those who do not turn to God from their ungrateful, impenitent life be saved?
>
> A.   Certainly not! Scripture says, "Surely you know that the unjust will never come into possession of the kingdom of God. Make no mistake: no fornicator or idolater, none who are guilty either of adultery or of *homosexual perversion*, no thieves or grabbers or drunkards or slanderers or swindlers, will possess the kingdom of God."[20]

That seemed to be clear evidence in favor of the denomination's current policy of calling all homosexual behavior sinful and, on that basis, of barring gay and lesbian people from office in the church.

That would have been the end of the discussion, except for my memory that when people began using the *Book of Confessions* in arguments against homosexuality, Johanna Bos, a professor at Louisville Presbyterian Theological Seminary, had noted that the text of Answer 87 of the Heidelberg Catechism was not authentic.[21] In fact, a footnote in the *Book of Confessions* indicates that this translation of the Heidelberg Catechism had its origin in the early 1960s, when the North American Area Council of the World Alliance of Reformed and Presbyterian Churches authorized a four-hundredth-anniversary edition of the Heidelberg Catechism, originally written in 1563.[22] The text of the Heidelberg Catechism in our *Book of Confessions* was taken from that anniversary translation.

Johanna Bos noticed a difference between earlier translations and the 1962 edition because she was born and raised in the Netherlands. There, as a youth, she received rigorous training in the Heidelberg Catechism, along with the Belgic Confession and the Canons of Dort, which together comprise the three doctrinal statements of the Dutch Reformed churches. It was common practice in the Reformed churches of the Netherlands for pastors to spend several years taking young people carefully through the catechism in preparation for their joining the church, usually at about age eighteen. Furthermore, Dutch Reformed pastors were obliged to preach through the catechism each year at the evening service. Bos said that, despite all of her study in the Netherlands, she had never heard any mention of homosexuality. My interest and curiosity were aroused.

At the Huntington Library in San Marino, California, I discovered a significant number of editions of the Heidelberg Catechism available only in the rare book room. I read Question and Answer 87 in an early Latin version of Ursinus, published in 1586.[23] I followed that with a German version attributed to Olevianus from 1795.[24] Then I went to more familiar territory and read a Dutch version of the catechism, published along with a Psalm book, from 1591.[25] I found and consulted a 1645 English edition published in London during the meeting of the Westminster Assembly,[26] and I concluded my catechism inquiry by studying a 1765 English translation of the catechism prepared for the Dutch Reformed Church in New York.[27]

Answer 87 was the same in all of these early editions and translations. The list of those impenitent sinners excluded from the kingdom of God was always, in the same order, "unchaste person, idolater, adulterer, thief, covetous man, drunkard, slanderer, robber, or any such like." In *none* of the texts was there even a word where the 1962 version of the Heidelberg inserted the phrase "homosexual perversion." In every case the list went from adulterer to thief, with no intervening word or phrase which could have been rendered "homosexual perversion."

The early editions of the catechism provide Scripture references in the margin. For Question and Answer 87 the texts are always 1 Corinthians 6:9–10; Ephesians 5:5; 1 John 3:14–15; and Galatians 5:21. At this point, I remembered that some years ago I had heard that the phrase "homosexual perversion" in the 1962 version of Answer 87 in the Heidelberg Catechism was taken from the translation of 1 Corinthians 6:9–10 in the New English Bible.[28] Indeed, I discovered that the two translators of the 1962 version had inserted into the catechism the wording of 1 Corinthians 6:9–10 as it appears in the New English Bible, which had been published in 1961 and was at the time the newest available translation. The phrase "homosexual perversion" was used for the first time in that 1961 NEB translation.

The words in Greek that were translated in the 1961 NEB as "homosexual perversion" are *malakoi* and *arsenokoitai* (discussed at length in chapter 5). They appear together only in this one passage in the New Testament. In the NRSV they are rendered as "male prostitutes, sodomites." In chapter 5, I presented a body of scholarly opinion that refutes the translation in the NEB, but I must make two additional points. First, from a scholarly perspective, it is inexcusable to insert words, from another source, that were not in the original text of the catechism. Second, from a Christian perspective it is inexcusable to create a mid-twentieth-century rendition of the catechism that appears to condemn all same-sex relations when that condemnation is not present in the sixteenth-century original. The 1988 translation of the Heidelberg Catechism, published by the Reformed Church in America, removed the phrase "homosexual perversion" from Question and Answer 87, relied upon the NRSV translation instead of the NEB, and in a footnote acknowledged that there was no word in the original text of the Heidelberg Catechism that corresponded to the phrase "homosexual perversion."[29] Unfortunately, it is the earlier, 1962 translation of the catechism, without any footnote, that appears in our *Book of Confessions.* The confessions included in the Presbyterian *Book of Confessions* were chosen soon after the 1962 edition of the Heidelberg Catechism was published, and that version was chosen as the newest available.

The authors of the Heidelberg Catechism, Answer 87, did not intend that it be based on a quotation from a single biblical text. Note that the other biblical texts cited in the margin of the catechism (Eph. 5:5; 1 John 3:14–15; Gal. 5:21) focus in quite different directions from the New English Bible version of 1 Corinthians 6:9–10.[30] Ephesians 5:5 reads, "For be very sure of this: no one given to fornication or indecency, or the greed which makes an idol of gain, has any share in the kingdom of Christ and of God." What is most interesting in this passage is that it is not homosexuality (as some modern authors claim) but covetousness, greed, and striving for financial gain that are defined as idolatry. First John 3:14–15 says, "For everyone who hates his brother is a murderer, and no murderer, as you know, has eternal life dwelling within him." The focus is on the sin of lacking love for one's brothers. Galatians 5:21 has a long list of sins, including "quarrels, a contentious temper, envy, fits of rage, selfish ambitions." On the basis of these four biblical texts in the margin, one could hardly argue that Answer 87 was meant to focus on homosexuality.[31]

I wondered if perhaps the word translated as "indecency" in Ephesians 5:5 in the NEB might have supported the insertion of a reference to homosexuality. So I checked the Greek text on which the NEB was based.[32] The Greek word is *akathartos*, which, according to Liddell and Scott's *Greek-English Lexicon*, means "uncleanness," as of a wound, moral depravity, or ceremonial impurity.[33] There is no suggestion of an application specifically to same-sex practice. I checked Ephesians 5:5 in various translations. The Geneva Bible of 1560, which could conceivably have influenced the Heidelberg Catechism of 1563, rendered *akathartos* as "unclean person."[34] The RSV and the NRSV use the word "impure" in this place. In no instance is any application to same-sex practice indicated.

In my research I discovered that the 1962 version of the Heidelberg Catechism was translated by Allen O. Miller and M. Eugene Osterhaven. I had previously met Osterhaven, so I decided to contact him to try to understand what had happened. We had an exchange of letters and one phone call. He sent me material he had published in response to the criticism of Bos and Elwood. In one article he wrote: "When Allen Miller and I worked on the translation in 1962, the sexual revolution had already begun. . . . We believed that it would be well to be more specific in question 87 than Ursinus had been in his day."[35] In a phone conversation with Osterhaven, when I asked, again, why they chose to insert the phrase "homosexual perversion" when in fact there was no corresponding phrase in the original, he replied: "We just thought it would be a good idea."

Edward Dowey, professor at Princeton Seminary, was the chair of the Special Committee on a Brief Contemporary Statement of Faith, which put together the *Book of Confessions* and included the 1962 Miller and Osterhaven translation of the Heidelberg Catechism. It turns out that Dowey himself was not advised of the change and was stunned when it was discovered many years after the catechism was officially adopted. In an e-mail to Johanna Bos and Christopher Elwood on October 21, 1996, Dowey wrote, "A Presbyterian elder asked me a question during a leadership training school in New Brunswick Presbytery. I told him confidently there was no reference to homosexuality in the document. Sometime later I telephoned Gene Osterhaven, and he readily (and somewhat triumphantly as I recall) said they had made this change, holding that the subject was taboo in the sixteenth century, hence would not be named, even in a biblical text. . . . Our committee, and I especially, as chair are guilty of negligence; . . . no one dreamed of such chicanery as this; . . . I am dumbfounded that I and such careful scholars as Trinterud, Hendry, Smart, et al. failed to discover the illicit change."

The condemnation of homosexuality is not an essential teaching of our *Book of Confessions*. Indeed, except for this inaccurate insertion, there is no mention of homosexuality at all. One of the difficulties of translating any text is to use language that is faithful to the intent of the original and yet meaningful in our present cultural context. Unfortunately, our contemporary biases—the ones that we usually do not think to question—can influence a contemporary rendition of an older text. In this case, the Heidelberg Catechism found in the Presbyterian Church (U.S.A.) *Book of Confessions* is flawed by an inaccurate and unjustified insertion in Answer 87. The fact that this error condemns a whole class of church members makes it all the more grievous.

Steps Toward Correcting the Flaw in the *Book of Confessions*

Since the publication of the first edition of *Jesus, the Bible, and Homosexuality*, the church has taken a huge step toward restoring the Heidelberg Catechism to its original text.

In fact, the unauthorized tampering with Question and Answer 87 was just one of a number of errors in the document. Christopher Elwood, professor of historical theology at Louisville Presbyterian Theological Seminary, has documented four other passages (in addition to Q&A 87) in which the meaning of the original was significantly changed by the Miller and Osterhaven translation. Furthermore, the Christian Reformed Church, the Protestant Reformed Church in America, and the Reformed Church of Canada all use translations that avoid the problems discovered in the 1962 Miller and Osterhaven translation.[36]

Seven overtures to the 2008 Presbyterian General Assembly asked for the PC(USA) to restore the catechism to its original text. Prior to the Assembly, thirty-two Presbyterian scholars signed a petition asking for such a change. After much debate, the majority of the Theological Issues and Institutions Committee of the 218th General Assembly approved an overture from Newark Presbytery that spelled out the five errors in the translation and proposed revised language to restore the catechism to its original text. The full assembly then approved this overture by a vote of 60 percent (436) to 39 percent (280).[37]

The vote of the assembly starts the lengthy and complex process required for any change to the *Book of Confessions*. In brief, the Moderator of the 218th General Assembly in 2008 was required to appoint a committee of no less than fifteen elders and ministers to study the matter of restoring the Heidelberg Catechism to its original 1563 text. This committee has two years to study and must report its recommendations to the next General Assembly, in 2010. That second General Assembly must approve the recommendation of the Committee of fifteen (or change it), and then recommend the confession, as amended, to the presbyteries. Two-thirds of the 173 presbyteries (regional bodies of ministers and elders) must approve the recommendation of the 2010 assembly by the summer of 2011. If two-thirds of the presbyteries have voted in the affirmative, then a third General Assembly, in 2012, must approve and enact the new confession as part of the *Book of Confessions*.[38] Presbyterians take amending their confessional documents seriously (and proceed slowly). But the process to restore the Heidelberg Catechism to its original text has begun.

Principles of Our *Book of Order*

Like the *Book of Confessions*, the Presbyterian *Book of Order* embodies a trajectory toward ever-greater inclusiveness of people. The *Book of Order* stipulates that we should not deny membership with its full rights and privileges to anyone for "any other reason not related to profession of faith."[39]

The Articles of Agreement, which were the basis for the 1983 reunion of American Presbyterians, north and south, added four important new chapters to the *Book of Order*, none of which had been in the book of government of either of the predecessor denominations. These new chapters present the basic principles by which Presbyterians have governed and wish to govern themselves. Those principles point in the direction of increasing inclusiveness.

Chapter 3, "The Church and Its Mission," makes this principle of inclusiveness very clear. It calls the church "to a new openness to its own membership . . . becoming in fact as well as in faith a community of women and men of all ages, races, and conditions, and by providing for inclusiveness as a visible sign of the new humanity."[40] Chapter 4, "The Church and Its Unity," makes inclusiveness even more explicit:

> The Presbyterian Church (U.S.A.) shall give full expression to the rich diversity within its membership and shall provide means which

will assure a greater inclusiveness leading to wholeness in its emerging life. Persons of all racial ethnic groups, different ages, both sexes, various disabilities, diverse geographical areas, different theological positions consistent with the Reformed tradition, as well as different marital conditions (married, single, widowed, or divorced) shall be guaranteed full participation and access to representation in the decision making of the church.[41]

This paragraph represents repentance for the previous explicit exclusion of people of color, women, and those who are divorced. It also evidences our increasing awareness that we have often functionally excluded from leadership people who are young, people with disabilities, people who are unmarried, and those who are not from our geographic region, or who do not fit with our particular school of theology. This paragraph will be even more complete when it is amended to include the phrase "different sexual orientations."

Prior to the insertion of a provision, now known as G-6.0106b (which I discuss at length below), which was intended to prohibit the ordination of gay and lesbian people to office in the church, the *Book of Order* had a perfectly adequate and appropriate definition of the qualifications of church officer: "In addition to possessing the necessary gifts and abilities, natural and acquired, those who undertake particular ministries should be persons of strong faith, dedicated discipleship, and love of Jesus Christ as Savior and Lord. Their manner of life should be a demonstration of the Christian gospel in the church and the world."[42] I know many people who are LGBT who qualify for leadership according to those criteria.

A Flaw in the *Book of Order*

In 1993 the Presbyterian General Assembly declared a three-year period of study regarding homosexuality. As the end of the three years drew near, the approaching 1996 assembly in Albuquerque received fifty-one overtures relating to ordination of gay and lesbian people. These overtures were assigned to a fifty-member assembly committee on Ordination and Human Sexuality. The committee held a day of open hearings. A crowd of 1,000 people came to listen, and 230 signed up to speak for or against ordination of people who are homosexual, although only 103 people were able to speak, because of the time limitations.[43]

The majority recommendation by thirty-one members of the committee contained three sentences:

> Those who are called to office in the church are to lead a life in obedience to Scripture and in conformity to the historic confessional standards of the church. Among these standards is the requirement to live either in fidelity within the covenant of marriage of *one man and one woman,* or *chastity* in singleness. Persons refusing to repent of any self-acknowledged practice *which the confessions call sin* shall not be ordained and/or installed as deacons, elders, or ministers of the Word and Sacrament. [emphasis added]

The majority report then noted a significant exception to the principles it had just enunciated: "It is not the intention of this committee, through this recommendation to the presbyteries, to change anything in the church's present standards and polity in relation to divorce and remarriage."

A minority report signed by the remaining nineteen members of the committee called for allowing each session and presbytery to decide whether to ordain people who are gay or lesbian.

When the amendment came to the floor, Friday, July 5, there was a forty-five-minute "informational presentation and prayerful reflection" on both the majority and minority reports, followed by ninety minutes of debate. Two minutes of prayer followed and then the vote. The final vote approving the majority report was 313 for, 236 against, with no abstentions—57 percent for and 43 percent against.[44]

James D. Anderson, a gay Presbyterian, noted that

> the original version of this amendment came from the Assembly Committee on Ordination and Human Sexuality with the phrase "marriage of one man and one woman." On the floor of the assembly, this was changed to "marriage of a man and a woman," in an attempt to circumvent clear prohibitions of divorce in the words of Jesus and in the confessions. It was thought that "a" rather than "one" would permit heterosexuals to continue to enjoy as many spouses as they wish, as long as they engage in their serial marriages one at a time. In contrast, lesbian and gay folks are held to a quite different standard. We are not allowed even a single life-long partner. Such is the morality of apartheid.[45]

Amendment B, as the three-sentence statement approved by the assembly was known, was sent to the presbyteries as a potential change in the *Constitution*. During the debates in the presbyteries, the text of Amendment B proved to be less than clear. Practically, what does "chastity in singleness" mean? What exactly are the practices that the confessions call sin?

But while the text was not clear, almost everyone knew that the *intent* of Amendment B was to find some sort of theological basis to bar people who are gay and lesbian from being ordained. Despite the ambiguity of Amendment B, by spring 1997, out of 172 presbyteries, 97 voted yes, 74 voted no, and 1 took no action. Amendment B was thus approved and became G-6.0106b in the *Book of Order*. Of all the individuals voting in presbyteries, a bare majority of 50.69 percent voted for Amendment B, and 48.91 percent against it. With this action, the majority felt that they had effectively barred people who are homosexual from ordained office in the Presbyterian church. It was, however, only the beginning of much confusion and controversy.

Fundamental Misunderstandings

On the surface, the amendment that came to be called G-6.0106b sounds great. Of course, everyone wants their church officers "to lead a life in obedience to Scripture and in conformity to the historic confessional standards of the church." But the inaccurate assumptions about the Bible and the confessions in the second and third sentences have caused enormous problems. I will highlight two problems in particular.

The first problem is that most Presbyterians incorrectly assume that "chastity" as it is used in the amendment means celibacy. The moderator of the assembly committee that produced Amendment B declared that "chastity" meant "restraint from engaging in sexual intercourse outside the bonds of marriage between a man and a woman."[46] However, the committee's report made the *Book of Confessions* the basis for its judgments. In the *Book of Confessions* "chastity" describes a responsible quality of life that applies to any Christian, married or single. Thus, chastity did not always mean sexual abstinence.

Since the Presbyterian *Book of Confessions* is the source referred to in the amendment, the definition of "chastity" should be taken from the context and use of the word there. Because all of the references to "chastity" in the *Book of Confessions* have application both to single and married people, "celibacy" cannot be the meaning, as the following selections from the *Book of Confessions* demonstrate [emphases added]:

Book of Confessions, 4.108, from the Heidelberg Catechism

Q.   108. What does the seventh commandment teach us?

A.   That all *unchastity* is condemned by God, and that we should therefore detest it from the heart, and live *chaste* and disciplined lives, whether in holy wedlock or in single life.

Q.   109. Does God forbid nothing more than adultery and such gross sins in this commandment?

A.   Since both our body and soul are a temple of the Holy Spirit, it is his will that we keep both pure and holy. Therefore he forbids all *unchaste* actions, gestures, words, thoughts, desires and whatever may excite another person in them.

Book of Confessions, 7.248, from the Westminster Larger Catechism

Q.   138. What are the duties required in the Seventh Commandment?

A.   The duties required in the Seventh Commandment are: *chastity* in body, mind, affections, words, and behavior, and the preservation of it in ourselves and others; watchfulness over the eyes and all the senses; temperance, keeping of *chaste* company, modesty in apparel, marriage by those that have not the gift of continency, conjugal love, and cohabitation; diligent labor in our callings; shunning of all occasions of uncleanness and resisting temptations thereunto.

Book of Confessions, 7.249, from the Westminster Larger Catechism

Q.   139. What are the sins forbidden in the Seventh Commandment?

A.   The sins forbidden in the Seventh Commandment, besides the neglect of the duties required, are: adultery, fornication, rape, incest, sodomy,[47] and all unnatural lusts; all unclean imaginations, thoughts, purposes, and affections; all corrupt or filthy communications, or listening thereunto; wanton looks, impudent or light behavior, immodest apparel, prohibiting of lawful, and dispensing with unlawful marriages; allowing, tolerating, keeping of stews, and resorting to them; entangling vows of single life, undue delay of marriage; having more wives or husbands

> than one at the same time; unjust divorce or desertion; idleness, gluttony, drunkenness, *unchaste* company; lascivious songs, books, pictures, dancings, stageplays, all other provocations to, or acts of, uncleanness either in ourselves or others.

Chastity is a very important concept in the *Book of Confessions*. It asks that we all live our sexual lives with a responsible modesty. Chastity is compatible with "conjugal love" according to the Westminster Larger Catechism. Furthermore, in every instance in these excerpts from the *Book of Confessions,* chastity applies to all people, single or married, and thus cannot be a synonym for celibacy.

The second problem, perhaps more important, is that the amendment is based on false assumptions about what exactly "the confessions call sin." In fact, all of us commit acts "which the confessions call sin," and we are not repentant either, since we no longer regard as sins many things that were forbidden in earlier times and circumstances.

The confessions are historical documents that reflect not only general biblical principles, but also the ethical standards of the time and culture in which they were written. General ignorance of the content of the confessions made it possible for Presbyterians to appear to honor the confessions without actually understanding or applying them to their daily lives. If the third sentence of G-6.0106b is taken literally, "Persons refusing to repent of any self-acknowledged practice which the confessions call sin shall not be ordained and/or installed as deacons, elders, or ministers of the Word and Sacrament," then *no* Presbyterian can be ordained or installed as deacon, elder, or minister of the Word and Sacrament.

Several examples may be helpful to illustrate my point:

1. In the seventeenth century as English Puritans reacted against the required celibacy of the Roman Catholic priesthood, "undue delay of marriage" was specified as a sin in the Westminster Larger Catechism. The Westminster Confession declared that it is "the duty of Christians to marry onely in the Lord."[48] The seventeenth-century English Puritan application of this principle was that "such as profess the true reformed Religion, should not marry with infidels, papists or other idolaters." In fact, the pope was branded the antichrist![49]

2. The Second Helvetic Confession mandates, "Let marriages be made with consent of the parents, or of those who take the place of parents."[50] In the sixteenth and seventeenth centuries, prearranged marriages were standard practice, and often at what we would think was a very young age.

3. Most Presbyterians today do not keep a Puritan Sabbath. The Westminster Catechisms enjoin us against "profaning the day by idleness, or doing that which is in itself sinful, or by unnecessary thoughts, words, or works, about our worldly employments or recreations."[51] Were we to follow this, we could not participate in sports nor watch them on television on Sunday. Nor may we even think about the work waiting for us on Monday.

4. Few of us are repentant of our "worldly amusements." Today it would be impossible to watch television and entirely avoid images that our Puritan ancestors would have categorized as sinful "lascivious songs, books, pictures, dancings, stageplays, and all other provocations to, or acts of, uncleanness either in ourselves or others."[52] We not only observe others but we ourselves dress in ways that the Puritans (and our grandparents) would have thought "immodest apparel."[53] The most modest bathing suit on our beaches today would not have passed Puritan muster.

5. Even some of our worship practices violate Puritan standards. We do not consider the display of religious art to be sinful today, but it was forbidden in seventeenth-century Puritan England. The Westminster Larger Catechism designates as sin "the making of any representation of God, of all, or of any of the three Persons, either inwardly in our mind, or outwardly in any kind of image or likeness of any creature whatsoever."[54]

6. Presbyterians influenced by the charismatic movement would no doubt be surprised to discover that they are unrepentant sinners according to the confessions. The confessions demand, "Therefore, let all strange tongues keep silence in gatherings for worship, and let all things be set forth in a common language which is understood by the people gathered in that place."[55] "Prayer . . . is to be made . . . if vocal, in a known tongue."[56]

There are at least 250 sins mentioned in the *Book of Confessions*, and we all practice at least some of them in good conscience. Since most people, both in the Presbyterian Church and in other denominations, are not familiar with the sixteenth- and seventeenth-century confessions,[57] the church, in practice, only bars people who are gay or lesbian from ordination and still claims to be following our confessional tradition.

The young man who crafted the third line in G-6.0106b, "Persons refusing to repent of any self-acknowledged practice which the confessions call sin shall not be ordained and/or installed as deacons, elders, or ministers of the Word and Sacrament," believed that his sentence would mean that decisions on ethical matters in the church would be made on confessional rather than polity grounds.[58] The result has been the exact opposite.

G-6.0106b is a nice-sounding amendment that is a theological and practical mess. Those who voted for it felt like they were standing up for the Bible and the confessions! In fact, by relying on false assumptions about the Bible and the confessions, the amendment actually distorts fundamental principles of both. Ordination of people who are homosexual can be perfectly consistent with the Bible and the confessions. It is only the biased cultural assumptions about the Bible and the confessions, as contained in the second and third sentences of the amendment, that prevent lesbian and gay people from being ordained in the church.

Steps toward Correcting the Flaws in the *Book of Order*

In 2001, when I was Moderator of the 213th General Assembly, the assembly approved an overture to create a Theological Task Force on the Peace, Unity, and Purity of the Church. There were four mandated topics: Christology, Scripture, ordination standards, and power. Two previous Moderators and I appointed a task force of twenty people selected from the over five hundred who were recommended or applied. The people we chose reflected the full theological and demographic diversity of the church.

The Task Force members worked together for four and a half years. They discovered that they shared in the essentials of the Christian faith, especially Christology and their commitment to Scripture. They never took a vote on the ordination of people who are homosexual. Instead, they crafted a compromise—an authoritative interpretation (AI) of an existing section of the *Book of Order*—in G-6.0108, which is appropriately titled "Freedom of Conscience." The idea behind the proposal was simple: The whole church sets national standards. The governing body closest to the candidate for ordination, the session or the presbytery, applies those standards. If a candidate has a "scruple," a dissent, then the presbytery decides if it is an essential of the Reformed faith. If it is not an essential, then the person can be ordained. The compromise restored the best of our Presbyterian tradition.

In 2006, the 217th General Assembly voted 298 to 221 to approve the report of the Theological Task Force on the Peace, Unity, and Purity of the PC(USA). In so doing, the General Assembly created a new authoritative interpretation of G-6.0108—"which would permit a candidate who disagrees with part of the church's ordination standards, such as those involving the ordination of gays and lesbians, to declare an objection or a 'scruple.' The local governing body [presbytery] would then decide whether that departure from the denomination's constitutional standards 'constitutes a failure to adhere to the essentials of Reformed faith and polity,' or can be tolerated."[59]

In the two years that followed, two highly qualified people who were gay moved forward as a result of this new legislative framework. The first was Lisa Larges, the Minister Coordinator for the nonprofit advocacy group That All May Freely Serve. Larges had been a candidate for ministry in 1985 in the Presbytery of the Twin Cities, but her ordination was blocked in 1992 by the General Assembly Permanent Judicial Commission (GAPJC), the highest court in the Presbyterian Church, because she is a lesbian. Under the terms of the new AI, in January 2008, Larges was permitted to move to examination for ordination by the San Francisco Presbytery. Also in early 2008, Paul Capetz's ordination was restored by the Presbytery of the Twin Cities. Captez is a gay man who was ordained in 1991 but who set aside his ordination in 2000 in response to G-6.0106b, which he considered a violation of Reformed theology and "a false kind of works righteousness."[60]

On February 11, 2008, the GAPJC overturned the work of the Peace, Unity, and Purity Task Force and the majority decision of the 2006 General Assembly. In a controversial ruling, the GAPJC declared that G-6.0106b was the one essential that no one could "scruple." This was an astonishing misinterpretation of what constitutes an essential tenet in the Reformed tradition. A helpful metaphor that reflects our Presbyterian understanding of essential tenets is to think of a series of concentric circles. According to our confessions, Jesus Christ is the center of our faith as the one in whom we meet the triune God. For Protestants, the next layer of our core values is a belief in Scripture and justification by grace through faith. The third layer in the circle is made up of the characteristically Reformed concepts of sovereignty, election, covenant, stewardship, sin, and obedience.[61] There are many additional rings that represent our attempts to understand the whole counsel of God. We are most sure that we are dealing with essentials as we move toward the center of the circle. The GAPJC decision took something from the periphery of our faith—in this case, a poorly written clause in our *Book of Order*, from 1996, that is still subject to intense theological debate—and made it the central tenet of our faith.

In response, the John Knox Presbytery Overture to the 218th General Assembly in 2008 called for the assembly to overturn the decision by the GAPJC. The overture stated: "The 218th General Assembly (2008) affirms the authoritative interpretation of G-6.0108 approved by the 217th General Assembly (2006). Further, the 218th General Assembly (2008), pursuant to G-13.0112, interprets the requirements of G-6.0108 to apply equally to all ordination standards of the Presbyterian Church (U.S.A.)."[62] The Church Orders and Ministry Committee approved the John Knox Presbytery Overture by a vote of 43 to 15, and the full assembly then approved it by a vote of 53 percent (374) to 46 percent (325). Thus the 218th General Assembly overturned the GAPJC decision and restored the right of the presbytery to make the determination as to whether a candidate's dissent represents a departure from an essential of the faith. This decision took effect immediately upon passage by the assembly.

The 218th General Assembly also made history by passing the Boston Presbytery Overture, which removed G-6.0106b and replaced it with new text that reads:

> Those who are called to ordained service in the church, by their assent to the constitutional questions for ordination and installation (W-4.4003), pledge themselves to live lives obedient to Jesus Christ the Head of the Church, striving to follow where he leads through the witness of the Scriptures, and to understand the Scriptures through the instruction of the Confessions. In so doing, they declare their fidelity to the standards of the Church. Each governing body charged with examination for ordination and/or installation (G-14.0240 and G-14.0450) establishes the candidate's sincere efforts to adhere to these standards.[63]

I believe this revised text regarding ordination puts the focus exactly where it should be—on Jesus, the Scriptures, and the Confessions—the essential values at the center of our theological tradition.

The Boston Presbytery Overture also deleted those prior Authoritative Interpretations, passed since 1978, that had been used to bar LGBT candidates from the ministry. The Boston Overture was approved by the Church Orders and Ministry Committee by a vote of 41 to 11. It was then approved by the full Assembly by a vote of 380 to 325, with 3 abstentions. The revisions to G-6.0106b, because they are a change to the *Book of Order*, require the approval of a majority of the 173 presbyteries by June 28, 2009 (one year from the adjournment of the last assembly). However, the removal of the discriminatory authoritative interpretations took effect immediately. The approval by the General Assembly of both the John Knox Presbytery Overture and the Boston Presbytery Overture represents a huge step toward LGBT equality in the PC(USA).

REAFFIRMING THE BIBLE
AND THE PRINCIPLES OF OUR FAITH

The best methods of interpretation, from the Reformation on down through today, call upon us to interpret the Scripture through the lens of Jesus Christ's life and ministry. Using this method, we see clearly that Jesus and the Bible, properly understood, do not condemn people who are homosexual. In fact, as I will show in the next chapter, the Bible contains an extravagant welcome for sexual minorities. In church governance, our confessions and *Book of Order* embody a trajectory of ever-greater inclusiveness. To bar people who are LGBT from ordination and marriage is a violation of these fundamental principles of our faith. In the last two years, the Presbyterian Church has taken important steps to uphold these biblical and confessional principles by welcoming our lesbian, gay, bisexual, and transgender sisters and brothers as full and equal members in our church and society. The Holy Spirit is at work in the church. Praise God.

8
All Are One in Christ Jesus

I first started to read the Bible every day when I was in junior high. I wanted to know God, and I knew that this book would show the way. Now retired, I realize I've been reading the Bible daily for over sixty years. What is so astonishing about that experience is that after all this time, there is still so much more to discover about God's revelation in Scripture.

I've been specifically studying the biblical texts as they relate to homosexuality since 1993, yet I still feel that I have just scratched the surface in terms of understanding all that is there. Through studying the increasingly rich scholarship in this field, I have come to believe that there are many biblical passages that are more helpful in understanding how Christians should relate to people who are LGBT than the verses that are commonly cited.

Jesus understood the sacred texts and God's intention for humanity. So when we read the Bible through the lens of Jesus' redemptive life and ministry, we are better able to discern God's revelation. Jesus welcomed every kind of person into God's community—especially the outcast, the alien, the marginalized, the forgotten, and the foreigner. Reading the Bible through the lens of Jesus' redemptive life and ministry we see over and over again, God's radically inclusive grace that welcomes all who have faith. Let us examine three passages that show how Jesus' teachings illuminate God's extravagant welcome.

THE PARABLE OF THE GOOD SAMARITAN
(LUKE 10:25–37)

In the parable of the Good Samaritan a religious lawyer stands up to test Jesus. "'Teacher,'" he asks, "'what must I do to inherit eternal life?'" Jesus replies by asking the man what is written in the Jewish law. The lawyer responds by quoting Deuteronomy 6:5 and Leviticus 19:18: "'You shall love the Lord your God with all your heart, and with all your soul, and with all your strength, and with all your mind; and your neighbor as yourself.'"[1] Jesus simply says to the lawyer, "'You have given the right answer; do this, and you will live'" (Luke 10:27–28).

Let us stop and note: this is all the justification we need for accepting people who are lesbian, gay, bisexual, or transgender as full and equal members of the church. Love God, and love your neighbor as yourself—that is the heart of the Christian message. Everything else is commentary.

However, the lawyer, "wanting to justify himself," continues by asking Jesus, "'And who is my neighbor?'" Jesus responds by telling the story of a man who, while going down a notoriously dangerous road, fell into the hands of robbers, who stripped and beat him and went away leaving him half dead. Both a priest and a Levite saw the man but passed by on the other side of the road.

Then Jesus adds a surprising element to the story: "'A Samaritan while traveling came near him; and when he saw him, he was moved with pity. He went to him and bandaged his wounds, having poured oil and wine on them. Then he put him on his own animal, brought him to an inn, and took care of him. The next day he took out two denarii [equivalent to several days' wages], gave them to the innkeeper, and said, "Take care of him; and when I come back, I will repay you whatever more you spend."'" (Luke 10:33–35).

This is a remarkable story. Jews wanted nothing to do with the Samaritans.[2] Indeed, the lawyer with whom Jesus is speaking studiously avoids even saying "the Samaritan," referring to him simply as "the one who showed him kindness."[3] Jesus himself had been refused hospitality by the Samaritans when he attempted to pass through their land. His disciples had wanted to call down fire from heaven to consume them. But Jesus "turned and rebuked" his disciples (Luke 9:52–55).

The Samaritan did what the priest and Levite refused to do. New Testament scholar and Middle East expert Kenneth Bailey points out that "a Samaritan would not be safe in a Jewish town with a wounded Jew over the back of his riding animal. Community vengeance may be enacted against the Samaritan, even if he has saved the life of the Jew. . . . The overlooked reality of the Samaritan's final act is that he risks his life to care for this man in a Jewish inn."[4]

In this familiar story, Jesus uses a hated, alien outsider who showed kindness as the model for how we are to act as neighbors. This one story, based in Jesus' understanding of God's command in Leviticus 19 that we love both the alien (19:33) and our neighbor (19:17) as ourselves, should be sufficient to motivate Christians to grant equal rights to people who are LGBT.

JESUS' TEACHING ON MARRIAGE AND DIVORCE
(MATTHEW 19:10–12)

Matthew 19:10–12 appears in the midst of a lengthier discussion of marriage and divorce between Jesus and the disciples. Here, the disciples complain that because Jesus' policy on divorce and remarriage is so strict, perhaps it would be better not to marry. Jesus replies,

> "Not everyone can accept this teaching, but only those to whom it is given. For there are eunuchs who have been so from birth, and there are eunuchs who have been made eunuchs by others, and there are eunuchs who have made themselves eunuchs for the sake of the kingdom. Let everyone accept this who can." (Matt. 19:11–12)

This is an extraordinary passage. Many commentaries focus on the discussion about divorce and miss the larger point of this passage. But look carefully: Jesus is asked a question about heterosexual marriage and divorce, and he immediately broadens the conversation to acknowledge three different types of sexual minorities in that culture ("eunuchs who have been so from birth, eunuchs who have been made eunuchs by others, and eunuchs who have made themselves eunuchs for the sake of the kingdom"). That is stunning, especially given that "the eunuch was *persona non grata* both socially and religiously" in that culture.[5]

Notice especially that Jesus recognizes that some people are eunuchs "from birth." New Testament scholar Thomas Bohache asks, "Could Jesus not be referring to a broad category of people who from their birth, have not 'fitted' the predominant expectations of gender and sexuality?"[6] And theologian, psychotherapist, and former Jesuit priest John J. McNeill puts it more boldly: "The first category—those eunuchs who have been so from birth—is the closest description we have in the Bible of what we understand today as a homosexual."[7] It is clear that Jesus did not see humanity as universally heterosexual. Jesus recognized and acknowledged many types of sexual difference—even in a society in which such difference would have been downplayed, hidden, or even punished.[8]

Notice too, that in Matthew 19:3–9, the text that immediately precedes Jesus' discussion of eunuchs, Jesus stands up for women. As Boheche observes, "Jesus counsels mutuality between a husband

and wife, rather than affirming the traditional laws of divorce that favoured the husband."[9] And in Matthew 19:13, which immediately follows our text, Jesus blesses the little children, another group who would have been largely ignored at the time. Indeed, "the disciples spoke sternly to those who brought them; but Jesus said, 'Let the little children come to me, and do not stop them; for it is to such as these that the kingdom of heaven belongs'" (Matt.19:13). Jesus consistently subverted the patriarchal religious and social hierarchy and extended egalitarian welcome to everyone, not just the privileged few at the top of the social order.

Moreover, it seems plausible that the word "eunuch" could have been used by Jesus' opponents as a derogatory epithet against him and his followers "to cast aspersions on their masculinity."[10] Theologian Halvor Moxnes suggests that "'eunuch' in Matthew's contextual world could have been a slur leveled against those young men in the Jesus Movement who left home and household and followed him, thus putting themselves 'out of place' and 'represent[ing] a provocation to the very order of the community.'"[11] As an unmarried man in a traditional culture, Jesus may have been subject to many of the same slurs as people who were sexual minorities in his culture. Yet, as Moxnes observes, "Jesus picked up the word [eunuch] and accepted it."[12]

In Matthew 19:10–12, Jesus acknowledges three different types of sexual minorities. Jesus acknowledges that some people are sexual minorities from birth. And Jesus himself may have been subject to many of the same slurs as sexual minorities in his culture. The men around him wanted to talk about the law. Instead, Jesus showed that God's grace and love extends to everyone—especially those people who are disenfranchised, overlooked, or forgotten by traditional culture.

PHILIP AND THE ETHIOPIAN EUNUCH
(ACTS 8:26–39)

Acts 8:26–39 is another biblical story that involves Samaritans, sexual minorities, and God's radically inclusive grace. Acts 8 reports that after Stephen's death a severe persecution began against the church in Jerusalem. Saul (who later became Paul) was a leader in that persecution. The disciples were forced to flee Jerusalem and were scattered throughout the countryside of Judea and Samaria. Philip went down to Samaria, where he proclaimed the gospel with great effectiveness.

Then an angel of the Lord said to Philip, "'Get up and go toward the south to the road that goes down from Jerusalem to Gaza'" (Acts 8:26). There he encountered an Ethiopian eunuch, a court official of the Queen of the Ethiopians, who was in charge of her entire treasury.[13] This man had come to Jerusalem to worship and was now returning home. He was seated in his chariot, reading the prophet Isaiah. The Holy Spirit directed Philip to go to the chariot and join its occupant. Philip asked the man, "'Do you understand what you are reading?'" The eunuch replied, "'How can I, unless someone guides me?'" (Acts 8:30–31). He then invited Philip to sit beside him in his chariot.

"Then Philip began to speak, and starting with this scripture, he proclaimed to him the good news about Jesus" (Acts 8:35). "The eunuch said, 'Look, here is water! What is to prevent me from being baptized?' . . . Philip and the eunuch went down into the water, and Philip baptized him" (Acts 8:36–38).

This text is significant in several ways. First is the prominent role of the Holy Spirit. "An angel of the Lord" directed Philip to go down the road that leads to his encounter with the Ethiopian eunuch. Philip was not acting on his own. Rather, his outreach was being directed by God. When Philip encountered the eunuch, the Holy Spirit intervened once again and said, "'Go over to this chariot and join it'" (8:29). Reaching out to the Ethiopian eunuch might not have been Philip's first instinct—the eunuch was a foreigner, of a different race and ethnicity, and belonged to a sexual minority who was not fully welcome in the worship community of Israel.[14] Previously, such outreach would have been unthinkable. But the Holy Spirit directed Philip to reach out nonetheless. After the eunuch has been baptized and joined in the faith, Philip's work was done, and the Spirit of the Lord whisked him away to Azotus to continue to spread the good news. Clearly the Holy Spirit was watching over Philip every step of the way—directing his actions, pushing him outside his comfort zone, and keeping him safe on a wilderness road as he takes one of the most radical actions of this fledging Jesus movement.

Second, it is significant that the eunuch was reading the prophet Isaiah. Theodore Jennings Jr., professor of biblical and constructive theology at Chicago Theological Seminary, writes at length about the significance of this fact. "The Isaiah being read by the eunuch is the same prophet who specifically includes eunuchs in the divine dispensation. Moreover the passage the eunuch was pondering is one that he may well have connected to his situation as a eunuch:"[15]

Let us read the passage from Isaiah that the eunuch was reading:

> By a perversion of justice he was taken away.
>   Who could have imagined his future?
> For he was cut off from the land of the living,
>   stricken for the transgression of my people.
> (Isa. 53:8)

Jennings comments,

> In his lifelong humiliation and marginalization (for which his responsibilities as court treasurer could not entirely compensate), he was in a position to receive the "good news of Jesus," who was himself humiliated and marginalized by the respectable and the powerful. Through some such recognition the African eunuch is moved to join himself more intimately with Jesus and his Way, and so requests baptism. Being thus joined with Jesus, he, though separated from Philip, "went on his way rejoicing" (8:39).[16]

The relevance of this passage from Isaiah is echoed by others as well. Nancy Wilson, moderator of the Metropolitan Community Church, similarly believes, "It is not *incidental* that Luke quotes this passage of Isaiah or that the eunuch wanted to understand it. The term 'cut off' is a reference to the curse that was placed on anyone who was *exiled, executed by capital punishment,* or *did not reproduce.* The Ethiopian eunuch was reading a prophecy of a Messiah *with whom he could identify!*"[17]

In a closely related passage, Isaiah 56, the prophet Isaiah reversed prior Old Testament prohibitions against eunuchs and foreigners. Leviticus 21:16–23 said that eunuchs, along with anyone who had a blemish, "shall not come near the curtain or approach the altar." Deuteronomy 23:1 went even further, denying such "blemished" persons not only the priesthood but any participation in the worshiping community.[18]

But in Isaiah 56, the Lord specifically welcomes eunuchs:

> For thus says the LORD:
> To the eunuchs who keep my sabbaths,
>   who choose the things that please me
>   and hold fast my covenant,
> I will give, in my house and within my walls,
>   a monument and a name
>   better than sons and daughters;
> I will give them an everlasting name
>   that shall not be cut off.
> (Isa. 56:4–5)

And in the next sentence God extends that welcome to foreigners as well:

> For my house shall be called a house of prayer
>   for all peoples.
>
> (Isa. 56:7)

In reference to Isaiah 56:1–8, Frederick J. Gaiser, professor of Old Testament at Luther Seminary, asserts, "The move here is radical. While there are many places where scripture reinterprets or reactualizes the tradition, using an old word to say something surprisingly new to a new generation, at least one scholar [Herbert Donner] counts this as the only case in the Old Testament of the outright abrogation of one divine word by another."[19]

Finally, and perhaps of greatest significance, the Ethiopian eunuch is believed to be the first Gentile to convert to Christianity. The Holy Spirit could have chosen anyone to be the first Gentile convert. And the Holy Spirit chose a black, African, sexual minority who showed faith. McNeill writes, "I like to think of this eunuch as the first baptized gay Christian."[20]

Old Testament scholar Mona West remarks on the importance of this text for the LGBT community:

> It is a significant story for queer people of faith because the eunuch is a sexual minority in the context of Jewish religion during this time. . . . Queer people of faith would read this story as our own. We are kept from full participation in the Church because of what is perceived as our outsider sexual status. We have been denied ordination and communion. Our relationships are also not blessed by the Church. At best we are allowed to attend worship if we "leave our sexuality at the door." We are allowed marginal participation in the body of Christ if we adopt a "don't ask, don't tell" policy, or if we promise not to be a "practising" homosexual.[21]

Jennings notes the considerable impact of this text:

> The preservation of this story in Acts has had the result that those who identify with this Ethiopian eunuch, whether as African, under conditions of colonialism, or racism, or as sexually marginalized, under conditions of heterosexism and homophobia, have been enabled to recognize their own significance in the history of God's dealings with humanity.[22]

So too Wilson comments that the conversion of the Ethiopian eunuch represents "the most clear and complete fulfillment of the prophecy of Isaiah 56, that God's house would become a 'house of prayer for all people.'"[23]

Notice, when Philip baptized this man, they did not have to have a presbytery meeting to discuss his sexual orientation or whether he had a partner. At no point was the eunuch asked to change who he was or treated as someone who needed to be cured of some affliction. The Ethiopian eunuch showed faith and was baptized.

The repeated and direct involvement of the Holy Spirit, the significant reference to the liberating prophecies of Isaiah, and the fact that the first Gentile convert to Christianity is from a sexual minority and a different race, ethnicity, and nationality together form a clarion call for inclusiveness, radical grace, and Christian welcome to all who show faith.

ALL ARE ONE IN CHRIST JESUS

Look at what Jesus does in each of the three passages. In Luke 10:25–37, Jesus is asked a legalistic question about differing interpretations of the holiness code, and he immediately expands the circle of those who are our neighbors to include the Samaritan—a hated, alien, outcast. In Matthew 19:10–12, Jesus is asked a question about laws concerning heterosexual marriage, and he immediately broadens the conversation to include sexual minorities. In Acts 8:26–39, the Holy Spirit, the Spirit of Christ, intercedes three times to guide Philip to reach out to a black, African, Gentile eunuch so that he too could be included! In each case, the formerly marginalized are welcomed and honored just as they are. That is the gospel message. That is Jesus' call to us—to love God with all our heart, soul, strength, and mind, and to love our neighbor as ourself.

Jesus is the center of Scripture. It is to Christ that the church witnesses. Jesus taught that to love God and love our neighbor is the heart of the gospel. Jesus welcomed society's outcasts. He reached out to women, children, people of all races and ethnicities, the poor, the disabled, the sick, Gentiles, and, yes, sexual minorities. When we read the Bible through the lens of Jesus' redemptive life and ministry, we can see that both the Old and New Testaments command us to accept those who are different from ourselves.

One of the astonishing things about the Bible is the way our understanding of it continues to unfold. Think of the remarkable story in

Acts 15. All of the earliest Christians were first Jews. They had grown up being taught that Gentiles—non-Jews—were by nature unclean and by practice polluted by idolatry. But Acts 15 shows that as the apostles came to know Gentiles, they discovered something that now seems obvious—God had always intended the Gentiles' conversion. It was not until the apostles had the real-world experience of knowing Gentiles that they were able to see what had always been there in the Scriptures. Usually we cannot see what we have been conditioned not to see. But experience can sometimes dissolve mistaken assumptions or dispel prejudices that previously prevented us from seeing deeper truths in Scripture.[24]

Over the years, "black theology" has brought profound new insights about race to our understanding of the biblical texts. "Feminist theology" opened our eyes to the prominent role of women in the Bible. "Liberation theology" focused our attention on the Bible's liberating gospel for the poor and oppressed. Today, "queer theology" is illuminating our understanding of the role of sexual minorities in the biblical text. In each case, the theological insights of formerly marginalized groups have enriched the whole church's understanding of Scripture. In the process, these liberating theologies have helped to bring many Christians into a closer relationship with God.

Once we remove heterosexist assumptions from our reading of the biblical texts, a whole new world of depth and meaning emerges. The more deeply we delve into the biblical word, the more instances we find of God's radical welcome for all who have faith.

May it be so.

Appendix
Progress toward LGBT Equality in other Denominations in the United States

While I have, until now, focused primarily on the Presbyterian Church (U.S.A.), in this appendix I discuss the movement for LGBT equality in other denominations across the United States. Every denomination is working through this process in its own time and in its own way. Furthermore, each denomination will write its own story in a way that reflects the particular tradition and theology of that denomination. It is instructive, however, to look at the remarkable progress being made across a wide range of denominations.

Increasing numbers of people across the religious spectrum in the United States are seeing support for LGBT equality as consistent with, and in some cases even mandated by, their faith. Almost every major denomination has an active advocacy group working for LGBT equality.[1] Forty years ago there were none. That is extraordinary progress in a short space of time. Furthermore, several major denominations in the United States have already embraced LGBT equality as official denominational policy—and others have taken important initial steps in that direction.

In other denominations, the conflict over differing views on homosexuality is intense. It is extremely painful to witness many otherwise tolerant denominations continue to engage in discrimination in spite of the growing biblical and theological scholarship in support of equality. As some denominations dig in, equivocate, or move toward equality at a glacial pace, hate crimes continue against people who are LGBT, and Christian families with LGBT members are torn apart. I believe the soul of the wider church family is wounded anytime the church fails to testify to God's extravagant welcome for everyone. I do not want to minimize that painful reality. But looking back over the past forty years, I think the signs of progress are considerable and show once again the arc of history bending toward justice.

METROPOLITAN COMMUNITY CHURCHES

As recently as the mid 1960s, there were no openly gay clergy in the United States. At the time, police routinely arrested gay, lesbian, bisexual, and transgender people under a range of antigay civil statutes. But the civil rights movement was a catalyst for a dramatic shift in how formerly disenfranchised people saw themselves and the world.

On October 6, 1968, a former Pentecostal preacher and openly gay man named Troy Perry gathered twelve people for a Christian worship service in his living room in Huntington Park, California. This marked the start of "the world's first church group with a primary, positive ministry to gays, lesbians, bisexual and transgender persons."[2] The Rev. Perry called it the Metropolitan Community Church (MCC). Now, forty years later, the MCC has grown to 44,000 members and adherents in 300 congregations in 22 countries.[3] From the beginning, MCC has woven equality into the very fabric of the church. The MCC Statements of Vision, Purpose, and Direction declare a commitment to "proclaim God's inclusive love for all people." Their core-values statement emphasizes that "love is our greatest moral value and resisting exclusion is a primary focus of our ministry." Their approach is ecumenical as well—an estimated 40 percent of their members come from conservative or fundamentalist Protestant denominations, and another 40 percent come from a Roman Catholic background.[4]

UNITARIAN UNIVERSALIST ASSOCIATION

On July 4, 1970, the Unitarian Universalist Association (UUA) General Assembly in Seattle passed a resolution written by the Rev. Richard Nash condemning discrimination against homosexuals and bisexuals.[5] The UUA resolution called on "all peoples"—both society at large and UUA fellowships themselves—to "end all discrimination against homosexuals in employment practices."[6] In many ways, support for gay and lesbian civil rights was a natural fit for the UUA. Unitarians and Universalists were leaders in the abolitionist movement and in the struggle for women's rights and welcomed interracial couples long before the California Supreme Court declared antimiscegenation laws unconstitutional in 1948.[7] Unitarian Universalists were also actively involved in the civil rights movement and were among the first to make the connection between civil rights and gay and lesbian rights. Since then, the UUA has continued to be a pioneer for LGBT equality. In 1973 they created a national office for gay concerns; in 1984 they passed a resolution in support of gay and lesbian civil unions; in 1996 they became the first major U.S. denomination to support the right to marry for same-sex couples; and in 2002 they made history once again when the Rev. Sean Parker Dennison was called by South Valley UU Society of Salt Lake City, Utah—thus becoming the first out transgender person called to serve as a parish minister.[8]

UNITED CHURCH OF CHRIST

From the earliest days of the movement, the United Church of Christ (UCC) has shown extraordinary leadership on equal rights for people who are LGBT. On April 12, 1969, two months before the Stonewall riots signaled a profound national shift in gay consciousness, the UCC Council for Christian Social Action adopted a resolution declaring "its opposition to all laws which make private homosexual relations between consenting adults a crime."[9] The council also opposed the exclusion of gay and lesbian people from the armed forces. In 1972 the UCC's Golden Gate Association ordained the Rev. William R. Johnson, making him the first openly gay person ordained to mainline Protestant ministry. The 1975 General Synod declared that sexual orientation is not a legitimate ground to deny civil liberties.[10] In 1977, in Virginia, the Rev. Anne Holmes became the first openly lesbian woman ordained in the UCC.[11] In 1985 the General Synod called on all UCC congregations and bodies to study homosexuality and declare that they are "open and affirming."[12] In 2005 the General Synod passed a resolution in support of equal marriage rights for all people, regardless of gender. In so doing, the UCC became the first mainline church to express support for complete marriage equality for LGBT persons. Unlike other denominations where the decision often comes down to a handful of votes on either side, in the UCC the vote was overwhelmingly in favor of full marriage equality. The Associated Press reported 80 percent in favor while those in the room reported that it was closer to 90 percent approval.[13]

EPISCOPAL CHURCH

The Episcopal Church also welcomes gays and lesbians as members, and some Episcopal dioceses permit the blessing of same-sex unions and same-sex marriage ceremonies. The Episcopal Church ordained its first openly gay priest in 1989. In 1994, the Episcopal Church passed a resolution explicitly affirming that gay, lesbian, and bisexual people could not be refused ordination in the Episcopal Church. It stated, "No one shall be denied access to the selection process for ordination in this church because of race, color, ethnic origin, age, national origin, marital status, sexual orientation, disabilities or age, except as otherwise specified by these canons."[14]

In 2003, the Episcopal Church made history by electing its first openly gay bishop. The Rev. V. Gene Robinson, who lives with his partner, was consecrated as bishop of the Diocese of New Hampshire. The Worldwide Anglican Communion later rebuked the Episcopal Church for this decision. While a request from the Archbishop of Canterbury has led to a de facto moratorium on the consecration of new gay Episcopal bishops, many leaders of the Episcopal Church are clear that ordination of LGBT clergy and blessings for same-sex marriages are an essential part of their ministry.[15]

EVANGELICAL LUTHERAN CHURCH IN AMERICA

Even in some denominations that officially prohibit ordination of LGBT pastors or blessing of same-sex unions, there is movement toward allowing individual congregations to exercise freedom of conscience on the matter. For example, on the one hand, the Evangelical Lutheran Church in America (ELCA) states in its "Definition and Guidelines for Discipline" (revised 1993) that "practicing homosexual persons are precluded from the ordained ministry of this church."[16] The "Vision and Expectations: Ordained Ministry in the ELCA" specifies that "ordained ministers who are homosexual in their self-understanding are expected to abstain from homosexual sexual relationships."[17] The "Vision and Expectations: Commissioned Associates in Ministry" (1990) makes the same requirement for commissioned ministers.[18]

On the other hand, many clergy members and churches have blessed same-sex unions and called LGBT candidates as pastors. Prior to the ELCA's 2007 Churchwide Assembly, eighty-two LGBT Lutheran ministers chose "to introduce themselves to their denomination" and spoke out against the denomination's policy that prohibits them from entering into lifelong, loving family relationships.[19] Furthermore, an organization called Extraordinary Lutheran Ministries (ELM) credentials and rosters qualified candidates of all sexual orientations and gender identities for ministry, connects them with congregations and ministries, and provides financial resources for these ministries. Although the ELM has no official connection to the ELCA, "sixteen ELCA congregations, two ELCA synod offices, and one Evangelical Lutheran Church in Canada are served by pastors on the ELM roster."[20]

The 2007 Churchwide Assembly (CWA) reflected the ELCA's evolving views on LGBT equality. Several "memorials" (what Presbyterians call overtures or other denominations call resolutions) to approve LGBT ordination or blessings for same-sex unions were defeated or were directed to a committee for further study. Yet there was also an historic breakthrough. By a vote of 538 to 431 the CWA passed what is known as the Landahl motion (after Bishop Paul Landahl, from Metro Chicago Synod, who offered the motion), which, while leaving the church's historic prohibition on the books, "encourages synods, synodical bishops, and the presiding bishop to refrain from or demonstrate restraint in disciplining those congregations and persons who call into the rostered ministry otherwise-qualified candidates who are in a mutual, chaste, and faithful committed same-gender relationship."[21] Emily Eastwood, executive director of Lutherans Concerned North America, wrote, "The dam of discrimination cracked as the church looked itself in the face and said it is no longer 'mete [meet], right, and salutary' that we should remove our LGBT ministers simply for having a family."[22]

AMERICAN BAPTIST CHURCHES USA

Like the polity in the UCC, local congregations in the American Baptist Churches USA are autonomous, responsible for articulating their own doctrine, style of worship, and mission.[23] This results in a diversity of theological viewpoints on homosexuality within the denomination.

On the one hand, in 1992 the General Board of ABCUSA, passed an antigay resolution "through a never-before-used referendum process using mail ballot without discussion."[24] The resolution stated, "We affirm that the practice of homosexuality is incompatible with Christian teaching."[25] At the same time, however, local congregations are charged with setting their own course on these matters. In 1992 University Baptist Church in Minneapolis, Minnesota, called Nadean Bishop as the first open lesbian to pastor to an ABC church.[26] Today, twenty-five openly gay and lesbian people serve as pastors in ABCUSA congregations.[27] The Association of Welcoming and Affirming Baptists has seventy-two member congregations and promotes LGBT equality within the ABCUSA and other moderate-to-progressive Baptist denominations. Furthermore, seven of the thirty-five ABCUSA geographic regions are welcoming and affirming of people who are LGBT—which includes a commitment to ordination and placement of qualified LGBT candidates for ministry.

UNITED METHODIST CHURCH

Theologically, the United Methodist Church (UMC) is guided by what has come to be known as the Wesleyan Quadrilateral: "Wesley believed that the living core of the Christian faith was revealed in Scripture, illumined by tradition, vivified in personal experience, and confirmed by reason."[28] For many members of the UMC, Scripture, tradition, experience, and reason are pointing toward support for LGBT equality.

The UMC *Book of Discipline*, ¶161G, explicitly states that "homosexual persons no less than heterosexual persons are individuals of sacred worth" and should be welcomed into United Methodist families and congregations.[29] The church also supports "certain basic human rights and civil liberties" for gays and lesbians, including some limited recognition of same-sex relationships.[30] At the same time, the General Conference explicitly prohibits LGBT ordination and blessings for same-sex unions.[31]

While the General Synod of the UCC "speaks to the church, not for the church," in the United Methodist Church the opposite is the case: only one body may speak for the UMC, and it is the General Conference, which is held every four years. The United Methodists General Conference is an international gathering with one thousand delegates from the United States, Europe, Africa, and the Philippines. In an unusually asymmetrical polity, General Conference decisions are binding on U.S. congregations, but "central conferences" (UMC regional bodies in Europe, Africa, and the Philippines) have the right to amend the decisions of the General Conference, as those decisions apply to their region.[32] Although the General Conference has opposed equal rights for people who are lesbian, gay, or bisexual (the church has, to date, not ruled on transgender members), it is important to note that *a majority of the U.S. representatives to the General Conference consistently vote in favor of LGBT equality.*[33]

SUPPORT FOR LGBT EQUALITY WITHIN AFRICAN AMERICAN CHURCHES

Two African American church organizations have formed to meet the needs of African Americans who are LGBT. In 1985, Bishop Carl Bean founded Unity Fellowship Church in California. Unity Fellowship has since grown to fourteen congregations across America.[34] And in June 2003 Rev. Yvette Flunder was consecrated as presiding bishop of Refuge Ministries/Fellowship 2000, a multidenominational fellowship of over fifty primarily African American Christian leaders and laity who represent churches and faith-based organizations from all parts of the country and Africa.[35] The leaders involved in the fellowship range "from ultra conservative to liberal" but they have all embraced the goal of implementing "'radical inclusivity' within their congregations."[36]

GROWING SUPPORT EVEN IN TRADITIONALLY CONSERVATIVE DENOMINATIONS

The Seventh-day Adventist Church is an international, conservative Christian denomination that currently prohibits the ordination of women and people who are LGBT. [37] Yet within the American branch of the fellowship "are dedicated, active members of Adventist congregations and at the same time partners in committed, long-term homosexual relationships—persons who are, in effect, incurably Adventist and incurably gay."[38] In the 1970s several of these members founded Seventh-day Adventist Kinship International, incorporated as a nonprofit in 1981. It now has a membership of over one thousand in twenty countries on five continents. Indeed, SDA Kinship International has produced a helpful book titled *Christianity and Homosexuality: Some Seventh-day Adventist Perspectives,* which contains a collection of essays that examine what it means to be both gay and Adventist, with new insights drawn from personal experience, biology, medicine, behavioral science, Scripture, theology, and Christian social perspectives.[39]

The Roman Catholic Church actively opposes ordination of women, LGBT ordination, and same-sex marriage. Under Pope Benedict XVI the church has become even more pronounced in its discrimination against people who are LGBT. In 2005, Pope Benedict XVI approved a document that denies even *celibate* gay men the right to attend seminary and be ordained.[40]

In spite of official policy, it is clear that there is a diversity of opinions on the matter within the larger church family. For example, in 1996 the National Coalition of American Nuns issued a "Statement on Same-Sex Marriage," which read, "The National Coalition of American Nuns believes that the State's failure to recognize same-sex marriage is an unambiguous discrimination based on sexual orientation and is politically and morally wrong."[41]

Catholics and former Catholics, including John Boswell, John J. McNeill, and Daniel Helminiak, have produced excellent biblical and theological scholarship in support of LGBT equality. Furthermore, Catholic clergy, such as Professor Charles Curran, theologian James Alison, and Bishop Thomas John Gumbleton, have shown tremendous courage in speaking out against official church policies on homosexuality.

New Ways Ministry lists over two hundred "gay-friendly" Catholic parishes in the United States and Canada and seventy-nine gay-friendly Catholic colleges and universities that have some type of lesbian/gay student group, support group, or ally group.[42] Founded in 1977 by Rev. Robert Nugent and Sr. Jeannine Gramick, New Ways Ministry provides a gay-positive ministry of advocacy and justice for lesbian and gay Catholics. The ministry was condemned by the Vatican, and both founders were forced to resign from New Ways Ministry in 1984. But New Ways Ministry nevertheless continues their support and advocacy for people who are LGBT. Other groups working to reform the Roman Catholic Church from within include the Catholic Pastoral Committee on Sexual Minorities, the Conference of Catholic Lesbians, Dignity USA, Fortunate Families, and the National Association of Diocesan Lesbian/Gay Ministries.

CONCLUSION

We are witnessing a profound transformation in attitudes toward people who are LGBT throughout many American denominations. In the 1950s very few people knew any "out" LGBT people. Today, most

Americans do. They are friends and coworkers; parents, children, and siblings; neighbors, elected officials, and fellow church members. For many people, as ignorance has been replaced with real-world knowledge of people who are LGBT, myths and preconceptions have vanished. This remarkable transformation has given us the opportunity to read the biblical texts anew, through the lens of Jesus' redemptive life and ministry, free from some of the mistaken assumptions that had previously obscured our understanding of God's revelation for our lives. Like growing numbers of Christians across the United States and around the world, I believe that support for LGBT equality is consistent with and indeed mandated by my faith.

Study Guide

by David Maxwell

INTRODUCTION

This study guide for *Jesus, the Bible, and Homosexuality: Explode the Myths, Heal the Church* (Westminster John Knox Press, 2009, www.wjkbooks .com) provides plans for seven units of approximately one-hour duration. Participants should have a copy of the book or easy access to one. The study guide assumes that all participants have read the material before each session.

By clarifying the facts relating to the topic at hand, the author attempts to explode many of the myths and distorted historical and biblical perceptions dominant in our society and many of our churches. For many participants, this book offers a reminder of information they have heard in bits and pieces throughout their lives. For others, this information may be new. Therefore, having a copy of the book is advisable so that participants can easily refer to what they have read. They should feel free to write in the book, underlining or highlighting places they wish to remember. Writing notes in the margins is okay too.

With this book, Jack Rogers gives a gift to the church and a challenge to all who consider themselves disciples of Jesus Christ. The gift comes from a fellow Christian who is, among other things, a minister, a scholar, and a teacher. He makes available to his readers his own faith journey, his careful study of Scripture and theology, and the results of careful research that most of us could not do for ourselves.

As mentioned, this guide is for seven sessions:

Session 1: Preface and chapter 1

Session 2: Chapter 2

Session 3: Chapter 3

Session 4: Chapter 4

Session 5: Chapter 5

Session 6: Chapters 6 and 7

Session 7: Chapter 8 and Appendix

General Guidelines

1. Encourage people to buy the book. If cost or habit makes this unlikely, then as you prepare, be alert to information that might be put on newsprint/chalkboard/handout.
2. Acknowledge at the beginning what is in the paragraph above about the author. People don't have to agree, but they cannot argue about another person's telling of her or his own life experience. Likewise, historical documentation should be accepted and not debated. Rogers is a recognized scholar and has done painstaking research.
3. Assurances should be given that expressions of feelings about what is read or heard or about one's own fear of exposing oneself and one's thoughts will not be rejected or ridiculed. Learning something new or making a confession can be frightening, and people need to know that they can share their thoughts and feelings without fear of being ridiculed or labeled, or becoming the subject of gossip.
4. Acknowledge that the topic of the book is a large one. Encourage people to talk with each other and help each other stay open to God's presence and leading. If the group is large, consider encouraging people to chat via e-mail or phone during the days between sessions (as an attempt to clarify what they have heard or to share their perspectives) or even to meet during the week for further discussion.
5. It is important to pay close attention to language and assumptions in this debate. One's choice of terms often reflects an entire worldview. For example, Rogers never uses the word "homosexuals" in the book. Rather he always uses the term "people who are homosexual" or "people who are gay and lesbian"—to highlight the humanity of every person and to reflect the fact that everyone is more than just their sexuality. The terms "queer," "fag," or "dyke" are often considered terms of empowerment when used by people who are LGBT (lesbian, gay, bisexual, or transgender) but are considered pejorative when used against people who are LGBT. See note 1, "Preface to the First Edition," page 177, for a more complete discussion of the challenge of finding appropriate terms. It is recommended that leaders follow Rogers's model and use the phrase "people who are LGBT" in referring to this population. Generalizations, unquestioned assumptions, unsupported suppositions, or stereotypes should be identified as inappropriate. Participants should be instructed to speak to their own direct experience and avoid generalizations that fall outside of their direct experience (i.e., "these people," "of course," "it's obvious

that," etc....) If any participant is unable to speak respectfully, it may even be necessary to suggest that a person should excuse himself or herself from the series. Leaders should strive to create a safe space for dialogue, and every participant should agree to strict confidentiality as to who is in the group and what is said in the group. In talking with others outside of the group, participants should be directed to speak only about their own experience.

6. Encourage careful listening and discourage the habit of trying to create a rebuttal or counterargument while someone else is speaking.

7. People will receive a great deal of information, and you should stop every time you are ready to go on to new information to ask questions that will help people articulate what they are learning or wondering about. Try not to ask questions that can be answered with just a yes or no. Questions such as the following may encourage participants to ask their own questions or claim their own new ideas or insights:

- What new thoughts came to you in this section of our conversation?
- What do you think about this recounting of historical events?
- If any of this makes you feel uneasy or bewildered, would you like to tell the rest of us about that?
- Can you imagine how people felt when they realized there was another way to look at this issue?
- Often when we change our belief about something, we not only learn to swim in new waters, but we also feel we're abandoning others with whom we formerly agreed. If you change your belief, what are you risking?

8. Opening the session with prayer helps people to know that their hopes and fears are put into God's hands as you pray for the Spirit to guide the group and to help everyone see more clearly what is God's will for the church and for themselves. In addition to the prayers in this study guide, you may find suitable prayers in the *Book of Common Worship* (Westminster/John Knox Press, 1993) or you may compose them yourself. If praying in public is difficult for you, some people, when asked ahead of time, may be willing to lead the group in prayer.

So often, we are unwilling to open ourselves to the possibility that what we think or even believe might benefit from a more thorough examination. Even reading or considering ideas other than those upon which we have built our positions and shaped our convictions seems to be too threatening or a waste of time. This approach to a subject, of course, contradicts our beliefs that God still acts in history and that the Spirit continues to reveal to us that which may have previously been hidden from us.

In your role as leader of a study of this book, you should ask yourself if openness to revelation and to facts not known before is experienced as threat or possibility. Coming to grips with one's own answers to those questions should make all leaders more sensitive and responsive to the learners' reactions to the book. Those we teach need to be assured that honest responses, expressed without accompanied derision of what others say and think, are essential to learning and to the work of the Spirit in and among the participants. Encouraging people to name and explore their fears and their reluctance to entertain new possibilities will make the time together more supportive of new insights and understandings of both God's will and the church's life as a community of faith.

You might ask the participants a question like this: In this situation, where you may be confronted by ideas that are contrary to your own, what fears or discomforts might you have? Following their responses, assure them that no one's thoughts will be dismissed or ridiculed. Disagreeing with someone opens a possibility for growth in both people. Language that is considerate of others' viewpoints can be heard far more easily than language that condemns or accuses.

Each session is designed to fill an hour. You may easily stretch this to a longer period of time if you choose. In fact, you will need to choose the questions you most want the group to discuss before the session begins as well as decide how much time to give to each of them. The structure of each session is as follows:

- Session Theme
- Opening
- Key Ideas and Questions
- Responding Activity
- Closing Prayer

Most of the time in each session is spent discussing the Key Ideas and Questions. The ideal size for a group discussion is five to eight persons. Groups larger than eight persons make it difficult for everyone to have a chance to speak. Consider alternatives, such as breaking the group into smaller groups for part of the sessions. Reporting back to the larger group can be helpful during some discussions and not necessary in others.

A first and second reading of this book seems essential for all leaders. In the first reading, marginal comments or question marks will capture what has struck you in positive or negative ways. In the second reading, you may see more clearly what was murky before and recognize the critical moves the author makes that you want to address in the sessions. An outline of key ideas (those items that brought insight to you) in each chapter enables you to make your own outline for the sessions if you prefer. Be sure to include time for questions or comments from the participants.

Finally, use the material that is most helpful for your group. Some groups that are already in agreement with Jack Rogers's position will study this book. Others will study this book out of a desire to understand someone with whom they disagree. The questions you select to discuss obviously need to reflect the context of your own situation.

PREFACES AND CHAPTER 1: STUDYING HOMOSEXUALITY FOR THE FIRST TIME

Session Theme

Jack Rogers shares his personal journey as a Christian, scholar, and minister in the Presbyterian Church (U.S.A.). While he did not seek to be involved in advocating ordination of people who are LGBT, through his experiences and study he has come to this position. The first chapter also shares some of the history of the movement for ordaining people who are LGBT in the PC(USA).

Opening

1. Open with the following prayer:

   Almighty God, as we join together to study this book, we thank you for the gifts of healthy minds that enable us to grasp ideas; the company of others who teach us, console us, and struggle through life with us; and your Holy Spirit who moves through us and guides us. Open our hearts and minds as we begin this conversation, remembering that you are the giver of all knowledge and wisdom. Amen.

2. Welcome participants. If members of the group do not know each other, consider spending some time having people introduce themselves and sharing their reasons for participating in this study. Beginning to feel comfortable in the group will make this study much more satisfying for everyone.

Depending on your group, you may need to set some ground rules. Congratulate participants for being willing to discuss a topic that is so controversial in our society and churches. Suggest spending some time to agree on rules for how to discuss sensitive issues in a respectful manner. Invite participants to list some rules they would like the group to follow when the conversation gets heated. You may want to have handy a helpful list found at http://www.pcusa.org/peacemaking/guidelines .pdf. Whatever rules you create or use, make sure they are visible during the entire time of studying this book. That way, if someone gets out of line, you can always gently remind that person of the ground rules that the group sets.

Key Ideas and Questions

1. In the preface to the first edition, page xvii, paragraph 4, Rogers says that the issue of lesbian, gay, bisexual, and transgendered people (LGBT) is "a defining issue of our time. For some it is an issue of maintaining traditions and customs that have given order to our society. For others, it is an issue of justice—all citizens should be entitled to equal rights under the law. For me, it is a moral and spiritual issue. How can the church live up to the highest ideals of Jesus Christ? How can we most faithfully act according to the central principles of the Bible? How can we most honestly and equitably share the love of God with all people?"

   • Do you agree that this is a defining issue of our time? Should it be? If not, what should be the defining issue?
   • Rogers gives three concerns people state in the issue. For some it is an issue of maintaining traditions and customs. For others, it is justice. For him, it is a moral and spiritual issue. Which concern do you believe is the most important issue? Why?
   • Discuss briefly his three moral and spiritual questions. Can you think of other moral and spiritual questions he did not mention?

2. On page xviii, paragraph 3, Rogers shares his reason for writing this book. Ask participants to read that paragraph aloud. No matter if they end up agreeing or disagreeing with Rogers, can they agree with his purpose? Does everyone have the same desire?

3. In chapter 1, Rogers describes his unwillingness to become involved in his local church's discussion of inclusion of LGBT people. Invite a participant to summarize Rogers's experience to remind the group of his journey. Jack says, "It just was not a problem that I wanted to take on." Allow time for comments.

4. The experience in his church leading to the decisions by the session not to become a More Light Church (one that welcomes LGBT

persons) and the gay member to leave the church surely affected Rogers. Many find that when we get to know people who are LGBT, what was once an "issue" becomes personal. What has your experience been personally and as a church?

5. In the end Rogers believes the church grew in its comfortableness with the issue. Do you agree that the process was a helpful one in the long run even though some people felt hurt?

6. Invite someone to summarize the section beginning on page 3 titled "My Formation as an American Evangelical Christian." Allow time for comments regarding anything people find important to note.

7. The section on pages 6–8 titled "Teaching at Fuller Theological Seminary" is full of information regarding evangelicals, fundamentalists, and the doctrine of inerrancy. Make sure participants understand the definitions of and differences between each of these terms.

8. Pages 8–13 describe some of the recent history in the Presbyterian Church (U.S.A.) regarding ordination of people who are homosexual. Depending on time and interest, invite participants to summarize and discuss items of interest in this section.

9. Give participants a chance to reread the final section (pages 15–16), "How My Mind Changed." At this point the goal of the group is to understand the author's process and not argue with it. Make sure participants understand where Rogers is coming from and have an appreciation for his journey.

Responding Activity

1. Allow participants a few minutes of silence to either think quietly or write in a journal (that they can bring to other sessions) the main points they wish to remember about today's session. They can also finish these sentences:

   - I didn't know that . . .
   - I hope in future sessions we discuss . . .
   - My goal from this study is . . .

2. If there is time, invite a few people to share anything they wish about the three sentences.

Closing Prayer

Invite the group to pray for the church and pray that God will lead everyone to the truth that has been promised to set us free. If it is customary to close with prayer, do that in accord with what is expected and include the hope that God's truth will be revealed.

CHAPTER 2: A PATTERN OF MISUSING THE BIBLE TO JUSTIFY OPPRESSION

Session Theme

This session traces some of the ways the Bible has historically been used to justify slavery and the subordination of women. Rogers shows how leading theologians from a previous era used Scottish Common Sense philosophy, the theology of Francis Turretin, and appeals to "natural law" to justify their own cultural prejudices. Rogers makes an analogy between the way the Bible was misused to justify slavery and the subordination of women and the way that it is being used today to deny equal rights to people who are LGBT.

Opening

1. Welcome any newcomers and open the session with prayer for illumination and for the ability to hear what the author is saying and also what members will say to each other.
2. Briefly summarize the last session either verbally or by outline on newsprint or chalkboard.
3. Prepare a listing of the various names by which the former Presbyterian churches were known and the dates of their mergers or splits. (You can download a chart showing all the many changes of name among Presbyterians throughout history. Go to www.history .pcusa.org/pres_hist/. The chart is more extensive than is needed for this discussion. However, if you enlarge it, a greater perspective is provided.) Whenever the church has faced serious issues about what it stood for or against, the threat of split was often present. But at other times, separate churches discovered that they could be more faithful to God's expectations by joining forces and working together in witness and mission.

Key Ideas and Questions

1. This chapter may trigger some strong emotions from the participants. First, give some time for people to summarize what the chap-

ter says and what they learned. You may find the entire session is taken by this first activity!

2. Rogers begins by saying that homosexuality is not the first social issue with which the Presbyterian Church has wrestled. Sabbath observance, prohibition, use of tobacco, slavery, segregation, the role of women, divorce, and remarriage are others. What is his point?

3. Rogers argues (page 17) that the issue is what American Christiians thought about slavery and the subordination of women *at the time* when slavery was an active institution and women were still barred from leadership in the church and voting in society. "How could Christians for more than 200 years accept slavery and the subordination of women with not a hint that there was any other view in the Bible? Why did good, intelligent, devout Christian people not see what we now recognize as mitigating factors in the biblical record? Why did we change our minds?" Allow time for discussion.

4. How was the Bible used to justify slavery? The goal here is partly to recap some of the history, but just as importantly, you are trying to understand the method of interpretation that Rogers later argues is being used against people who are homosexual today. You might divide the group into two and assign one group James Henley Thornwell (pages 19–22) and the other group Robert Lewis Dabney (pages 22–25). Ask each group to reread the section and summarize the steps in the thinking of the influential theologian and pastor.

5. How was the Bible used to justify the subordination of women? (Depending on time available, you may need to choose either the slavery issue or women's subordination. You can use the same process for each since they are similar.)

6. How did church and society get it wrong (pages 29–32)? If time permits, allow participants to review and summarize these pages. Try to create a short list of phrases or one-liners that demonstrate the mistakes people made.

7. How did abolitionists come away with such a different interpretation of Scripture?

8. Read out loud or allow time for participants to reread the conclusion of this chapter, beginning on page 33. Can participants see Rogers's logic in comparing the biblical interpretation methods (now considered erroneous) used to justify slavery and the subordination of women with those used for excluding people who are homosexual from ministry? People in the class may or may not agree, but it is important to understand Rogers's logic at this point.

Responding Activity

Distribute paper and pens and ask people to write out their responses to the following questions:

> Describe an experience where you had a change of heart and mind (in any area of your personal or professional life):
>
> What did you initially believe?
>
> What challenged that belief?
>
> How did your views begin to shift?
>
> What do you believe now?
>
> How did you feel at each stage of the process?
>
> How did you feel after the fact—looking back on your experience and former belief?
>
> What are the emotional risks and benefits involved in the process?

Ask participants to share and discuss what they wrote.

Closing Prayer

> *O God,*
> *Light of the minds that know you,*
> *Life of the souls that love you,*
> *Strength of the thoughts that seek you:*
> *Help us so to know you*
> *That we may truly love you,*
> *So to love you*
> *That we may fully serve you,*
> *Whose service is perfect freedom;*
> *Through Jesus Christ our Lord. Amen.*
> *(Book of Common Worship,* p. 19)

CHAPTER 3: A BREAKTHROUGH
IN UNDERSTANDING THE WORD OF GOD

Session Theme

The church went through some radical changes due to a couple of historical events in the twentieth century and a theological movement from Europe that opened a new understanding of Scripture that was both Christ-centered and open to scholarly study of the texts. These factors impacted the church as it looked anew at issues such as slavery, women's role in the church, divorce, and so on.

Opening

1. Welcoming and prayer. Welcome all participants and allow a few minutes for introduction of any new members. You may offer a prayer of your own or use the one that follows:

   Gracious Creator, we are such creatures of habit, resistant to change. New thoughts challenge us to question what we've always known to be true. Yet of course we want to do what's right in your eyes and seek the courage to follow your Spirit, wherever the Spirit leads us; Lead us, give us an inner calm so that we might follow Christ's footsteps more faithfully. Amen.

2. Provide an opportunity for feedback from the previous session and comments on what they have read this week in chapter 3. Since much of this session will be reviewing the content, don't spend too much time in the opening on this. One way to review last week is to read the first paragraph of chapter 3 on page 35.

Key Ideas and Questions

1. How did the church change its mind (pages 35–39)? Depending on your group, simply raising this question and allowing participants to reply may be enough. If you need some leading questions, consider the following:

- What were the two crucial events that occurred by the middle of the nineteenth century and divided the mainstream Protestant churches into two camps? (the Civil War and the publication of Darwin's *The Origin of Species*)
- What did the modernists believe?
- What did the fundamentalists believe?
- What were the five "essential and necessary doctrines," and what is a "scruple"?
- What happened in the 1927 General Assembly?

2. What was neo-orthodoxy, and how did it change the conversation? (This discussion begins on page 37 and continues through the chapter.) The main point to make is that the new approach turned people's attention to Jesus Christ as revealed in Scripture and didn't shy away from biblical research but rather encouraged it.
3. The section on "Social Change" beginning on page 39 discusses the influence of neo-orthodoxy on the church as it looked at oppressive social institutions. Most of the participants in your group grew up after the 1927 General Assembly and so may not be too impressed with the radical changes that occurred as a result of neo-orthodoxy. Review the new looks at race, women, and divorce and remarriage found on pages 40–44.
4. Read aloud paragraphs 1–4 on page 44. This is a key argument. How does it resonate with you? Allow plenty of time for discussion.
5. If you have time and there is interest, summarize Rogers's "Personal Note" on pages 44 and 45. How would the church be different now if the same standards for divorced people were still used as those for people who are homosexual? How many of our excellent ministers who have suffered through divorce would be ineligible for leadership?
6. In the final sections Rogers tells the story of the Confession of 1967 and the Brief Statement of Faith in 1991. What is important about the church putting into writing what it believes about certain issues?

Responding Activity

Invite the participants to think in silence for a minute or two about the future. What groups of people continue to be excluded or treated unjustly in our world who may at some time (perhaps now) merit the church writing a special Confession to clarify its position regarding their role or rights?

Closing Prayer

Gracious God, we thank you for continuing to shed light on your people, making your Word known more fully and for all those who follow you, spreading your love to all your children. May we continue to learn to share the grace you so freely have given us. Amen.

CHAPTER 4: INTERPRETING THE BIBLE
IN TIMES OF CONTROVERSY

Session Theme

Rogers reviews the seven guidelines for interpreting the Bible that are commonly agreed upon by mainline Protestants today. After tracing their roots in various confessions, he discusses how each principle might help us in our current discussion regarding homosexuality and the church.

Opening

1. Welcome participants and provide time to introduce any new people. Provide your own prayer or use this one:

   O Lord our God, you are always more ready to bestow your good gifts upon us than we are to seek them. You are more willing to give than we desire or deserve. Help us so to seek that we may truly find, so to ask that we may joyfully receive, so to knock that the door of your mercy may be opened for us; through Jesus Christ our Lord. Amen.
   (*Book of Common Worship*, p. 18)

2. Allow a few minutes to review last week and see if people wish to discuss any leftover questions.

Key Ideas and Questions

1. Both the northern and southern Presbyterian churches adopted guidelines for the interpretation of Scripture (in 1982 and 1983). The guidelines are similar to those used by most mainstream Christian denominations today. Consider providing a copy of the seven guidelines to participants.
2. Use most of your time to go through each guideline. Ask the participants to say what they believe it means, and then focus on a question or two, such as those that are suggested here. There may be several interpretations. Accept them, and then have the participants reread and decide together their meaning.

- *Guideline 1.* Read the third paragraph of the Commentary section on page 55 to sum up what the Bible is. After comments from the group, read the next two paragraphs. Allow discussion.
- *Guideline 2.* Read the first sentence of the Commentary on page 56 and then the three directions for reading the plain text on pages 56–57. Use the next paragraph to explain "plain."
- *Guideline 3.* Go to the first paragraph of the Commentary following the guideline and then the second paragraph, beginning with the sentences after footnote number 27. Ask for reactions to this guideline. Do people see that changes in interpreting Scripture have led us to the understandings that most of us have today? They may recall earlier discussions about the changes of mind regarding slavery and women's place in the church. If not, you can remind them.
- *Guideline 4.* The Commentary can help us understand the importance of its meaning. Use the second paragraph to evoke questions or comments from group members.
- *Guideline 5.* This guideline is also deceptively simple, but reading the first two paragraphs of the Commentary will flesh out its importance. As always, allow for comments and questions as these guidelines are presented. Be sure that the participants know that the book contains significant material from biblical scholars and from the confessions of our church to support the meaning of the guidelines.
- *Guideline 6.* Read the third paragraph of the Commentary on page 63 ("God's message . . .") and welcome questions.
- *Guideline 7.* This can best be understood by reading the two paragraphs of the Commentary.

Responding Activity

Invite a general discussion around the following questions. Depending on time, you may choose from these:

- Which of the guidelines is the most helpful and why?
- Which are unclear?
- Does the church really need to establish guidelines and rules? Why or why not?
- Can you think of an erroneous interpretation you previously held that has been changed in light of these guidelines?

Closing Prayer

Before closing in prayer, remind people that for the next session they are to read chapter 5, a very dense chapter, filled with much information. In order to make the best use of time in the next session, it is imperative that people read the chapter before they arrive.

A closing prayer might express thanks for the help that has been given by these guidelines to the church and to our better understanding of what God is saying to us in Scripture.

CHAPTER 5: WHAT THE BIBLE SAYS AND DOESN'T SAY ABOUT HOMOSEXUALITY

Session Theme

Rogers reviews the eight passages in the Bible that have been used to condemn homosexuality, especially Romans 1. He then explores non-biblical theories that have been imposed on Romans 1. He concludes by discussing Acts 10–15, in which the early church decided to admit Gentiles, and argues that it provides a helpful model for resolving the current debate over the role of people who are LGBT in the church.

Opening

1. Welcome participants and spend just a few minutes reviewing any questions from last session.
2. Either invite a participant to pray or offer a prayer yourself to open the session. A possible prayer follows.

> *Lord, open unto me*
> *Open unto me—light for my darkness.*
> *Open unto me—courage for my fear.*
> *Open unto me—hope for my despair.*
> *Open unto me—peace for my turmoil.*
> *Open unto me—joy for my sorrow.*
> *Open unto me—strength for my weakness.*
> *Open unto me—wisdom for my confusion.*
> *Open unto me—forgiveness for my sins.*
> *Open unto me—love for my hates.*
> *Open unto me—thy Self for my self.*
> *Lord, Lord, open unto me! Amen.*
> (*Book of Common Worship*, p. 23)

Key Ideas and Questions

- What is natural law (page 77), and how does Rogers say it is being misused in this debate?

167

- Scientists have shown that part of the nonhuman animal population in the world is indeed homosexual. Most people who are LGBT do not view their sexuality as a choice. A growing number of scientists are convinced that homosexuality in humans is genetic. How do scientific studies influence the way you think about homosexuality?
- On pages 76–85, what are the nonbiblical theories that Rogers says are imposed on the biblical texts? What does it mean to "impose a theory upon a text" or to "read something into a text"? How do we account for the way our own biases inevitably change our interpretation of any text?
- The Genesis creation story is often used to argue that monogamous, heterosexual marriage is God's intention for humanity. Yet, as Rogers shows, that was not the intention of the passages. Indeed, the earliest generations mentioned in Genesis practiced polygamy. What, in your view, is the purpose of marriage? How should we understand marriage customs like polygamy in Scripture?
- Rogers finds that Acts 10–15 provides a helpful analogy to our current debate. What happens in Acts 10–15? Why was it such a big deal at the time? How did the events described in Acts 10–15 change the world? What is the relevance of these passages to our discussion of ordination and marriage for people who are LGBT today?

Responding Activity

Invite participants to spend a few minutes in silence, thinking about all that has been said today. Then allow them five minutes to write down some notes in their journals about what they will take with them from today's session. These will not be shared but may be helpful when they later wish to discuss the book with friends or family. If you have a talkative group that doesn't need or want a quiet activity, you can invite people to simply call out, in brief phrases or sentences, what they wish to remember from today's session. No response is needed from other participants.

Closing Prayer

O loving God,
To turn away from you is to fall,
To turn toward you is to rise,
And to stand before you is to abide forever.
Grant us, dear God,
In all our duties your help;
In all our uncertainties your guidance;
In all our dangers your protection;
And in all our sorrows your peace;
Through Jesus Christ our Lord. Amen.
(Book of Common Worship, p. 23)

CHAPTER 6: REAL PEOPLE AND REAL MARRIAGE

CHAPTER 7: RECOMMENDATIONS FOR THE PRESBYTERIAN CHURCH (U.S.A.)

Session Theme

Chapter 6 discusses and refutes many of the arguments made against people who are homosexual and their relationships and shares Rogers's own experience with gay and lesbian persons. Chapter 7 includes significant actions taken by his denomination, the Presbyterian Church (U.S.A.), which may lead to real change for persons called to ordained ministry who are LGBT.

Opening

If there is time, you can certainly spread this session into two sessions, treating chapter 6 and chapter 7 in separate sessions. Enough questions are provided to do that. However, if you have just one session, make sure you pick the questions below that are most pertinent to your group. Ask everyone to read the two chapters before the session.

1. Welcome the participants and provide a few minutes for anyone to share briefly any thoughts or questions they have had since the last session.
2. Provide a prayer of your choice, or say the following:

> *God of grace,*
> *You have given us minds to know you,*
> *Hearts to love you,*
> *And voices to sing your praise.*
> *Fill us with your Spirit,*
> *That we may celebrate your glory*
> *And worship you in spirit and in truth;*
> *Through Jesus Christ our Lord. Amen.*

Key Ideas and Questions

1. Rogers criticizes stereotyping groups of people, especially with negative images and moral values when they are not necessarily true. What is a stereotype? Have you ever been stereotyped?

2. In the section on "Clergy Sexual Misconduct" beginning on page 89, Rogers mentions the fact that clergy abuse has been unmasked and the Roman Catholic Church and many mainline churches are facing increasing lawsuits for heterosexual and homosexual sexual misconduct. While he commends the steps the denomination has taken to crack down on sexual misconduct, he questions the blanket law that people who are LGBT are all unworthy of ordination simply for their sexual orientation. What do you think of that? Is it fair?

3. As we see in "The Evolution of the Purpose of Marriage" (pp. 90–91), marriage has not been a stagnant institution by any means. The church has changed its understanding of who can marry and the purpose of marriage multiple times. Is it inevitable that eventually the church will include people who are LGBT in the list of those whose relationships are acknowledged and celebrated?

4. Allow a few minutes to review "Male Gender Superiority and Opposition to Same-Sex Marriage" on pages 91–95. Rogers states that many religious fundamentalists view a patriarchal family structure as the key to the health of the church and the nation. This view usually includes the submission of women to men. Rogers talks about the strong link between opposition to equality between men and women and opposition to homosexuality. Is allowing people who are homosexual the right to marry and raise children really a threat to our society? Why or why not? Is this really about male heterosexual privilege and dominance?

5. In the "Opposition to Science" section on pages 95–97, Rogers cites the growing number of professional medical organizations that have declared homosexuality not to be a mental illness or gender-identity disorder. In fact, they have found that same-sex couples or families do not vary significantly from heterosexual families. Yet some religious leaders are the most vocal about refusing to see people who are homosexual as whole persons. What do you think?

6. Read aloud paragraphs 4 and 5 of "Violent Rhetoric" on page 98. Do you believe religion is provoking some to violence against

LGBT people? How would you respond to Coretta Scott King or Lewis B. Smedes?

7. What is the irony in the debate over marriage found on pages 98–100?

8. Rogers shares his experience of knowing gay and lesbian people and says (p. 103), "In my experience, they are just human beings with the normal hopes and fears, struggles and challenges of others in the population" (page 103). How does that compare with your own experience? How do you think people who are LGBT feel while watching this debate in the church?

9. In chapter 7 Rogers shares his recommendations for the Presbyterian Church (U.S.A.). He begins by stating that the first step for the church is to apologize—institutionally, collectively, and personally. Much harm has been caused to LGBT persons for centuries. Do you think an apology to people who are LGBT would help to heal the church? There is precedent for this, and if we come to believe that our interpretation and policies are indeed wrong, isn't the next step to apologize?

10. On pages 111-17 Rogers shows that the Heidelberg Catechism was mistranslated in 1962 and that the words "homosexual perversion" were inserted even though they are not in the original Catechism. How did that happen?

11. On page 116 (Steps toward Correcting the Flaw in the *Book of Confessions*) Rogers shares the action taken by the 2008 Presbyterian General Assembly to restore the Heidelberg Catechism to its original language. Do you agree that it should be restored? Why is this so important for Rogers? Do you agree?

12. If your group has not followed the history of G-6.0106b, you will want to spend some time reviewing that section (pages 119–24). Would your group change G-6.0106b? Would they simply remove it? Or would they leave it as is?

13. In the next-to-last section in chapter 7 (Steps toward Correcting the Flaws in the *Book of Order*), Rogers shares the creation and work of the Theological Task Force on the Peace, Unity, and Purity of the Church (PUP). An extremely diverse group of people spent considerable time together over a period of four and a half years. Allow time to review that section (pages 124–27) and discuss:

a. To what extent does finding agreement on controversial issues depend on people knowing each other?

b. Has your presbytery or church implemented the recommended process of gathering as the PUP committee did? Do you think this is an effective way to achieve justice for persons who are LGBT?

c. Do you agree with the changes suggested by the 2008 General Assembly? If so, how can you support the passage of this amendment in your presbytery?

14. Read aloud the final section of chapter 7 (on page 127) and allow a few minutes for participants to comment.

Responding Activity

1. After reading chapter 7, one realizes how slow change comes in the life of the church. For some, this is disheartening because individual hearts and minds change quicker and those who have changed become impatient with the larger group. Invite participants to name specific actions that they might take right now on the change to the *Book of Confessions* or the *Book of Order* if they feel these are important issues.

2. Spend a few minutes in quiet reflection, thinking about all the groups in the world today who live in situations of injustice. What light can the church offer to these situations?

CLOSING PRAYER

Eternal God, your patience with us is amazing. Who would think that our attempts to be faithful to you might result in causing suffering for our brothers and sisters? Let your light shine on our imperfect minds as we seek to be salt for your earth. Amen.

CHAPTER 8: ALL ARE ONE
IN CHRIST JESUS, AND APPENDIX

Session Theme

In chapter 8 Rogers examines the parable of the Good Samaritan (Luke 10:25–37), Jesus' teaching on marriage and divorce (Matt. 19:10–12), and Philip and the Ethiopian eunuch (Acts 8:26–39) and shows how they relate to the debate over LGBT equality in the church. These stories show Jesus welcoming every kind of person into God's community. The appendix provides information about how the movement for LGBT equality is growing in other denominations besides the PC(USA).

During this session consider providing time to react to both the final chapter and the appendix, and also provide time for an evaluation of the book and your time together.

Opening

1. Welcome participants and remind them that this will be the last session of this study. There will be time to evaluate the book and your time together at the end of the session. Take care of any housekeeping tasks (such as planning for whatever comes next) at this time.
2. Provide a prayer of your choice, or say the following:

> *Eternal God,*
> *our beginning and our end,*
> *be our starting point and our haven,*
> *and accompany us in this day's journey.*
> *Use our hands*
> *to do the work of your creation,*
> *and use our lives*
> *to bring others the new life you give this world.*
> *In Jesus Christ, Redeemer of all,*
> *Amen.*
> (*Book of Common Worship*, p. 500)

Key Ideas and Questions

1. Chapter 8 focuses on three Scripture texts that Rogers believes are more helpful in understanding how Christians should relate to people who are LGBT than the verses that are commonly cited. Depending on the size of your group, either divide into smaller groups and assign one of the passages (the parable of the Good Samaritan, Jesus' teaching on marriage and divorce, or Philip and the Ethiopian eunuch) to each group, or choose one passage to discuss as a large group. Allow participants time to review the section of the book that examines the Scripture text, and then discuss how this text sheds light on the issue of LGBT equality. What was new or surprising to you in each section? What are the common threads that unite these three passages?

2. On page 136 Rogers says, "Usually we cannot see what we have been conditioned not to see. But experience can sometimes dissolve mistaken assumptions or dispel prejudices that previously prevented us from seeing deeper truths in Scripture." Can you think of an experience you have had with someone that dissolved a mistaken assumption? What happened?

3. The appendix offers updates from other denominations where the movement for LGBT equality continues as well. Allow participants who have experience with those denominations to share any information that is helpful to the group. How is the debate similar or different? How do differences in polity (church laws/structure) impact the debate in these other denominations?

Responding Activity

1. Since this is the last session, you might want to make a list of things people still find unclear or wish to discuss. If there is enough to merit an additional session, see if the group wants to do so. If not, perhaps a few people who so desire can agree to meet and continue the discussion.

2. Spend a few minutes evaluating the book as a whole. Even if people don't come out where Rogers does, do they understand and appreciate his position? What are the strengths of his argument? What are

the weaknesses? This can be a helpful time for clarification, and it does not need to cause tension in the group if everyone doesn't agree.
3. Invite participants to share one thing they will take from this experience and book. No response is needed from other participants, except to listen attentively to one another.

Closing Prayer

Close with a prayer that gives thanks to God for the presence and leading of the Holy Spirit. Acknowledgment should be made of feelings of discomfort, of being stretched, of repentance, of hope, and of despair. The struggles that may have been felt by participants—the struggle to understand, or their weariness of waiting for liberation from the restraints that keep some from full recognition and participation in the life of the church—can be committed to God's mercy and care.

Feel free to invite group members to voice their own prayers and conclude with the following sentence: *"May our prayers be pleasing to you, God, our Rock and our Redeemer. Amen."*

Notes

Preface to the Second Edition

1. Tavia Simmons and Martin O'Connell, "Married-Couple and Unmarried-Partner Households: 2000," Census 2000 Special Reports, U.S. Department of Commerce Economics and Statistics Administration, U.S. Census Bureau, February 2003. Accessed at http://www.census.gov/prod/2003pubs/censr-5.pdf.

2. Gary J. Gates and Jason Ost, *The Gay and Lesbian Atlas* (Washington, DC: The Urban Institute, 2004), 13, cited in Timothy Palmer and Rev. Debra W. Haffner, *A Time to Seek: Study Guide on Sexual and Gender Diversity* (New York: The Religious Institute on Sexual Morality, Justice, and Healing, 2007), 20.

3. Refusing to take the matter to the session was a violation of the pastors' responsibilities under the Constitution of the Presbyterian Church (U.S.A.) (*Book of Order*, Directory for Worship W.2.3011 and W.2.3012).

Preface to the First Edition

1. The first known use of the word "homosexual" in English was in 1892, in C. G. Chaddock's translation of Krafft-Ebing's *Psychopathia sexualis* 3:225. While the use of the word homosexual originated in a medical context where it was linked to pathology, I show in this book that contemporary science finds no such link.

Since finishing this book, I have become aware that bisexual and transgender people do not recognize themselves in the term "homosexual." It is a problem of my social location and that of the audience I am addressing that we do not yet fully understand and have not yet incorporated into our vocabulary distinctions that are essential to members of the LGBT community.

Finding the right word to describe real people who embody an array of human gender expression is difficult. We learned the importance of changing nomenclature in the civil rights struggle when identifying terms changed from "colored" to "Negro" to "black" to "African American." I am helped by the recent study by Mark D. Jordan, professor of religion at Emory University, and a gay man, in his recent book *Blessing Same-Sex Unions: The Perils of Queer Romance and the Confusions of Christian Marriage* (Chicago: University of Chicago Press, 2005), 20, where he struggles to find an appropriate term of generalization. He opts for "queer," as do most LGBT folk and many in the academic community. While "queer" has become a symbol of empowerment within the LGBT community, I do not use that term because, for the heterosexual community I am addressing, "queer" still sounds pejorative.

This book is meant to support full inclusion in the church and society of all LGBT people. When I use the word "homosexual," I mean it in the way that it is used in the press, and in church documents, as a general term for people who self-identify as not being in the majority population of those who think of themselves as heterosexual. Indeed, I am primarily addressing a church culture of people who think that everyone is heterosexual and that those who express their sexuality in any other way are acting against their nature. That is a myth that I am trying to correct.

I hope that in a few years those of us in the heterosexual community, including myself, will become more skilled in describing the realities of the LGBT community. I long ago learned that "man" was not a word that included women. I hope to be as sensitive to appropriate terms in the LGBT community in the future. My desire is that this book will help to erase any pejorative connotation that clings to words describing people whose sexual orientation is different than the majority. The time will come when all people are recognized as created by God and acceptable just as they have been created.

2. Beginning in 2004, the term has been extended to two years.

3. Addison Hardie Leitch.

4. In this chapter and the next, I present research I did, some of which has already been published in my earlier book *Reading the Bible and the Confessions: The Presbyterian Way* (Louisville, KY: Geneva Press, 1999).

Chapter 1: Studying Homosexuality for the First Time

1. In Presbyterian government the session is the governing body of a congregation, composed of elected elders and the ministers of Word and Sacrament.

2. More Light is a Presbyterian designation for a congregation that is willing to elect qualified lesbian, gay, bisexual, and transgender persons to all offices in the church. Other denominations have similar movements with different names.

3. In Presbyterian polity, deacons are ordained to a ministry of service. They have no governance or other ministry function. Elders are members who have been ordained to a ministry of governance and general spiritual oversight in collaboration with the pastors, who are ministers of Word and Sacrament.

4. There was a cost, however. The congregation lost at least ten members and $40,000 in pledges from people who were uncomfortable with the study.

5. Much of the material in this chapter has been previously published in Jack Rogers, *Confessions of a Conservative Evangelical*, 2nd ed. (Louisville, KY: Geneva Press, 2001).

6. For a historical sketch of this period see Jack Rogers, *Claiming the Center: Churches and Conflicting Worldviews* (Louisville, KY: Westminster John Knox, 1995), 29–39.

7. For a detailed discussion of the Old Princeton interpretation of Scripture, see Jack B. Rogers and Donald K. McKim, *The Authority and Interpretation of the Bible: An Historical Approach* (San Francisco: Harper & Row, 1979), chaps. 5 and 6. A 1999 reprint edition, with a new epilogue, is available from Wipf & Stock Publishers, 150 West Broadway, Eugene, OR 97401.

8. Reformed is the theological name for that Protestant tradition with roots in the Calvinism that began in what we now call Switzerland. It is one of the Reformation strands, along with Lutheranism, Anglicanism, and Anabaptism.

9. Jack Bartlett Rogers, *Scripture in the Westminster Confession: A Problem of Historical Interpretation for American Presbyterianism* (Grand Rapids: Eerdmans, 1967).

10. G. C. Berkouwer, *Holy Scripture*, trans. and ed. Jack Rogers (Grand Rapids: Eerdmans, 1975).

11. See George Marsden, *Reforming Fundamentalism: Fuller Seminary and the New Evangelicalism* (Grand Rapids: Eerdmans, 1987).

12. Richard N. Ostling, "Evangelicals' Platform Shows Complex Political Profile," *Pasadena Star-News*, January 28, 2005, D5. University of Akron political scientist John C. Green asserts that the National Association of Evangelicals represents evangelicalism's pragmatic center. For Green, the progressive, or left, wing of evangelicalism is represented, for example, by Jim Wallis of *Sojourners* magazine in his new book *God's Politics: Why the Right Gets It Wrong and the Left Doesn't Get It* (San Francisco: Harper & Row, 2005), and leaders of the right wing include not only Jerry Falwell and Pat Robertson but also James Dobson of Focus on the Family and Southern Baptist executive Richard Land. This extreme right would more properly be known as fundamentalists.

13. Jerry Falwell, ed., with Ed Dobson and Ed Hindson, *The Fundamentalist Phenomenon: The Resurgence of Conservative Christianity* (Garden City, NY: Doubleday & Co., 1981).

14. George Marsden in *Fundamentalism and American Culture: The Shaping of Twentieth-Century Evangelicalism: 1870–1925* (New York: Oxford University Press, 1980), 4, describes fundamentalism as "militantly anti-modernist Protestant evangelicalism."

15. See Jack Rogers, "Inerrancy," in *A New Handbook of Christian Theology*, ed. Donald W. Musser and Joseph L. Price (Nashville: Abingdon Press, 1992), 254–56.

16. Harold Lindsell, *The Battle for the Bible* (Grand Rapids: Zondervan, 1976).

17. Jack Rogers, ed., *Biblical Authority* (Waco, TX: Word Books, 1977). My article was "The Church Doctrine of Biblical Authority," 15–46.

18. Rogers and McKim, *The Authority and Interpretation of the Bible*.

19. See, for example, John D. Woodbridge, *Biblical Authority: A Critique of the Rogers/McKim Proposal* (Grand Rapids: Zondervan, 1982).

20. The editor of *Christianity Today*, Kenneth Kantzer, referred to me as a "black beast."

21. The United Presbyterian Church in the United States of America was the result of a merger in 1958 of the United Presbyterian Church of North America and the Presbyterian Church in the U.S.A.

22. "The Church and Homosexuality," *Blue Book I, 190th General Assembly (1978) of the United Presbyterian Church in the United States of America, San Diego, California, May 16–24, 1978*, pp. D-1-D-201.

23. For further discussion, see Jack B. Rogers and Donald K. McKim, "Pluralism and Policy in Presbyterian Views of Scripture," in *The Confessional Mosaic: Presbyterians and Twentieth-Century Theology*, ed. Milton J Coalter, John M. Mulder, and Louis B. Weeks (Louisville, KY: Westminster/John Knox Press, 1990), 37–58.

24. *Minutes* of the General Assembly, UPCUSA, 1978b, 61–62.

25. Tom Gillespie, chair of the assembly committee, announced that the committee was recommending that the assembly "not exercise its right to render a constitutional interpretation." He said that to do so would call into question the constitutional rights of the presbyteries in the ordination process. The committee proposed, "rather, that it offer the 'definitive guidance' requested." See *Church and Society* 68, no. 5 (May–June 1978): 22–24.

26. See *The Constitution of the Presbyterian Church (U.S.A.), Part II, Book of Order, 2003–2004* (Louisville, KY: Office of the General Assembly, 2003), G-14.0207 and G-14.0405.

27. "Report of the Committee on Pluralism in the Church to the 190th General Assembly (1978) of the United Presbyterian Church in the United States of America," *Minutes*, 1978, Part I, p. 293.

28. For a discussion of the three mandates of the task force, see Jack B. Rogers and Donald K. McKim, "Pluralism and Policy in Presbyterian Views of Scripture," in *The Confessional Mosaic*, 49–52.

29. For the result, see *Presbyterian Use and Understanding of Scripture, a Position Statement of the General Assembly, Presbyterian Church (U.S.A.)* (New York and Atlanta: Office of the General Assembly, 1983), n.p.

30. A booklet named for and containing the two reports was published in Louisville by the Office of the General Assembly of the Presbyterian Church (U.S.A.) in 1992. Both the PCUS report, "Presbyterian Understanding and Use of Holy Scripture," and the UPCUSA report, "Biblical Authority and Interpretation," are printed in this booklet, published by the Office of the General Assembly in 1992 and available from Presbyterian Distribution Service, Louisville, KY, as #OGA-92-003.

31. Jeffrey S. Siker, ed., *Homosexuality in the Church: Both Sides of the Debate* (Louisville, KY: Westminster John Knox, 1994), 195–208, provides an appendix with the relevant documents. He includes earlier statements of the Episcopal Church and the Southern Baptist Convention as well. The definitive statement of the Roman Catholic Church to that time is found on 39–47.

32. The Coalition now has a variety of objectives, all concerned with reform and renewal of the Presbyterian Church in a generally conservative direction.

33. "Correction," *Presbyterian Outlook* 179, no. 8 (March 3, 1997): 2. Five percent, or 620 congregations, undertook the study, but in half of these only the ses-

sion studied the matter. Thus only 2.5 percent of the congregations conducted a congregational study.

34. Personal conversation, but in a public setting.

35. *Book of Order,* The Form of Government, G-6.0106b. This section is popularly referred to as G-6.0106b.

36. See J. Gordon Melton, *The Churches Speak on Homosexuality: Official Statements from Religious Bodies and Ecumenical Organizations* (Detroit: Gale Research, 1991). Siker, ed., *Homosexuality in the Church*, "Appendix: Selected Denominational Statements on Homosexuality," 195–208, cites recent statements by the Episcopal Church, the Evangelical Lutheran Church in America, the Presbyterian Church (U.S.A.), the Southern Baptist Convention, the United Church of Christ, and the United Methodist Church.

37. The definition of "sodomy" has changed over time. In the Middle Ages it referred to any form of sexual expression that was not open to procreation. Then it focused on anal intercourse. Until the twentieth century, such sexual expression was viewed as wrong and often made illegal, whether by heterosexual or homosexual couples. Then the law was narrowed in the United States to apply only to homosexuals. See Alan A. Brash, *Facing Our Differences: The Churches and Their Gay and Lesbian Members* (Geneva, Switzerland: WCC Publications, 1995), 37.

38. *Boston Globe*, November 18, 2003. See http://www.boston.com/news/specials/gay_marriage/gallery/timeline/.

39. *Boston Globe*, January 20, 2005. See http://www.boston.com/news/specials/gay_marriage/gallery/timeline?pg=2.

40. *Boston Globe*, February 24, 2004. See http://boston.com/news/specials/gay_marriage/gallery/timeline?pg=10.

41. The pastor of a large Presbyterian Church wrote to me in those terms. Alan Keyes, a candidate for United States Senate, declared that the definition of marriage "will determine the life and death of the freedom and morality of our country" (cited in Emma Schwartz and Kathleen Hennessey, "A Marriage-Minded Protest," *Los Angeles Times*, October 16, 2004, A8).

42. Dr. James Dobson, *Focus on the Family Newsletter,* April 2004, and read on his March 24, 2004, radio broadcast; cited in Jeff Lutes, *A False Focus on My Family* (Lynchburg, VA: Soulforce, 2005), 8, http://www.soulforce.org/pdf/false_focus.pdf.

43. See *Book of Order*, G-5.0202: "An active member is entitled to all the rights and privileges of the church, including the *right* to . . . vote and hold office." It is that *eligibility* for office that we are unconstitutionally denying to our faithful gay and lesbian members.

Chapter 2: A Pattern of Misusing the Bible to Justify Oppression

1. Jack Rogers, "Should the United Presbyterian Church Ordain Homosexuals?" (Boston: The Case Study Institute, 1976), 18.

2. Robert A. J. Gagnon, in Dan O. Via and Robert A. J. Gagnon, *Homosexuality and the Bible: Two Views* (Minneapolis: Fortress Press, 2003), 44–47. For

Gagnon's argument in more detail, see Robert A. J. Gagnon, *The Bible and Homosexual Practice: Texts and Hermeneutics* (Nashville: Abingdon Press, 2000), 442–52; Thomas E. Schmidt, *Straight and Narrow: Compassion and Clarity in the Homosexuality Debate* (Downers Grove, IL: InterVarsity Press, 1995), 26–27; Christopher Seitz, "Sexuality and Scripture's Plain Sense: The Christian Community and the Law of God," in *Homosexuality, Science, and the "Plain Sense" of Scripture,* ed. David L. Balch (Grand Rapids: Eerdmans, 2000), 182; Ray S. Anderson, "Homosexuality and the Ministry of the Church: Theological and Pastoral Considerations," in *More Than a Single Issue: Theological Considerations concerning the Ordination of Practising People Who Are Homosexual,* ed. Murray A. Rae and Graham Redding (P.O. Box 504, Hindmarsh SA 5007: Australian Theological Forum, 2000), 75.

3. John D'Emilio and Estelle B. Freedman, *Intimate Matters: A History of Sexuality in America* (New York: Harper & Row, 1988), xvi: "Whites imposed on blacks an image of a beastlike sexuality to justify both the rape of black women and the lynching of black men."

4. *Authorized Version of the English Bible*, 1611, commonly known as the King James Version. This translation of the Bible was the standard one in English from the time of colonization until the late 1950s.

5. *City of God* 19.15; cited in Stephen R. Haynes, *Noah's Curse: The Biblical Justification of American Slavery* (New York: Oxford University Press, 2002), 225 n. 14.

6. Haynes, *Noah's Curse,* esp. chap. 2.

7. Ernest Trice Thompson, *Presbyterians in the South,* vol. 1, *1607–1861* (Richmond: John Knox Press, 1963), 530. Some of the material in this chapter can be found as well in my book *Reading the Bible and the Confessions: The Presbyterian Way* (Louisville, KY: Geneva Press, 1999).

8. James Oscar Farmer Jr., *The Metaphysical Confederacy: James Henley Thornwell and the Synthesis of Southern Values* (Macon, GA: Mercer University Press, 1986), 222; and Thompson, *Presbyterians in the South,* 1:536.

9. *Address of the General Assembly of the Presbyterian Church in the Confederate States of America to All the Churches of Jesus Christ Throughout the Earth, Adopted Unanimously at the Organization of the General Assembly in Augusta, Ga., December, 1861* (n.p.: Published by order of the Assembly, n.d.), 5.

10. Ibid., 11.

11. Ibid., 15.

12. Ibid., 14.

13. Ibid., 11.

14. Ibid.

15. Ibid., 12.

16. Ibid., 15.

17. Ibid.

18. Cited in Eugene D. Genovese, "An Uncertain Trumpet: How Christians in the South Sought to Reconcile Slavery with Scripture," in *Books & Culture,* January/February 1999, 36. In December 1861, the Reverend J. Henry Smith of

North Carolina had used almost the same words: "If we fail, the progress of civilization will be thrown back a century."

19. S.v. "Dabney, Robert Lewis," in Randall Balmer and John R. Fitzmier, *The Presbyterians*, Denominations in America 5, ed. Henry Warner Bowden (Westport, CT: Greenwood Press, 1993), 147.

20. Ernest Trice Thompson, *Presbyterians in the South*, vol. 2, *1861–1890* (Richmond: John Knox Press, 1973), 200.

21. Ibid., 200.

22. Cited in Haynes, *Noah's Curse*, 71; quoting Dabney, *A Defence of Virginia (and through Her of the South), in Recent and Pending Contests against the Sectional Party* (New York: E. J. Hale & Son, 1867).

23. Thompson, *Presbyterians in the South*, 2:217.

24. Cited in Thomas Cary Johnson, *The Life and Letters of Robert Lewis Dabney* (Richmond: Presbyterian Committee of Publication, 1903), 320.

25. "Ecclesiastical Relation of Negroes," *Speech of Rev. Robert L. Dabney, in the Synod of Virginia, Nov. 9, 1867; Against The Ecclesiastical Equality of Negro Preachers in Our Church, and Their Right to Rule Over White Christians* (Richmond: Printed at the Office of the "Boys and Girls' Monthly," 1868), 8. Cf. Thompson, *Presbyterians in the South*, 2:218.

26. Dabney, "Ecclesiastical Relation," 8.

27. Ibid., 10.

28. Ibid., 8.

29. Ibid.

30. Thompson, *Presbyterians in the South*, 2:218–19.

31. Robert L. Dabney, "Anti-Biblical Theories of Rights," *Presbyterian Quarterly* 2, no. 2 (July 1888): 215–42, 219.

32. Ibid., 232–33.

33. Ibid., 223–24.

34. Cited in Genovese, "An Uncertain Trumpet," 36.

35. D'Emilio and Freedman, *Intimate Matters*, 28: "Western culture had traditionally feared the sexual voraciousness of women. As the 'weaker vessel,' woman supposedly had less mastery over her passions and had to be carefully controlled."

36. Cited in *Minutes*, PC(USA), 1987, 643.

37. Betty A. DeBerg, *Ungodly Women: Gender and the First Wave of American Fundamentalism* (Minneapolis: Fortress Press, 1990), 20.

38. Cited in ibid., 20.

39. *Extract from Minutes of the General Assembly*, PCUSA, 1803–1811, 310; cited in Karen (Bear) Ride Scott, "Expanding the Horizons of Ministry: Women of the Cloth in the Presbyterian Church, U.S.A." (DMin diss. project, San Francisco Theological Seminary, 1990), 84.

40. Lois A. Boyd and R. Douglas Brackenridge, *Presbyterian Women in America: Two Centuries of a Quest for Status*, Contributions to the Study of Religion 9, A Publication of the Presbyterian Historical Society (Westport, CT: Greenwood Press, 1983), 6.

41. Ronald W. Hogeland, "Charles Hodge, The Association of Gentlemen and Ornamental Womanhood: 1825–1855," *Journal of Presbyterian History* 53, no. 3 (Fall 1975): 245.

42. John W. Stewart, "Charles Hodge Revisited," *Princeton Seminary Bulletin* 18, no. 3 (November 1997): 287. An abridged edition of Hodge's *Systematic Theology*, edited by Edward N. Gross, was published in 1988 by Baker Book House in Grand Rapids.

43. Cited in Hogeland, "Charles Hodge," 247–48.

44. Dabney, "Rights," 223.

45. Ibid., 219.

46. Cited in Boyd and Brackenridge, *Presbyterian Women in America*, 208.

47. Cited in ibid., 217–18.

48. Ibid., 212.

49. Jack B. Rogers and Donald K. McKim, *The Authority and Interpretation of the Bible: An Historical Approach* (San Francisco: Harper & Row, 1979), 242–43.

50. Cited in ibid., 293.

51. Ibid., 235–42.

52. Ibid., 242.

53. Farmer, *Metaphysical Confederacy,* 138.

54. Ibid., 134–35.

55. See Morton H. Smith, *Studies in Southern Presbyterian Theology* (Amsterdam: Jacob Van Campen, 1962), 202 and 205. Smith, writing as a mid-twentieth-century Southerner, admired Dabney and agreed with his argument regarding slavery.

56. Cited in Rogers and McKim, *Authority and Interpretation*, 293.

57. William B. Gravely, "Christian Abolitionism," in *The Social Gospel: Religion and Reform in Changing America,* ed. Ronald C. White Jr. and C. Howard Hopkins (Philadelphia: Temple University Press, 1976), 18. In contrast to others who called for the gradual elimination of slavery, abolitionists called for its immediate end.

58. Aileen S. Kraditor, *Means and Ends in American Abolitionism: Garrison and His Critics on Strategy and Tactics, 1834–1850* (New York: Pantheon Books, 1967), 41 and 83.

59. John R. McKivigan, *The War against Proslavery Religion: Abolitionism and the Northern Churches, 1830–1865* (Ithaca, NY: Cornell University Press, 1984), 31.

60. Ibid., 20.

61. Gravely, "Christian Abolitionism," 18.

62. McKivigan, *War against Proslavery Religion*, 13.

63. Ibid., 58.

Chapter 3: A Breakthrough in Understanding the Word of God

1. For further discussion, see Jack Rogers, *Claiming the Center: Churches and Conflicting Worldviews* (Louisville, KY: Westminster John Knox, 1995), 15–17.

2. Ibid., 34–35.

3. For the full and original wordings of these "essentials," see *The Presbyterian Enterprise: Sources of American Presbyterian History*, ed. Maurice W. Armstrong, Lefferts A. Loetscher, and Charles A. Anderson (Philadelphia: Westminster Press, 1956), 281. The nondenominational fundamentalist movement took these five essentials and modified them to make #2 the deity of Christ, and #5 the premillennial return of Christ. These came to be called the "five fundamentals."

4. According to usual parliamentary rules, the person who is moderating, or chairing, a meeting cannot make a motion. Therefore, Erdman, following proper procedure, turned the chair, or the moderating of the meeting, over to his vice-moderator, and Erdman was then, himself, permitted to make a motion.

5. See further, Jack B. Rogers and Donald K. McKim, *The Authority and Interpretation of the Bible: An Historical Approach* (San Francisco: Harper & Row, 1979), 366–67.

6. Jack Rogers, *Reading the Bible and the Confessions: The Presbyterian Way* (Louisville, KY: Geneva Press, 1999), 92–98.

7. The group comprised approximately 13 percent of the ministers in the church. Many of them were pastors of large churches, who thus exercised considerable influence. See Charles E. Quick, "A Statistical Analysis of the Signers of the Auburn Affirmation," *Journal of Presbyterian History* 43, no. 3 (Fall 1965): 182–96, esp. 183 and 193.

8. "An Affirmation designed to safeguard the unity and liberty of the Presbyterian Church in the United States of America," Auburn, NY, n.d., p. 6, cited in Rogers, *Reading the Bible and the Confessions*, 96.

9. Donald McKim, *Westminster Dictionary of Theological Terms* (Louisville, KY: Westminster John Knox, 1996), s.v. "Neo-orthodoxy."

10. For a recent exposition and appraisal of the thought of Barth, Brunner, and five other theologians usually designated as neo-orthodox, see Douglas John Hall, *Remembered Voices: Reclaiming the Legacy of "Neo-Orthodoxy"* (Louisville, KY: Westminster John Knox, 1998).

11. McKim, *Dictionary*, s.v. "Kierkegaardian."

12. *Presbyterian Understanding and Use of Holy Scripture* [and] *Biblical Authority and Interpretation* (Louisville, KY: Office of the General Assembly, 1992), 38–44.

13. See chap. 1, p. 9 above, for theologians identified with neo-orthodoxy.

14. W. Eugene March, "'Biblical Theology,' Authority and the Presbyterians," *Journal of Presbyterian History* 59, no. 2 (Summer 1981): 118.

15. "Presbyterian scholars such as G. Ernest Wright, Floyd V. Filson, James D. Smart, John Wick Bowman, John A. Mackay, Joseph Haroutunian, Otto Piper, Arnold Rhodes, John Bright, Donald G. Miller, Balmer H. Kelly, and others, led the way in the '40s and '50s in advocating a new 'biblical theology'" (ibid., 118).

16. Ibid., 118–19.

17. Ibid., 119.

18. Ibid., 121.

19. Ibid., 121–22.

20. E. T. Thompson, *Presbyterians in the South,* vol. 3, *1890–1972* (Richmond: John Knox Press, 1973), 336.

21. Ibid., 3:338.

22. Ibid., 3:339.

23. Ibid., 3:539.

24. Ibid., 3:540.

25. "Report of the Ad Interim Committee on a Biblical Study of the Position of Women in the Church," *Minutes,* PCUS, 1956, 141.

26. *Book of Confessions,* 6.009; cited in "Report . . . Women," *Minutes,* PCUS, 1956, 139.

27. "Report . . . Women," *Minutes,* PCUS, 1956, 139.

28. *Minutes,* PCUSA, 1929; cited in James G. Emerson Jr., "The Remarriage of Divorced Persons in the United Presbyterian Church of the United States of America" (PhD diss., Divinity School of the University of Chicago, 1959), 125.

29. *Minutes,* PCUSA, 1930, 86–87.

30. Ibid., 87.

31. Ibid., 88.

32. James G. Emerson Jr., *Divorce, the Church, and Remarriage* (Philadelphia: Westminster Press, 1961), 127.

33. *Minutes,* PCUS, 1938, 110. Cf. Thompson, *Presbyterians in the South,* 3:516.

34. *Minutes,* PCUS, 1946, 104.

35. *Minutes,* PCUS, 1953, 89.

36. Ibid., 90.

37. Ibid.

38. Ibid.

39. *Minutes,* PCUS, 1959, 68–70; Thompson, *Presbyterians in the South,* 3:518–19.

40. *Minutes,* PCUS, 1959, 69; *Book of Confessions,* 6.137–6.138.

41. Eric Mount Jr. and Johanna W. H. Bos, "Scripture on Sexuality: Shifting Authority," *Journal of Presbyterian History* 59, no. 2 (Summer 1981): 224.

42. See especially John 7:53–8:11, the story of the woman taken in adultery.

43. Jack Rogers, "The Day before Christmas," in *On Speech and Speakers: An Anthology of Writings and Models,* ed. H. Bruce Kendall and Charles J. Stewart (New York: Holt, Rinehart & Winston, 1968), 233.

44. Ibid., 234.

45. Jack Rogers, "Biblical Authority and Confessional Change," *Journal of Presbyterian History* 59, no. 2 (Summer 1981): 136–37.

46. For a complete list of the committee at all stages, see *Report of the Special Committee on a Brief Contemporary Statement of Faith* (Philadelphia: Office of the General Assembly, 1965), 10.

47. Rogers, "Biblical Authority and Confessional Change," 142–43.

48. Edward A. Dowey Jr., *A Commentary on the Confession of 1967 and an Introduction to the Book of Confessions* (Philadelphia: Westminster Press, 1968), 40–41.

49. *Book of Confessions*, 9.44.

50. "A Declaration of Faith (Presbyterian Church in the United States)," in *The Proposed Book of Confessions with Related Documents*, Approved by the 116th General Assembly and Recommended to the Presbyteries for Their Advice and Consent (Atlanta: Presbyterian Church in the United States, 1976), chap. 6, lines 65–67. The declaration did not receive the necessary three-quarters vote to become part of the PCUS *Constitution*, but it was used widely in the congregations.

51. "Declaration of Faith," chap. 2, lines 122–25.

52. Jack Rogers, "The Kenyon Case," in *Women and Men in Ministry*, ed. Roberta Hestenes (Pasadena, CA: Fuller Theological Seminary, 1985), 148.

53. For a brief discussion of the Adopting Act of 1729, see Rogers, *Reading the Bible and the Confessions*, 91–92.

54. Rogers, "Kenyon Case," 148.

55. Ibid., 157–58.

56. Ibid., 150.

57. *Book of Confessions*, 9.44.

58. Rogers, "Kenyon Case," 150.

59. Jack Rogers, *Presbyterian Creeds: A Guide to the Book of Confessions* (Louisville, KY: Westminster John Knox Press, 1991), 231–32.

60. *Book of Confessions*, 10.3, lines 29–32.

61. *Book of Confessions*, 10.4, line 64.

62. *Book of Confessions*, 10.3, lines 47–51.

63. Rogers, *Presbyterian Creeds*, 268–69.

Chapter 4: Interpreting the Bible in Times of Controversy

1. I discussed these guidelines in my earlier book *Reading the Bible and the Confessions: The Presbyterian Way* (Louisville, KY: Geneva Press, 1999). Some of the material in this chapter, especially citations from the Reformed confessions, will overlap with that earlier publication.

2. *Presbyterian Understanding and Use of Holy Scripture and Biblical Authority and Interpretation* (Louisville, KY: Office of the General Assembly, 1992), preface. These two reports were gathered into one booklet with the following comment: "The two papers were written in response to the need for a common basis in a diverse church for understanding and using Scripture." Hereafter cited as Guidelines.

3. See chap. 3 above for more specifics on the context of this discussion.

4. Guidelines, 41–44.

5. Ibid., 43.

6. Ibid., 51.

7. Ibid., 52.

8. Cited in *Presbyterian Understanding and Use of Holy Scripture, Position Statement Adopted by the 123rd General Assembly (1983) of the Presbyterian Church in the United States* (Louisville, KY: Office of the General Assembly, 1992), 17.

9. Guidelines, 17, The Geneva Confession of 1541.

10. Guidelines, 17, The Synod of Bern of 1528.

11. *Book of Confessions*, 3.18. Cited below as *BC*.

12. *BC*, 8.11.

13. *BC*, 9.29.

14. Guidelines, 18, A Declaration of Faith.

15. See the brave and painfully honest admission of a pastor, Joanna Adams, that even without intending it she caused another great pain in the Covenant Network–sponsored film *Turning Points*.

16. Calvin, *Institutes of the Christian Religion* 4.16.23; cited in Jack B. Rogers and Donald K. McKim, *The Authority and Interpretation of the Bible* (San Francisco: Harper & Row, 1979), 97.

17. *BC*, 5.010.

18. *BC*, 9.29.

19. Guidelines, 12.

20. Guidelines, 11–12.

21. Guidelines, 11.

22. Richard B. Hays, "Awaiting the Redemption of Our Bodies," *Sojourners* 20 (July 1991): 18.

23. The first known use of the word "homosexual" in English was in 1892. C. G. Chaddock's translation of Krafft-Ebing's (1886) *Psychopathia sexualis* 3:255 referred to a patient: "He had been free from homo-sexual inclinations."

24. *BC*, 6.006.

25. *BC*, 6.010.

26. *BC*, 9.30.

27. Guidelines, 21.

28. For an application of this to homosexuality, see Jeffrey S. Siker, "Homosexual Christians, the Bible, and Gentile Inclusion: Confessions of a Repenting Heterosexist," in *Homosexuality in the Church: Both Sides of the Debate,* ed. Jeffrey S. Siker (Louisville, KY: Westminster John Knox Press, 1994), 187–91.

29. *BC*, 4.022.

30. *BC*, 5.010.

31. *Presbyterian Understanding and Use*, 21.

32. The recent (1962) insertion of the phrase "homosexual perversion" in the Heidelberg Catechism, Answer 87, is without historical justification, as I will show in chapter 7.

33. *BC*, 4.108.

34. *BC*, 5.246.

35. *BC*, 7.49.

36. *BC*, 7.48.

37. *BC*, 9.44–46.

38. *BC*, 9.47.

39. Ibid.

40. *BC*, 3.18.

41. *BC*, 5.010.

42. Guidelines, 20.

43. Walter Wink, "Homosexuality and the Bible," in *Homosexuality and Christian Faith: Questions of Conscience for the Churches,* ed. Walter Wink (Minneapolis: Fortress Press, 1999), 44.

44. *BC*, 6.007.

45. *BC*, 6.008.

46. *BC*, 6.175.

47. Guidelines, 22.

48. *The Oxford Dictionary of the Christian Church*, ed. F. L. Cross, 3rd ed., ed. E. A. Livingstone (Oxford: Oxford University Press, 1997), s.v. "Textual Criticism": "The belief that textual criticism has radically altered the text lying behind the traditional translations of the Bible has been one of the factors prompting the production of modern versions in recent times. . . . But the resulting changes in the text, at least so far as the NT is concerned, are by no means so fundamental as is often supposed." Cf. Eldon Jay Epp, "Ancient Texts and Versions of the New Testament," in *The New Interpreter's Bible*, vol. 8 (Nashville: Abingdon Press, 1995), 1–11.

49. Martti Nissinen, *Homoeroticism in the Biblical World: A Historical Perspective*, trans. Kirsi Stjerna (Minneapolis: Fortress Press, 1998), 43.

50. Phyllis A. Bird, "The Bible in Christian Ethical Deliberation concerning Homosexuality: Old Testament Contributions," in *Homosexuality, Science, and the "Plain Sense" of Scripture*, ed. David L. Balch (Grand Rapids: Eerdmans, 2000), 157.

51. Victor Paul Furnish, "The Bible and Homosexuality: Reading the Texts in Context," in Siker, *Homosexuality in the Church*, 31.

52. *BC*, 5.010.

53. *BC*, 6.009.

54. Guidelines, 52; Guideline 1.

55. In Presbyterian government, election to office is a privilege, but eligibility for election is a *right* according to the church constitution. See *Book of Order*, G-5.0202: "An active member is entitled to all the rights and privileges of the church, including the right . . . to vote and hold office."

Chapter 5: What the Bible Says and Doesn't Say about Homosexuality

1. Richard B. Hays, "Awaiting the Redemption of Our Bodies: The Witness of Scripture concerning Homosexuality," in *Homosexuality in the Church: Both Sides of the Debate,* ed. Jeffrey S. Siker (Louisville, KY: Westminster John Knox Press, 1994), 5. Hays views homosexuality as evidence of human sinfulness, based on his reading of Romans 1. I deal with his view later in this chapter.

2. Daniel A. Helminiak, *What the Bible Really Says about Homosexuality,* millennium edition, updated and expanded (Tijaque, NM: Alamo Square Press, 2000), 46.

3. Some writers believe that the statement by the men of Sodom, "Bring them out to us, so that we may know them" (Gen. 19:5), has a homosexual connotation.

That is not necessarily the case. The Hebrew word *yada*, meaning "to know," appears almost 1,000 times in the Hebrew Scriptures. It is used to refer to sexual intercourse only ten or eleven times. In each case the reference is to heterosexual intercourse. Therefore we should be cautious in attributing any homosexual connotation to it. See Don Blosser, "Why Does the Bible Divide Us? A Conversation with Scripture on Same-Gender Attraction," in *To Continue the Dialogue: Biblical Interpretation and Homosexuality*, ed. Norman Kraus (Telford, PA: Pandora Press, 2001), 121–47; cited in David G. Myers and Letha Dawson Scanzoni, *What God Has Joined Together? A Christian Case for Gay Marriage* (San Francisco: HarperSanFrancisco, 2005), 86.

4. Helminiak, *What the Bible Really Says*, 46.

5. Dale B. Martin, "*Arsenokoites* and *Malakos*: Meanings and Consequences," in *Biblical Ethics and Homosexuality: Listening to Scripture,* ed. Robert L. Brawley (Louisville, KY: Westminster John Knox Press, 1996), 129.

6. Ibid., 127.

7. Martti Nissinen, *Homoeroticism in the Biblical World: A Historical Perspective*, trans. Kirsi Stjerna (Minneapolis: Fortress Press, 1998), 48. Cf. Phyllis A. Bird, "The Bible in Christian Ethical Deliberation concerning Homosexuality: Old Testament Contributions," in *Homosexuality, Science, and the "Plain Sense" of Scripture*, ed. David L. Balch (Grand Rapids: Eerdmans, 2000), 148.

8. Choon-Leong Seow, "Textual Orientation," in Brawley, *Biblical Ethics and Homosexuality*, 22.

9. Ibid., 22. Cf. Helminiak, *What the Bible Really Says*, 48–49. Other OT references include Isa. 1:10–17 and 3:9; Jer. 23:14; Ezek.16:49; and Zeph. 2:8–11.

10. Nissinen, *Homoeroticism*, 47.

11. Ibid., 47.

12. Bird, "The Bible in Christian Ethical Deliberation," 149–50.

13. Victor Paul Furnish, "The Bible and Homosexuality: Reading the Texts in Context," in Siker, *Homosexuality in the Church*, 20.

14. Helminiak, *What the Bible Really Says*, 52–53.

15. Furnish, "The Bible and Homosexuality," 20.

16. Bird, "The Bible in Christian Ethical Deliberation," 157.

17. Nissinen, *Homoeroticism*, 42. Cf. Bird, "The Bible in Christian Ethical Deliberation," 151.

18. Myers and Scanzoni, *What God Has Joined Together?* 90. They note that Tim and Beverly LaHaye, conservative Christians who insist that same-sex acts are an abomination, nonetheless counsel modern married couples to have intercourse during the wife's menstrual period.

19. Marion L. Soards, *Scripture and Homosexuality: Biblical Authority and the Church Today* (Louisville, KY: Westminster John Knox, 1995), 17. He says that discerning relevance is impossible "given the historical setting and purpose of the Holiness Code in which Lev. 18:22 and 20:13 occur, and more, given that we confess in faith that Christ is the end of the law (Rom. 10:4)."

20. Brian Blount, "Reading and Understanding the New Testament on Homosexuality," in *Homosexuality and Christian Community,* ed. Choon-Leong Seow (Louisville, KY: Westminster John Knox Press, 1996), 33.

21. Ibid. Blount comments regarding 1 Cor. 6:9: "Chronologically, this is Paul's first statement on this issue, and it is also his least understandable." Cf. Nissinen, *Homoeroticism,* 113.

22. Nissinen, *Homoeroticism,* 113.

23. Ibid., 115.

24. Martin, "*Arsenokoites* and *Malakos,*" 119.

25. Ibid., 119.

26. Ibid., 121.

27. Ibid., 123. Martin, in the notes to his article, seems to treat these quoted words as a general claim made by antigay scholars.

28. Nissinen, *Homoeroticism,* 118.

29. Martin, "*Arsenokoites* and *Malakos,*" 128–29.

30. Nissinen, *Homoeroticism,* 114.

31. Furnish, "The Bible and Homosexuality," 19. The OT references in the KJV are Deut. 23:17–18; 1 Kgs. 14:22–24; 15:12; 22:46; 2 Kgs. 23:7; Joel 3:3. The NT references in the NRSV are in 1 Cor. 6:9 and 1 Tim. 1:10. Myers and Scanzoni, *What God Has Joined Together?* 96, list thirteen different English translations of the two words since 1961.

32. Alice Ogden Bellis and Terry L. Hufford, *Science, Scripture, and Homosexuality* (Cleveland: Pilgrim Press, 2002), 110. Martin, "*Arsenokoites* and *Malakos,*" 119–22.

33. Nissinen, *Homoeroticism,* 118.

34. Soards, *Scripture and Homosexuality,* 20.

35. See Thomas E. Schmidt, *Straight and Narrow: Compassion and Clarity in the Homosexuality Debate* (Downers Grove, IL: InterVarsity Press, 1995), 96–97.

36. Ibid., 97.

37. Seow, "Textual Orientation," 32 n. 15.

38. Ibid., 22. Seow notes that Jude, in the Greek text, indicates that the people of Sodom and Gomorrah have "practiced immorality in the same way [as the angels in Gen. 6] and pursued other flesh (*sarkos heteras*)." The flesh that the men of Sodom pursued was angelic, "other, different," the word from which we get "hetero," as in "heterosexual."

39. Blount, "Reading and Understanding," 34: "The worst thing is that they worship and serve not the Creator, but the creature. Their problem was idolatry."

40. Alan Brash, *Facing Our Differences: The Churches and Their Gay and Lesbian Members* (Geneva, Switzerland: WCC Publications, 1995), 44.

41. Nissinen, *Homoeroticism,* 105.

42. Ibid., 105.

43. Helminiak, *What the Bible Really Says,* 80.

44. Nissinen, *Homoeroticism,* 107.

45. See ibid., 104, for the Greek words.

46. Ibid., 107.

47. Ibid, 107. See, e.g., Robert A. J. Gagnon, *The Bible and Homosexual Practice: Texts and Hermeneutics* (Nashville: Abingdon Press, 2000), 364.

48. Nissinen, *Homoeroticism*, 107.

49. Ibid., 108.

50. Ibid.

51. Myers and Scanzoni, *What God Has Joined Together?* 98. They refer to John Boswell, *Christianity, Social Tolerance, and Homosexuality* (Chicago: University of Chicago Press, 1980), 158, 203–5.

52. See Robert Jewett, "The Social Context and Implications of Homoerotic References in Romans 1:24–27," in Balch, *Homosexuality, Science,* 229–30.

53. David E. Fredrickson, "Natural and Unnatural Use in Romans 1:24–27: Paul and the Philosophical Critique of Eros," in Balch, *Homosexuality, Science,* 204.

54. Ibid., 205.

55. Ibid., 216.

56. Jeffrey S. Siker, "Gentile Wheat and Homosexual Christians: New Testament Directions for the Heterosexual Church," in Brawley, *Biblical Ethics and Homosexuality*, 143.

57. Ralph McInerny, "Are There Moral Truths That Everyone Knows?" in *Common Truths: New Perspectives on Natural Law,* ed. Edward B. McLean (Wilmington, DE: Intercollegiate Studies Institute, 2000), 1. The *New Catholic Encyclopedia* defines natural law as "a law or rule of action that is implicit in the very nature of things. . . . More properly, however, it is applied exclusively to man and proceeds from human nature as rational. . . . For St. Thomas Aquinas, 'natural law' is nothing other than the participation of eternal law in rational creatures." *New Catholic Encyclopedia* (New York: McGraw-Hill, 1967), vol. 10, s.v. "Natural Law." Charles E. Rice claims that "morality is governed by a law built into the nature of man and knowable by reason. Man can know, through the use of his reason, what is in accord with his nature and therefore good. . . . The natural law is therefore a rule of reason, promulgated by God in man's nature, whereby man can discern how he should act"; see *50 Questions on the Natural Law: What It Is and Why We Need It* (San Francisco: Ignatius Press, 1999), 30, 31, and 51.

58. *Oxford English Dictionary (OED)*, s.v. "Prejudice," offers these, among many, definitions of prejudice: "a judgment formed before due examination; a premature or hasty judgment; a prejudgment . . . a preconceived idea of what will happen."

59. Stephanie Rosenbloom, "Religious Leaders Clash on 'Meet the Press,'" *New York Times*, November 28, 2004, www.nytimes.com/2004/11/28/politics/28cnd-talk.html.

60. See Marlene Zuk, *Sexual Selections: What We Can and Can't Learn about Sex from Animals* (Berkeley: University of California Press, 2002), 176. The original source is Bruce Bagemihl, *Biological Exuberance: Animal Homosexuality and Natural Diversity* (New York: St. Martin's Press, 1999).

61. Gagnon, *The Bible and Homosexual Practice.*

62. Ibid., 488.

63. Ibid., 364.

64. Ibid., 157.

65. Ibid., 142.

66. Ibid., 391.

67. See Dan O. Via and Robert A. J. Gagnon, *Homosexuality and the Bible: Two Views* (Minneapolis: Augsburg Fortress, 2003), 103.

68. Nissinen, *Homoeroticism*, 120–21.

69. David G. Myers, excerpt from *Psychology*, 7th ed. (New York: Worth Publishers, 2004). Available at www.davidmyers.org

70. Via and Gagnon, *Homosexuality and the Bible*, 103.

71. Schmidt, *Straight and Narrow*, 155.

72. Andrew Comiskey, *Pursuing Sexual Wholeness: How Jesus Heals the Homosexual* (Lake Mary, FL: Creation House, 1989), 44.

73. Myers, excerpt from *Psychology*.

74. Gagnon, *The Bible and Homosexual Practice*, 254.

75. Ibid., 493.

76. Ibid., 470.

77. Hays, "Awaiting the Redemption," 8.

78. Ibid. Marion Soards also treats Romans 1 as relevant to contemporary Christian people who are homosexual. His rationale is much the same as that of Hays. Indeed, he agrees with Hays on the two criteria for condemning homosexual intercourse: It is a graphic example of human fallenness, and it rejects the created order of heterosexual marriage. See Soards, *Scripture and Homosexuality*, 21–23.

79. See, for example, the research of Hershberger, Levay, Allen and Gorski, Gladue, Mustanki and Bailey, and others, in Myers, excerpt from *Psychology*. Available at www.davidmyers.org.

80. Hays, "Awaiting the Redemption," 13.

81. Nor is there any cultural agreement on the nature of marriage. Stephanie Coontz in *Marriage, a History: From Obedience to Intimacy or How Love Conquered Marriage* (New York: Viking Penguin, 2005), 24, says, "So it ought to be easy to cut through all the historical and cultural differences to find marriage's common features and explain why the institution is so ubiquitous. But talk about opening a can of worms! . . . After a half a century there is still no definition everyone accepts."

82. Stanley J. Grenz, *Sexual Ethics: An Evangelical Perspective* (Louisville, KY: Westminster John Knox, 1997), 230.

83. Schmidt, *Straight and Narrow*, 39. Cf. Ulrich W. Mauser, "Creation and Human Sexuality in the New Testament," in Brawley, *Biblical Ethics and Homosexuality*, 3–15.

84. Bird, "The Bible in Christian Ethical Deliberation," 167 n. 55, emphasis added.

85. Furnish, "The Bible and Homosexuality," 22.

86. Ibid.

87. Ibid. Furnish notes, "The concern in these verses is much narrower: to explain why, ordinarily, a man is moved to leave his own blood kin to join himself in sexual union with a woman."

88. Ibid., 23.

89. David L. Balch, "Concluding Observations by the Editor," in *Homosexuality, Science*, 288.

90. Ibid.

91. See Coontz, *Marriage, a History*, 24.

92. Gagnon, in Via and Gagnon, *Homosexuality and the Bible*, 61.

93. Cited in Herman C. Waetjen, "Same-Sex Relations in Antiquity and Sexuality and Sexual Identity in Contemporary American Society," in Brawley, *Biblical Ethics and Homosexuality*, 107–8.

94. The authors of the Confession of 1967 were not yet sensitive to the issue of women's rights. However, in the Kenyon Case in 1974, as we discussed in chap. 3, the Permanent Judicial Commission of the General Assembly affirmed that the equality of all people before God that the Confession of 1967 had applied to people of color was also applicable to women.

95. In June 1968, Barth's assistant, Eberhard Busch, drafted a letter under Barth's direction that constituted a partial, and only possible, retraction of his views on homosexuality. The letter was in response to a request that Barth join with others in protesting "defamation," and juridical "penalizing" of homosexuals who had committed no crime. Busch wrote, "Prof. Barth is today not completely satisfied any more with his former, incidental comments and would certainly formulate them today somewhat differently; . . . he could, in conversation with doctors and psychologists, come to a new judgment and exposition of the phenomenon." However, Busch continued, "Naturally you would gladly hear that from him. But since he must allow all kinds of restrictions befall him as an over-82-year-old man, he does not now have the requisite time left for it. That time he thinks he ought to deploy, with the powers remaining to him, to the work on themes and tasks that seem to him more important." See Karl Barth, "Freedom for Community," in *Theology and Sexuality: Classical and Contemporary Readings*, ed. Eugene F. Rogers Jr. (Oxford, UK: Blackwell Publishers, 2002), 114–15.

96. Karl Barth, *Church Dogmatics* [*CD*], vol. III, *The Doctrine of Creation*, part 4, ed. G. W. Bromiley and T. F. Torrance (Edinburgh: T&T Clark, 1961), 163.

97. Elouise Renich Fraser, "Karl Barth's Doctrine of Humanity: A Reconstructive Exercise in Feminist Narrative Theology" (PhD diss., Vanderbilt University, 1986), 123 n. 24: "The German phrase for both 'man and woman' as well as 'husband and wife' is *Mann und Frau.* . . . Barth's intention to use husband-wife as a paradigm for man-woman makes it difficult to determine which set of terms is more appropriate. In any case, it is not wrong to see husband-wife informing every reference to man-woman in this anthropological definition."

98. Ibid., 134. See Barth, *CD*, III/2 (1960): 314.

99. Fraser, "Barth's Doctrine of Humanity," 203. See Barth, *CD,* III/2:290. To feel the full power of Barth's earlier rejection of any form of natural theology, see *Natural Theology: Comprising "Nature and Grace" by Professor Dr. Emil Brunner and the Reply "No" by Dr. Karl Barth*, trans. Peter Fraenkel, intro. John Baillie (London: Geoffrey Bles at the Centenary Press, 1946), 74. Barth declares that "the image of God in man is totally destroyed by sin. Every attempt to assert a general revelation has to be rejected. There is no grace of creation and preservation. There are no recognizable ordinances of preservation. There is no point of contact for the redeeming action of God. The new creation is in no sense the perfection of the old but rather the replacement of the old man by the new."

100. Fraser, "Barth's Doctrine of Humanity," 221–22. It is significant that here, exegetically, Barth moves away from Jesus and the Gospels, on which he based his definition of humanity, and instead uses Gen. 2 and the Pauline Epistles, especially Eph. 5. Fraser notes that Barth appeals to Eph. 5 as the interpretive key to every Old and New Testament text on the relationship between man and woman. (Eastern Baptist Seminary was renamed Palmer Theological Seminary on July 1, 2005.)

101. Fraser, "Barth's Doctrine of Humanity," 217. See Barth, *CD,* III/4:166. Barth says, "The command of God shows him [a man] irrefutably—in clear contradiction to his own theories—that as a man he can only be genuinely human with woman, or as a woman with man. In proportion as he accepts this insight, homosexuality can have no place in his life, whether in its more refined or cruder forms."

102. Comiskey, *Pursuing Sexual Wholeness*, 40.

103. Jim Wallis, editor-in-chief of *Sojourners* magazine, said: "I can't ignore 3,000 verses in the Bible on poverty." See Leslie Scanlon, "'Monologue of the Religious Right' is over, Jim Wallis tells LPTS," *Presbyterian Outlook*, April 4, 2005, 4.

104. Luke Timothy Johnson, *Scripture and Discernment: Decision Making in the Church* (Nashville: Abingdon Press, 1996), 90, comments, "Luke has left his reader in no doubt concerning God's intention: From the beginning, God has willed the salvation of the Gentile world." See 89–90 on the many anticipations of Acts 10–15 in Luke and Acts. Johnson, 107, further comments, "The words of Jesus and the Scripture are normative for the believers, but in a way that allows new and deeper understanding of them."

105. Ibid., 147. Gagnon, in *Homosexuality and the Bible*, 43–44, fails to recognize the consistent biblical characterization of Gentiles as sinners, both in their being and in their behavior. Gagnon's rejection of the analogy of Gentile inclusion is further based on a series of false assumptions, such as the notion that homosexuality is a chosen condition. Thus he dismisses the analogy on grounds that are irrelevant.

106. Johnson, *Scripture and Discernment*, 147. See, further, 89–108 and 144–48.

107. Siker, "Gentile Wheat and Homosexual Christians," 146. For an expanded version of this testimony, see Jeffrey S. Siker, "Homosexual Christians, the Bible, and Gentile Inclusion: Confessions of a Repenting Heterosexist," in Jeffrey. S. Siker, ed., *Homosexuality in the Church*, esp. 187–90.

Chapter 6: Real People and Real Marriage

1. George Chauncey, *Why Marriage? The History Shaping Today's Debate over Gay Equality* (New York: Basic Books, 2004), 133: "One study had shown that of couples together for ten years, breakup rates were 4 percent for married heterosexual couples, 4 percent for gay men, and 6 percent for lesbians. Other comparative studies showed virtually no difference in the quality of relationships between gay couples and heterosexual couples."

2. David G. Myers and Letha Dawson Scanzoni, *What God Has Joined Together? A Christian Case for Gay Marriage* (San Francisco: HarperSanFrancisco, 2005), 68: "Regardless of the process, the consistency of the genetic, neural, and biochemical findings has swung the pendulum toward a greater appreciation of biological influences. If biology indeed proves critical (perhaps especially so in certain environments), such would explain why we do not experience our own sexual orientation as a choice."

3. Chauncey, *Why Marriage?* 153: "The belief that homosexuality is a sinful choice instead of a minority status is especially pronounced among people with a fundamentalist or evangelical worldview."

4. Ibid., 152: "A major Pew Foundation study conducted in early 2004 found that a person's belief or disbelief in the mutability of homosexual identity was a more powerful predictor of their attitudes toward gay people than education, knowing someone gay, or 'general ideological beliefs.'"

5. Paul in 1 Cor. 7:9: "If they are not practicing self-control, they should marry. For it is better to marry than to be aflame with passion." John Calvin, *Institutes of the Christian Religion* 2.8.41: "The companionship of marriage has been ordained as a necessary remedy to keep us from plunging into unbridled lust."

6. Heinrich Bullinger, writing in the Second Helvetic Confession (1566), commends those "who have the gift of celibacy from heaven," but wisely says, "But if, again, the gift be taken away, and they feel a continual burning, let them call to mind the words of the apostle: 'It is better to marry than to be aflame'" (I Cor. 7:9)" (*Book of Confessions*, 5.245).

7. See "Bishops Seek Easier Dismissal of Priests," *Los Angeles Times*, November 18, 1993. The story also says that "Jason Berry, who has written a book on the issue, estimated that the [R.C.] church spent $400 million from 1984 to 1992 to settle cases involving 400 priests."

8. A May 1991 survey of fifty presbyteries of the Presbyterian Church (U.S.A.) revealed that there were sixty-four ongoing or recent sexual misconduct cases reported, most involving ministers engaging in sexual intercourse outside of marriage. See "Policy and Amendments Aim to Combat Sexual Misconduct," *Presbyterian Outlook*, January 6–13, 1992, 6.

9. Westminster Confession of Faith, chapter 24, 3; in *The Confession of Faith of the Assembly of Divines at Westminster, From the Original Manuscript Written by Cornelius Burges in 1646*, ed. S.W. Carruthers (n.p.: Presbyterian Church of England, 1946).

10. *Minutes*, PCUSA, 1930, 87.

11. Jack Rogers, *Reading the Bible and the Confessions: The Presbyterian Way* (Louisville, KY: Geneva Press, 1999), 82 and 84.

12. "Three Gay Couples Argue for Right to Marry," *USA Today*, November 19, 1998, 7A.

13. Chauncey, *Why Marriage?* 62–63.

14. Stephanie Coontz, *Marriage, a History: From Obedience to Intimacy or How Love Conquered Marriage* (New York: Viking Penguin, 2005), 186: "In the thirteenth century the English jurist Henry de Bracton declared that a married couple is one person, and that person is the husband. When Lord William Blackstone codified English common law in 1765, he reaffirmed this principle. . . . This doctrine of coverture, in which the legal identity of a wife was subsumed ('covered') by that of her husband, was passed on to the colonies and became the basis of American law for the next 150 years." Cf. 115 and 194.

15. *Minutes*, PCUSA, 1930, 79–82.

16. Benton Johnson, "From Old to New Agendas: Presbyterians and Social Issues in the Twentieth Century," in *The Confessional Mosaic: Presbyterians and Twentieth-Century Theology*, ed. Milton J Coalter, John M. Mulder, and Louis Weeks (Louisville, KY: Westminster John Knox, 1990), 220.

17. CNN.com, November 18, 1998. "Three Gay Couples," 7A. Chauncey, *Why Marriage?* 131, notes that in a friend-of-the-court brief in the Massachusetts case "neither the ability nor willingness to procreate has ever been a condition for entering a marriage, nor has the inability to have children been a legal basis for ending a marriage. Statutory law and case law both showed that marriage instead established certain relational rights and obligations, which were designed to 'support individuals' expectations of emotional and sexual intimacy, vows of fidelity and commitment and sharing of economic assets and support.'"

18. Christopher Calhoun, Public Policy Advocate, L. A. Gay and Lesbian Center, in a letter to the *Los Angeles Times*, July 24, 1999, B7.

19. Chauncey, *Why Marriage?* 86.

20. "The particular form taken by modern heterosexism is largely derived from sexism." Dale B. Martin, "*Arsenokoites* and *Malakos*: Meanings and Consequences," in *Biblical Ethics and Homosexuality: Listening to Scripture,* ed. Robert L. Brawley (Louisville, KY: Westminster John Knox, 1996), 129.

21. Chauncey, *Why Marriage?* 147.

22. Anna Quindlen, "Now Available: Middle Ground," *Newsweek*, July 11, 2005, 74. Commenting on resistance to the "morning-after pill," to prevent pregnancy, Quindlen states, "The rise and righteous indignation of the powerful religious right have been fueled by the transformation of women's lives. . . . If easy access to a pill that has been shown to significantly decrease the number of abortions is not

a welcome development, what is the real point of the anti-abortion exercise? Is it to safeguard life, or to safeguard an outdated status quo in which biology was destiny and motherhood was an obligation, not an avocation? America leads the industrialized world in its abortion rate. Perhaps that is because it leads in hypocrisy as well."

23. Jerry Falwell, *Listen America!* (New York: Bantam Books, 1981), 159.

24. Cited in Chauncey, *Why Marriage?* 148.

25. Dobson first came to wide public notice while teaching child development at the University of Southern California with his book *Dare to Discipline*, which encourages parents to spank their children with "sufficient magnitude to cause the child to cry genuinely." See James Dobson, *Dare to Discipline* (Wheaton, IL: Tyndale House Publishers, 1970), 35.

26. Dan Gilgoff, "An Evangelical Leader Steps Squarely into the Political Ring," *U.S. News & World Report*, January 16, 2005, 62.

27. *U.S. News & World Report*, January 17, 2005, 69.

28. David Van Biema, "The Twenty-five Most Influential Evangelicals in America," *Time*, February 7, 2005, 36.

29. Dr. James Dobson, *Focus on the Family Newsletter,* April 2004 (mailed to more than two million people). Cited in Jeff Lutes, *A False Focus on My Family* (Lynchburg, VA: Soulforce, 2005), 6.

30. Focus on the Family, CitizenLink, *Q&A: The Homosexual Agenda*, July 25, 2003. Cited in Lutes, *A False Focus*, 6.

31. "The Battle for Marriage," television simulcast to more than 700 churches, May 23, 2004. Cited in Lutes, *A False Focus*, 6.

32. See Susan Olasky, "Femme Fatale," *World* 12, no. 2 (March 29, 1997): cover story. Cf. J. Lee Grady, "EPA Panel Rebukes *World*," *Christianity Today*, August 11, 1997, 58.

33. James C. Dobson, "Spooked by the Zeitgeist: Don't Give In to Feminist Pressure to Rewrite the Scriptures," *World* 12, no. 7 (May 3, 1997).

34. Doug Le Blanc, with Steve Rabey, "Bible Translators Deny Gender Agenda," *Christianity Today*, July 14, 1997, 62–63.

35. "Conservative Christians' Outcry Forces Cancellation of New Bible," *Los Angeles Times*, May 31, 1997, B4. *World* 12, no. 10 (June 14, 1997) ran a story headlined "Bailing Out of the Stealth Bible." In fact, Zondervan continued its translation work and in 2005 produced the TNIV, or Today's New International Version, in contemporary English, using gender-inclusive language. Moderate evangelicals praised the translation while Dobson and the more extreme fundamentalists remained relatively quiet. See "New Bible Woos Young Adults, Skirts Critics," in *Christian Century*, March 8, 2005, 14–15.

36. Aída Besançon Spencer, "Power Play," *Christian Century*, July 2–9, 1997, 618–19.

37. Ibid.

38. Michael G. Maudlin, "Inside CT," *Christianity Today* 41, no. 8 (July 14, 1997): 4.

39. Dobson, "Spooked by the Zeitgeist."

40. Cited in Martin E. Marty, "Doing It by the Book," *Christian Century*, May 3, 2005, 47.

41. Family.org: A Web site of Focus on the Family. http://www.family.org/welcome/bios/A0022947.cfm.

42. Focus on the Family joined with the following groups in sponsoring a full-page advertisement in *USA Today* to support their assertion that "Freedom from homosexuality *is possible*": National Association for Research and Therapy of Homosexuality; Exodus International, North America; Parents and Friends of Ex-Gays; Evergreen International; Transforming Congregations; International Healing Foundation; JONAH (Jews Offering New Alternatives to Homosexuality); and New Life Clinics.

43. James Dobson, "The Origins of Homosexuality," *Bringing Up Boys* (Wheaton, IL: Tyndale House Publishers, 2001), 115; cited in Lutes, *A False Focus*, 4. See the American Psychiatric Association, *Position Statement on Homosexuality*, 2000: "The APA affirms its 1973 position that homosexuality per se is not a diagnosable mental disorder. Recent publicized efforts to re-pathologize homosexuality by claming that it can be cured are often guided not by rigorous scientific or psychiatric research, but sometimes by religious and political forces opposed to full civil rights for gay men and lesbians."

44. H. Newton Malony, "Changes in Attitudes toward Homosexuality among Mental Health Professionals: What Pastoral Counselors Need to Know," in *Pastoral Care and Counseling in Sexual Diversity*, ed. H. Newton Malony (New York: Haworth Press, 2001), 24.

45. For further discussion, see "Gay and Lesbian Issues: Background and Ordering Information," http://www.psych.org/public_info/homose~1.cfm.

46. American Psychological Association Statement on Homosexuality, July 1994.

47. Dr. Joseph Nicolosi, Focus on the Family's "Love Won Out" conference, Oklahoma City, 2003; cited in Lutes, *A False Focus*, 4.

48. Ibid.

49. David G. Myers, excerpt from *Psychology*, 7th ed. (New York: Worth Publishers, 2004). Available at www.davidmyers.org, p. 2.

50. American Psychoanalytic Association, "Position Statement on the Treatment of Homosexual Patients," http://www.apsa.org/pubinfo/homosexuality.htm.

51. American Anthropological Association, "Statement on Marriage and the Family," http://www.aaanet.org/press/ma_stmt_marriage.htm.

52. Cited in Lutes, *A False Focus*, 7.

53. Joseph Nicolosi, *Reparative Therapy of Male Homosexuality* (Northvale, NJ: Jason Aronson, 1991). Freud is the most-cited author in the book. For further background, see Myers and Scanzoni, *What God Has Joined Together?* 72–73.

54. Nicolosi, "Love Won Out," 2003; cited in Lutes, *A False Focus*, 10.

55. Nicolosi, "Love Won Out," Focus on the Family Web site; cited in Lutes, *A False Focus*, 10. The American Psychiatric Association, *Position on Therapies Focused*

on Attempts to Change Sexual Orientation (Reparative or Conversion Therapies), approved by the assembly May 2000, states, "The American Psychiatric Association opposes any psychiatric treatment, such as 'reparative' or conversion therapy, which is based upon the assumption that homosexuality per se is a mental disorder or based upon the a priori assumption that a patent should change his/her sexual homosexual orientation."

56. Policy Statement: "Homosexuality and Adolescence," American Academy of Pediatrics, 1993, http://www.clgs.org/5/_6_1.html.

57. See the American Psychiatric Association, *Position on Therapies;* cited in Lutes, *A False Focus*, 11.

58. "Just the Facts about Sexual Orientation and Youth: A Primer for Principals, Educators, and School Personnel," APA Online (American Psychological Association, Public Interest Directorate), http://www.apa.org/pi/lgbc/publications/justthefacts.html.

59. Gil Alexander-Moegerle, *James Dobson's War on America* (Amherst, NY: Prometheus Books, 1997).

60. Nicolosi, Focus on the Family's "Love Won Out" conference; cited in Lutes, *A False Focus*, 12.

61. *Straight Answers, Exposing the Myths and Facts about Homosexuality*, Focus on the Family's Love Won Out series, p. 12; cited in Lutes, *A False Focus,* 12.

62. People for the American Way, "Right Wing Watch Online," November 12, 1999: "November: Attacks on Science, Homosexuality, and the APA," http://www.pfaw.org/pfaw/general/default.aspx?oid=3546.

63. See Jack B. Rogers and Donald K. McKim, *The Authority and Interpretation of the Bible: An Historical Approach* (San Francisco: Harper & Row, 1979), 296–97.

64. Focus on the Family, *Citizen* magazine, January 2003; cited in Lutes, *A False Focus*, 8. In another context, Dr. Maier, spokesperson for Focus on the Family, in an interview with Pete Winn said, "I think, as believers we always have to differentiate between that homosexual individual—whom God loves too dearly and who is made in His image—and the gay activist movement, which I believe is a tool of Satan" (*The Unhappy Truth about Being Gay*, Focus on the Family's *Citizenlink*, July 16, 2004).

65. Cited by David Batstone, "Jimmy Swaggart Tells Congregation He'd Kill Gays," September 22, 2004, http://www.sojo.net.

66. Chris Hedges, "Soldiers of Christ II: Feeling the Hate with the National Religious Broadcasters," *Harper's Magazine*, May 2005, 57. Frank Wright, the new president of the NRB, said, "We will fight the Fairness Doctrine, tooth and nail. It could be the end of Christian broadcasting as we know it, if we do not."

67. Coretta Scott King, in a speech at the Palmer Hilton Hotel, quoted in the *Chicago Defender*, April 1, 1998; cited in Lutes, *A False Focus*, 13.

68. Lewis B. Smedes, "Exploring the Morality of Homosexuality," in *Homosexuality and Christian Faith: Questions of Conscience for the Churches*, ed. Walter Wink (Minneapolis: Fortress Press, 1999), 77.

69. Barbara Kantrowitz, "State of Our Unions," *Newsweek*, March 1, 2004, 44. Cf. Coontz, *Marriage, a History*, 274.

70. *National and International Religion Report* 9, no. 9 (April 17, 1995): 8. Cf. Don S. Browning, Ronnie J. Miller-McLemore, Pamela D. Couture, K. Brynolf Lyon, Robert M. Franklin, *From Culture Wars to Common Ground: Religion and the American Family Debate* (Louisville, KY: Westminster John Knox, 1997), 52.

71. Leon Eisenberg, "Is the Family Obsolete?" *Key Reporter* 60, no. 3 (Spring 1995): 3. Cf. Browning et al., *From Culture Wars to Common Ground*, 52.

72. Browning et al., *From Culture Wars to Common Ground*, 53–54.

73. Sharon Jayson, "Divorce Drops, Along with Marriage," *USA Today*, July 18, 2005, notes that "divorce is on the decline in the USA, but a report to be released today suggests that may be due more to an increase in people living together than to more lasting marriages."

74. Cited in Ronald J. Sider, "The Scandal of the Evangelical Conscience," *Books & Culture*, January/February 2005, 9 and 39.

75. Cheryl Wetzstein, "Who's Happier Ever After?" *Insight* 14, no. 36 (September 28, 1998): 38; cited in *Current Thoughts and Trends*, March 1999, 13.

76. Browning et al., *From Culture Wars to Common Ground*, 3 and 53.

77. Chauncey, *Why Marriage?* 34. "The movement to come out was also profoundly shaped by the sexual revolution. . . . All around them, they [homosexuals] saw their heterosexual friends decisively rejecting the moral codes of their parent's generation, which had limited sex to marriage, and forging a new moral code that linked sex to love and common consent."

78. This material was provided by the Lambda Legal Defense and Education Fund to Ontario Consultants on Religious Tolerance Web site. I downloaded it on February 16, 2005.

79. Cited in Sider, "The Scandal," 9.

80. Ibid.

81. Pam Belluck, "To Avoid Divorce, Move to Massachusetts," November 14, 2004, www.nytimes.com/2004/11/14/weekinreview, printed November 17, 2004, p. 1.

82. Ernest Trice Thompson, *Presbyterians in the South,* vol. 2, *1861–1890* (Richmond: John Knox Press, 1973), 218.

83. Ronald W. Hogeland, "Charles Hodge, the Association of Gentlemen and Ornamental Womanhood: 1825–1855," *Journal of Presbyterian History* 53, no. 3 (Fall 1975): 248.

84. Chauncey, *Why Marriage?* 137. He cites *New York Times*, March 12, 2004, A12.

85. Chauncey, *Why Marriage?* 140: "In Massachusetts, two-thirds of the 752 couples to get marriage licenses on the first day were lesbian, and 40 percent of those couples had children living with them. This shouldn't be surprising, since having children raised the stakes for everyone."

86. "Bush Seeks Constitutional Ban on Same-Sex Marriage," *Los Angeles Times*, February 25, 2004, A1.

87. Cass R. Sunstein, "President versus Precedent," *Los Angeles Times*, February 26, 2004, B13.

88. "The Politics of Gay Marriage," *Los Angeles Times*, February 26, 2004, B12.

89. Chauncey, *Why Marriage?* 133.

90. Ibid. "In 1995, after conducting a comprehensive review of research studies, the American Psychological Association concluded that 'not a single study has found children of gay or lesbian parents to be disadvantaged in any significant respect relative to children of heterosexual parents.' But they were disadvantaged, the brief commented, by the fact 'that the State will not allow their parents to marry.'" [See note 27, American Psychological Association, *Lesbian and Gay Parenting: A Resource for Psychologists* (Washington, DC: APA, 1995).]

91. "Gays and the Gospel: An Interview with Troy Perry," *Christian Century*, September 25–October 2, 1996, 896.

92. Mel White, *Stranger at the Gate: To Be Gay and Christian in America* (New York: Simon & Schuster, 1994).

93. Soulforce, www.soulforce.org.

94. At the time of this writing, same-sex marriage was legal in the Netherlands, Belgium, Spain, and Canada.

95. Lewis Smedes, "Like the Wideness of the Sea," *Perspectives*, May 1999, 12.

Chapter 7: Recommendations
for the Presbyterian Church (U.S.A.)

1. Timothy C. Morgan, "Racist No More? Black Leaders Ask," *Christianity Today* August 13, 1995, 53.

2. *Minutes, 213th General Assembly, 2001, Part I, Journal* (Louisville, KY: Office of the General Assembly, 2001), Comment, p. 61, on Commissioners' Resolution 01-3, p. 487. "That the 213th General Assembly (2001) 1. Confesses the corporate guilt the Presbyterian Church (U.S.A.) shares for the evils of slavery and requests forgiveness from God and from all God's children whose lives have been damaged by these sins."

3. The General Assembly of the United Presbyterian Church in the U.S.A. gave definitive guidance against the ordination of "self-affirming, practicing" homosexuals. At the same time, the policy adopted called on United Presbyterians "to reject in their own lives, and challenge in others, the sin of homophobia," which was defined as "the irrational fear of and contempt for homosexual persons." For the larger context, see *Minutes*, UPCUSA, 1978b, 61–62 and 261–67.

4. "Confessional Nature of the Church Report," *Minutes,* PC(USA), 1986, Part I, 29.116.

5. Ibid.

6. A contemporary example would be a revision of the Southern Baptist Convention's "Faith and Message" (BFM) statement in 2000, which stated that "the office of pastor is limited to men as qualified by Scripture." On October 20, 2000, former President Jimmy Carter severed his lifelong connection with the Southern Baptist Convention in a letter that deplored the denomination's "increasingly rigid creed." Carter used as an example the denomination's declaration in May 2000 that women should no longer be called as senior pastors. The current convention stance left no room for individual interpretation of Scripture, Carter stated, and instead exalted the interpretations of the convention's leadership ahead of "Jesus Christ, through his words, deeds, and personal inspiration, as the ultimate interpreter of the Holy Scriptures" (Larry Stammer, "Carter Cuts Ties to Baptist Convention and Its 'Rigid' Conservatism," *Los Angeles Times,* October 21, 2000, A 13).

7. *Book of Confessions,* 6.175.

8. This flaw was based on erroneous interpretations of both the Bible and the *Book of Confessions.*

9. *Book of Order* [*BO*], G-2.0100.

10. Ibid.

11. *BO,* G-2.0300.

12. *BO,* G-2.0400.

13. *BO,* G-2.0500.

14. I have dealt with this in my book *Reading the Bible and the Confessions: The Presbyterian Way* (Louisville, KY: Geneva Press, 1999).

15. *BC,* 7.234–7.242.

16. *BC,* 10.3, lines 30–32.

17. *BC,* 8.11.

18. *BC,* 8.26, emphasis added.

19. *BC,* 9.44.

20. *BC,* 4.087, emphasis added.

21. Professor Bos then alerted her colleague at Louisville Presbyterian Theological Seminary, Christopher Elwood, professor of historical theology. Together they proposed a change back to the original text to the General Assembly but without success.

22. *The Heidelberg Catechism* (New York: United Church Press, 1962).

23. *DOCTRINAE CHRISTIANAE COMPENDIUM: seu COMMENTARII CATECHETICI,* ex ore D. ZACHARIAE VRSINI, vere Theologi (LONDINI: Excudebat Henricus Midoletonus impensis Thomae Chardi, 1586).

24. *Catechismus, oder Kurzer Unterict Christlicher Leher, wie derselbe in denen Reformirten Kirchen and Schulen in Deutschland wie auch in America, getrieben wird.* (Philadelphia: Gedruckt und zu haben bey Steiner und Kaemmerer, 1795).

25. *Het Boek Der Psalmen* (Middelbvrgh: Richard Schilders, druker der Staten s' landts van Zeelandt, 1591).

26. *THE SUMME OF CHRISTIAN RELIGION DELIVERED BY ZACHARIAS URSINUS First, by way of CATECHISM, and then afterwards more*

enlarged by a sound and judicious EXPOSITION, and APPLICATION of the same. First Englished by D. HENRY PARRY, and now again conferred with the best and last Latine Edition of D. DAVID PAREUS, sometime Professour of Divinity in Heidelberge (LONDON, Printed by James Young, and are to be sold by Steven Bowtell, at the signe of the Bible in Popes-head Alley. 1645). This commentary on the catechism by its primary author was translated into English in editions published in England in 1587, 1591, 1611, 1617, 1633, and the one cited in 1645. These would surely have been known to the Westminster Divines since they desired to be in harmony with the other Reformed churches.

27. *The Heidelbergh Catechism Or Method of Instruction IN THE CHRISTIAN RELIGION As The same is taught in the Reformed Churches and Schools of Holland and Germany. Translated for the Use of the Reformed Protestant Dutch Church, of the City of New-York, and others Schools in America* (New-York, Printed: PHILADELPHIA, Re-printed by ANTHONY ARMBRUSTER, in Race-Street, between Second and Third-Street, near the Sign of the Green Tree, 1765).

28. The translators used the NEB only for 1 Cor. 6:9–10. For the other three texts related to Answer 87, they used the Revised Standard Version.

29. The 1988 RCA translation of the Heidelberg Catechism is available online at http://www.rca.org/NETCOMMUNITY/Page.aspx?pid=377&srcid=372.

30. Cf. *The Holy Bible, containing the Old and New Testaments with the Apocryphal/Deuterocanonical Books*, New Revised Standard Version (New York: Oxford University Press, 1989). For the Revised Standard Version and a sample commentary, see Markus Barth, *Ephesians*, vol. 2, Anchor Bible (Garden City, NY: Doubleday, 1974).

31. *The New English Bible: New Testament* (New York: Oxford University Press, 1961; 2nd ed., 1970).

32. *The Greek New Testament: Being the Text Translated in the New English Bible, 1961,* edited with introduction, textual notes, and appendix by R.V. G. Tasker (London: Oxford University Press, 1964).

33. Henry George Liddell and Robert Scott, *A Greek-English Lexicon* (Oxford: Clarendon Press, 9th ed., 1940; with a revised supplement, 1996).

34. *The Bible and Holy Scriptures Conteyned in the Olde and Newe Testament* (Geneva: Printed by Rovland Hall, 1560).

35. M. Eugene Osterhaven, "Osterhaven Responds on Heidelberg Catechism," *Monday Morning*, February 17, 1997, 11.

36. Christopher Elwood, "Heidelberg Catechism Overtures: Joint Presentation by the Overture Advocates."

37. http://www.pcusa.org/ga218/news/ga08129.htm.

38. *BO*, G-18.0200.

39. *BO*, G-5.0103.

40. *BO*, G-3.0401.

41. *BO*, G-4.0403.

42. *BO*, G-6.0106a.

43. *General Assembly News*, vol. 1996, no. 3 (July 2, 1996): 1.

44. The same assembly, on the same day, voted to authorize the stated clerk to explore entering a friend-of-the-court brief in favor of the civil rights of same-sex couples. The assembly also voted to approve a budget that eliminated the only paid staff person supporting marriage and family life ministries. The assembly sent its prohibition of homosexual ordination for the vote of the 172 presbyteries as Amendment B.

45. James D. Anderson, "The Lesbian and Gay Liberation Movement in the Presbyterian Church (U.S.A.), 1974–1996," *Journal of Homosexuality* 34, no. 2 (1997): 57.

46. "'Fidelity and Chastity' Amendment Debate Clouded by Imprecise Definitions," *News Briefs,* December 13, 1996, 3–5.

47. The word "sodomy" is not a biblical word, as I have shown in chap. 5. It was used to describe sexual acts not open to procreation and as such applied to heterosexual as well as homosexual behavior.

48. Westminster Confession of Faith, chapter 24, 3; in *The Confession of Faith of the Assembly of Divines at Westminster, From the Original Manuscript Written by Cornelius Burges in 1646,* edited by S. W. Carruthers (n.p.: Presbyterian Church of England, 1946).

49. *BC,* 6.145, note concerning 1647 edition.

50. *BC,* 5.247.

51. *BC,* 7.061; cf. *BC,* 7.229.

52. *BC,* 7.249.

53. Ibid.

54. *BC,* 7.219.

55. *BC,* 5.217.

56. *BC,* 6.114.

57. I tried to remedy this problem in my book *Presbyterian Creeds: A Guide to the Book of Confessions* (Louisville, KY: Westminster John Knox Press, 1991).

58. Correspondence and personal discussion with Fred Beuttler. See his article "Making Theology Matter: Power, Polity, and the Theological Debate over Homosexual Ordination in the Presbyterian Church (U.S.A.)," *Review of Religious Research* 41 (1999): 239–61.

59. http://pres-outlook.net/index.php?option=com_content&view=article&id=2044.

60. Presbyterian News Service, "Two Gay Presbyterians Given the Green Light to Ordained Ministry," *Presbyterians Today,* March 2008, 27.

61. *BO,* chap. II, "The Church and Its Confessions," especially G-2.0500.

62. http://www.pc-biz.org/IOBView.aspx?m=ro&id=1497.

63. http://www.pc-biz.org/IOBView.aspx?m=ro&id=1461.

Chapter 8: All Are One in Christ Jesus

1. "The different forms which the love-command takes in the gospel tradition suggest finally that Jesus himself was the catalyst for the development of the

double command in the Christian tradition"; Joseph A. Fitzmyer, S.J., *The Gospel according to Luke* (X—XXIV), Anchor Bible (Garden City, NY: Doubleday, 1985), 879.

2. "Both sides claimed to be the true inheritors of the promises to Abraham and Moses; both sides, in consequence, regarded themselves as the rightful possessors of the land"; Tom Wright, *Luke for Everyone* (Louisville, KY: Westminster John Knox Press, 2004), 127.

3. Fitzmyer, *The Gospel according to Luke*, 883–87.

4. Kenneth E. Bailey, "The Parable of the Good Samaritan," chap. 22 in *Jesus through Middle Eastern Eyes: Cultural Studies in the Gospels* (Downers Grove, IL: InterVarsity Press, 2008), 295. Bailey comments, "The wounded man will never be the same. Jesus is demonstrating a part of the meaning of his own passion" (297).

5. Tom Horner, *Jonathan Loved David: Homosexuality in Biblical Times* (Philadelphia: Westminster Press, 1978), 124.

6. Thomas Bohache, "Matthew," in *The Queer Bible Commentary*, ed. Deryn Guest, Robert E. Goss, Mona West, and Thomas Bohache (London: SCM Press, 2006), 510.

7. John J. McNeill, *The Church and the Homosexual*, 4th ed.(Boston: Beacon Press, 1993;1st ed., 1976), 65.

8. Tom Horner, *Jonathan Loved David: Homosexuality in Biblical Times* (Philadelphia: Westminster Press, 1978), 123–24, "Eunuchs, however they became such, were not totally without sexual desires but were, in many cases, active homosexual practitioners. . . . Whatever Jesus meant by this saying [Matt. 19:10–12]—and it is a difficult one—there is no question that he is speaking of eunuchs in the most exalted terms." For a discussion of women sexual minorities in the ancient world, see Bernadette J. Brooten, *Love between Women: Early Christian Responses to Female Homoeroticism* (Chicago: University of Chicago Press, 1996), e.g., 140.

9. Bohache, "Matthew," 508.

10. See ibid., 510.

11. Halvor Moxnes, *Putting Jesus in His Place: A Radical Vision of Household and Kingdom* (Louisville, KY: Westminster John Knox Press, 2003), 72; cited in Bodache, "Matthew," 510.

12. Moxnes, *Putting Jesus,* 75; cited in Bohache, "Matthew," 510.

13. "The eunuch's homeland was nearly one thousand miles south of the Mediterranean coast, in the empire of Meroë, which flourished from 750 BCE to 350 CE. It was in an area about 75 miles northeast of modern Khartoum. Meroë, or Ethiopia, was ruled by queen mothers titled Candace." Queen Nawidemak ruled in the first half of the first century CE and was probably the Candace mentioned in Acts 8. See Edwin M. Yamauchi, "Why the Ethiopian Eunuch Was Not from Ethiopia," in *Interpreting the New Testament Text: Introduction to the Art and Science of Exegesis*, ed. Darrell L. Bock and Buist M. Fanning (Wheaton, IL: Cross-

way Books, 2006), 362–63. According to William Neil, the eunuch was apparently the queen's court chamberlain. *Acts,* New Century Bible Commentary (Grand Rapids: Eerdmans, 1987), 124.

14. According to Mona West, "It is possible that the eunuch could have been what is known in the Book of Acts as a 'God-fearer.'" See Mona West, "The Story of the Ethiopian Eunuch," in *The Queer Bible Commentary* (London: SCM Press, 2006), 572. Fitzmyer explains that the term "God-fearer" denoted "non-Jews sympathetic to Judaism, those who did not submit to circumcision or observe the Torah in its entirety, but who did agree with the ethical monotheism of the Jews and attended their synagogue services." See Joseph A. Fitzmyer, S.J., *The Acts of the Apostles: A New Translation with Introduction and Commentary*, Anchor Bible 31 (New York: Doubleday, 1998), 449–50.

15. Theodore W. Jennings Jr., *The Man Jesus Loved: Homoerotic Narratives from the New Testament* (Cleveland: Pilgrim Press, 2003), 155.

16. Ibid., 155. William Barclay writes, "Tradition has it that this eunuch went home and evangelized Ethiopia. We can at least be sure that, as he went on his way rejoicing, he would not be able to keep his new-found joy to himself." William Barclay, *The Acts of the Apostles* (Louisville, KY: Westminster John Knox Press, 2003; orig. pub., Edinburgh: St. Andrews Press, 1956), 80. Demetrius K. Williams notes the often overlooked significance of race in this story as well. The Ethiopian eunuch is clearly a black African, and many see his conversion as representing the fulfillment of Psalm 68:31, which declares, "Ethiopia will soon stretch out her hands to God." Demetrius K. Williams, "The Acts of the Apostles," in *True to Our Native Land: An African American New Testament Commentary*, ed. Brian K. Blount, Cain Hope Felder, Clarice J. Martin, and Emerson B. Powery (Minneapolis: Fortress Press, 2007), 226–28.

17. Nancy Wilson, *Our Tribe: Queer Folks, God, Jesus, and the Bible* (San Francisco: HarperSanFrancisco, 1995), 130.

18. Frederick Gaiser, "A New Word on Homosexuality? Isaiah 56:1–8 as Case Study," *Word & World* 14, no. 3 (Summer 1994): 282.

19. According to Herbert Donner, "This is nothing more and nothing less than a correction of Holy Scripture by the divine author himself." Herbert Donner, "Jesafa LVII-7: Ein Abrogationsfall innerhalb des Kanons—implikationen und Konsequenzen," in *Congress Volume: Salamanca 1983,* ed. J. A. Emerton, Supplements to Vetus Testamentum, 36 (Leiden: E. J. Brill, 1985), 92; cited in Frederick J. Gaiser, "A New Word on Homosexuality? Isaiah 56:1–8 as Case Study," *Word & World* 14, no. 3 (Summer 1994): 283.

20. John J. McNeill, *Freedom, Glorious Freedom* (Boston: Beacon Press, 1995),143; cited in West, "The Story," 573.

21. West, "The Story," 572–73. Also, a personal note: I am still uncomfortable using the word "queer" because it has been used as an epithet against LGBT people for so long. But it is now used by some people who are LGBT as a term of empowerment. Robert Goss, one of the editors of *The Queer Bible Commentary*, a

recent publication that I have found very insightful, gives a simple and helpful definition of "queer interpretation." It is "precisely the practice of making strange that which has been assumed to be familiar" (684). It is designed to jar us awake from traditional understandings to new possibilities. It is interesting to note that the word "Puritan" was originally a slur against Presbyterian reformers in sixteenth-century England that was then adopted by them as a badge of honor. Similarly, today many people who are gay, lesbian, bisexual, or transgender have taken what was once an epithet, transformed it into a term of empowerment, and now use it as a designation that includes all sexual minorities.

22. Jennings, *The Man Jesus Loved,* 155.

23. Wilson, *Our Tribe,* 131.

24. Note, for example, William Stacy Johnson's thoughtful analysis of the story of Ruth and Naomi: "The language used in the book of Ruth gives us a clue that covenant loyalty, as conceived within the precepts of biblical religion, is about something other than the narrow construct of 'gender complimentarity.' The bond described in Ruth is between two women. There is nothing overtly sexual about it, and yet the story being told uses the very same words that appear in the famous summary statement about the meaning of marriage from the book of Genesis." William Stacy Johnson, *A Time to Embrace: Same-Gender Relationships in Religion, Law, and Politics.* (Grand Rapids: Eerdmans, 2006), 145. Wilson, in the first edition of *Our Tribe,* lists twenty-nine passages in the OT and five passages in the NT that contain a direct or indirect reference to eunuchs. Furthermore, Norwegian Baptist minister, Ragnhild Schanke, finds that "48 *eunouchoi* are made invisible because translators have chosen to call them officers. This translation is obviously absurd when the term occurs in a context, and not only in a list. Matt. 19:12 is one such important scripture, since it is impossible to translate *eunouchoi* as officers. It demonstrates that the Bible is not as straight and narrow as many want to believe." Ragnhild Schanke, "Rituals and Same-sex unions," in *Same-sex Couples, Same-sex Partnerships and Same-sex Marriages: A Focus on Cross-national Differentials,* Proceedings from the Stockholm Conference, 25–26 September 2003, Documents de travail no 124, INED, 2004, 304, http://www-same-sex.ined.fr/WWW/04 Doc124Ragnhild.pdf.

Appendix: Progress toward LGBT Equality in other Denominations in the United States

1. For a list of advocacy groups in the United States, see http://www.religious institute.org/documents/TimetoSeekresources.pdf.

2. "How Did MCC Begin?" http://www.mccchurch.org/.

3. Eileen W. Linder, *Yearbook of American and Canadian Churches 2008* (Nashville: Abingdon Press, 2008), 381.

4. E-mail correspondence with the Rev. Elder Nancy Wilson, August 25, 2008.

5. Full text of the 1970 General Resolution available at http://www.uua.org/socialjustice/socialjustice/statements/14482.shtml.

6. See http://www.uua.org/socialjustice/socialjustice/statements/14482.shtml. It is important to note that the UUA held themselves to the same standard as they held society at large. Later antidiscrimination resolutions in the Presbyterian, Methodist, Lutheran, and American Baptist denominations called for an end to discrimination against people who are LGBT in secular society while permitting employment discrimination against people who are LGBT within the church.

7. Perez v. Sharp. Full text of the decision available at http://lmaw.org/freedom/docs/CA-Perez.pdf.

8. See http://www.uua.org/members/justicediversity/bisexualgay/20962.shtml.

9. Full text of the resolution available at http://www.ucc.org/assets/pdfs/1969-RESOLUTION-ON-HOMOSEXUALS-AND-THE-LAW.pdf.

10. See http://www.ucc.org/assets/pdfs/1975-A-PRONOUNCEMENT-CIVIL-LIBERTIES-WITHOUT-DISCRIMINATION.pdf.

11. See http://www.qrd.org/qrd/orgs/UCC/history.of.ucc.support.for.lgb.

12. Andy Lang, United Church of Christ, Office of Communication, http://www.qrd.org/qrd/orgs/UCC/history.of.ucc.support.for.lgb.

13. Phone interview with Rev. Michael Scheunemeyer, August 27, 2008.

14. See http://www.integrityusa.org/discrimination/index.htm.

15. See, for example, the work of Integrity USA: http://www.integrityusa.org/.

16. See http://archive.elca.org/legal/synods/guidelines.html.

17. See http://www.elca.org/Growing-In-Faith/Vocation/Rostered-Leadership/Ordained-Ministry/Vision-Expectations.aspx.

18. See http://www.elca.org/Growing-In-Faith/Vocation/Rostered-Leadership/Associates-in-Ministry/Vision-Expectations.aspx.

19. See http://www.lcna.org/lcna_news/2007–08-07a.shtm\#. The list of names was contained in a devotional booklet that was offered as a free gift to the voting members of the 2007 CWA and is available online at http://www.lcna.org/lcna_news/2007_cwa_apwmw/a_place_within_my_walls.htm.

20. E-mail correspondence with Amalia Vagts, Extraordinary Lutheran Ministries, October 10, 2008.

21. See http://archive.elca.org/assembly/pdf/E3_Landahl_substitution.pdf.

22. See http://www.lcna.org/lcna_news/2007–08-18a.shtm.

23. See http://www.abc-usa.org/resources/10facts.pdf.

24. "History of the Baptist LGBT Rights Movement," The Association of Welcoming & Affirming Baptists 1986–2006: http://www.wabaptists.org/who_we_are/history.htm.

25. See http://www.abc-usa.org/resources/resol/homosex.htm.

26. See http://www.wabaptists.org/who_we_are/history.htm.

27. Phone interview with Rev. Ken Pennings, Association of Welcoming and Affirming Baptists, September 22, 2008.

28. No author, *The Book of Discipline of the United Methodist Church 2004*, English ed. (Nashville: Abingdon Press, 2005), 77.

29. Ibid., ¶ 161G, 101.

30. Ibid., ¶ 162H, 107–108.

31. Ibid., ¶ 304.3, 197; ¶ 341.6, 241.

32. "A central conference shall have power to make such changes and adaptations of the *Book of Discipline* as the special conditions and the mission of the church in the area require." Ibid., ¶ 543.7, 331.

33. Phone interview with Rev. Troy Plummer, September 16, 2008.

34. See http://www.unityfellowshipchurch.org/wp2008/?page_id=4.

35. See http://www.arkofrefuge.org/flunder_bio_2004.shtml.

36. Herndon L. Davis, "Black Church History Comes Out of the Closet," http://www. operationrebirth.com/herndon2.html, 9/22/2008.

37. The Seventh-day Adventists and the Presbyterian Church (U.S.A.) are engaged in formal conversations using papers given by representatives of each body dealing with biblical, theological, and social issues. These conversations began in 2006 and are projected into 2010. See Jerry L. Van Marter, "Presbyterians, Adventists Continue Conversations," *PCUSANEWS*, August 29, 2008.

38. David Ferguson, Fritz Guy, and David Larson, eds., *Christianity and Homosexuality: Some Seventh-Day Adventist Perspectives* (Roseville, CA: Adventist Forum, 2008), xii.

39. Ibid.

40. Instruction concerning the Criteria for the Discernment of Vocations with regard to Persons with Homosexual Tendencies in View of Their Admission to the Seminary and to Holy Orders, available at http://www.vatican.va/roman_curia/congregations/ccatheduc/documents/rc_con_ccatheduc_doc_20051104_istruzione_en.html.

41. See http://www.equalitymaryland.org/pdfs/religion.pdf.

42. For a list of gay-friendly Catholic parishes, see http://www.newways ministry.org/GFP.html. For a list of gay-friendly Catholic colleges and universities, see http://www.newwaysministry.org/GFC.html.

Index